# Intermarriage

## The Challenge of Living with Differences Between Christians and Jews

*Susan Weidman Schneider*

THE FREE PRESS
*A Division of Macmillan, Inc.*
NEW YORK

The Free Press
A Division of Macmillan, Inc.
866 Third Avenue, New York, N.Y. 10022

Printed in the United States of America

printing number
2 3 4 5 6 7 8 9 10

*Library of Congress Cataloging-in-Publication Data*

Schneider, Susan Weidman.
  Intermarriage : the challenge of living with differences between Christians and Jews.

  Bibliography: p.
  Includes index.
  1. Interfaith marriage—United States.  I. Title.
HQ1031.S33  1989      306.8'43      88-33565
ISBN 0-02-927941-0

For Bruce

*who knows that endogamy isn't easy either*

# Contents

# Acknowledgments

The experiences of scores of interfaith couples across the United States and Canada make up the backbone of this book, and it is to these couples, whose life experiences are rendered anonymously here, that I owe my first thanks. Their willingness to talk about the details of their lives and their reflections on them provided me with the material on which I based my own observations.

The many social workers, psychologists, ministers, and rabbis who discussed with me their encounters with interfaith couples are acknowledged in the book itself, as their work is cited. But one must be singled out here for special gratitude: Esther Perel, psychotherapist, is quoted frequently in these pages, and it is because of her generosity in allowing me to follow several groups of interfaith couples she has worked with over the past three years that I was able to monitor how the couple dynamic can change through time. In our many discussions, and as she read earlier versions of this work, she helped me to refine my thinking on the complex issues that intermarriage raises in the lives of couples.

Informing all current work in the area of intermarriage are the studies of Egon Mayer, who for ten years has been providing fascinated consumers of such data (myself among them) with portraits of interfaith couples, their children, and converts to Judaism. His investigations, his understanding of the research that preceded his own, and the elegance with which he has written about his findings put all who are interested in couple relationships and in the future shape of the Jewish community greatly in his debt.

My gratitude extends, beyond these professionals in the field, to someone who has offered both professional counsel and warm friendship as this book was being written and long before. Vicki Rosenstreich, who has worked with interfaith families in many settings, provided invaluable personal support throughout this project, in addition to reading the manuscript in many different incarnations and sharing with me her own observations and conclusions about life and love.

Central to the book's conception and gestation was Victoria Pryor, my literary agent and patient adviser; Tory's most valuable contributions to this project were her chronic enthusiasm for the book and her willingness to listen to each new anecdote and insight over the telephone before it found its way into print. Arthur Drache, my collaborator in other projects, read an early version of this book, and spoke many kind words to me when I despaired of finishing it. Laura Wolff edited the manuscript with diligence; Susan Llewellyn and Edith Lewis shepherded the book through its final stages patiently and with good humor.

I thank my colleagues at *Lilith* magazine, especially Paula Gantz, for the grace with which they endured not only my absences while writing but also my somewhat distracted state when I was present. My husband, Bruce, and my children, Benjamin, Rachel, and Yael, were their usual tolerant and loving selves throughout, although Yael (now age six) says that she never wants to get married at all.

I alone am responsible for the observations and conclusions presented herein, but this book would have been a far poorer product without the contributions and support of all those named here.

# 1

## What We Talk About When We Talk About Intermarriage

Twenty years ago, according to the accepted wisdom, a person who married outside his or her faith group was likely trying to escape from it. This "rejectionist" analysis was almost always applied to Jews who married Christians. In fact, for Jews, as recently as 1963, the claim could be made that intermarriage was "the principal means of departure from Jewish life."[1] Today, by contrast, intermarriage is rising along with ethnic pride. A Jew today no longer marries a Christian in order to "pass" or assimilate; and an Italian Catholic, for example, does not necessarily want to give up strong ethnic or religious ties when marrying a Jew. Instead, they are looking for ways to harmonize their love for someone of a different faith with what may emerge as a strengthened desire to connect with their own religious or cultural identity. At the same time that social barriers between Jews and Christians are breaking down, there remains a strong tendency for individuals to maintain their ethnic and religious specificity.

The salient feature in the domestic lives of most of the interfaith couples introduced here is the desire of each partner to remain in contact with aspects of his or her birth culture and to transmit something of it to the next generation. Therefore, interfaith couples have to learn to live with their differences—differences that often persist in the couple's emotional life long after the outward manifestations of religious differences may have been resolved—even when one partner converts to the religion of the other.

There are currently more than 375,000 interfaith couples in the

United States. Of all the Jews marrying this year, between one-third and one-half will choose mates who were not born Jewish.[2] The overwhelming majority of these mates will be Christian. How will they live together? What meaning will religion have in their lives together? What identity issues will they face as they examine things about their own past lives that they consider too important to revise or cast off?

It seems almost too obvious to mention that all couples must adjust to sharing their lives with people different from themselves; part of the thrill of any close human connection is the discovery of where the similarities and the differences lie; these provide both comfort and challenge. For couples of different religious backgrounds—particularly when one is Christian and the other Jewish—the challenge can be very great. "Modern intermarriage," says one commentator, "has become revolutionary, particularly for Jews, precisely because the marriage partners are working at integrating different heritages, customs, memories, and histories that have been tragically at odds for thousands of years."[3]

No matter how many times we hear the misnomer "Judeo-Christian tradition," the two faiths are not one. There are very real differences between Judaism and Christianity, differences that may appear to have nothing to do with the couples themselves but that have shaped how each of them views life, death, morality, the relationship between self-sufficiency and community, and so on. These differences may be stimulating and enriching or they may be divisive; one of the tasks of interfaith couples is to determine the boundaries between their own unique relationship and the issue of religious differences. This book is an attempt to help couples find and negotiate that border.

A love relationship between people of two such radically different traditions becomes a kind of magnifying lens through which we can examine what religion may mean even to those who don't practice it, and why ethnic and family patterns sometimes masquerade as religious differences. Individuals learning to live as an interfaith couple often find themselves examining their own past and planning for their future in ways that few inmarried couples need to. Their searches and their accommodations can illuminate many issues that are buried or ignored in the lives of same-faith partners. Thus, the Christian-Jewish couple is at the center of this story. This book looks at who these people are, asks how and why they found each other, and examines the choices they face as they try to find creative ways of living with their differences. The concentric circles of those directly and indirectly affected appear here, too—the parents of the couple, the young and the adult children of interfaith marriages, and the community whose agencies may be called upon to serve any part of this population.

Interfaith marriage is a phenomenon viewed by some Jews and Christians with alarm, by some as a curiosity, and by the partners themselves as a name for their situation that represents only some of the many challenges they face in living together. The partners must at some level deal with their own and each other's feelings of loss of continuity, betraying ancestors, creating complexities in the lives of children alive and yet-to-be, of competition, anger, rejection. This book focuses on the expectations and emotions of both partners in a Jewish-Christian marriage, viewed mainly against the background of the Jewish community. So clear is the demographic assymetry between Jews and Christians that intermarriage has quite different meanings and implications for each group.

One might reposition the lens and look at these families, for example, against the background of North America's Christian majority. However, Christians, who twenty years ago were writing with anxiety about the complex dynamics of Protestant-Catholic intermarriage, are not nearly so concerned about Christian-Jewish unions as are Jews, primarily for demographic reasons. Although equal numbers of Jews and Christians make up these couples, their percentages of the religious communities they represent are vastly different (5 percent as compared with a fraction of 1 percent). There are fewer than 7 million Jews in all of North America, and more than 250 million Christians. The response of Christian families when a child is marrying someone whose background may be significantly different from theirs may be acceptance, joy, or dismay, but their response is first and last a personal one. The intermarriage will have no effect on the gross number of Christians in the world, nor will it tip the balance in churches or family groupings.

Jews, as a community, respond somewhat differently from Christians or members of other faith groups when their children marry out of their parents' faith, because of the historical realities of Jewish life through the ages and the current realities concerning the Jewish attrition rate as a consequence of intermarriage.

Most Jewish clergy and lay personnel do not support intermarriage (though they respond with varying degrees of insight and concern) unless the non-Jewish partner converts to Judaism. Christian clergy—especially liberal Protestants—are more encouraging. While not promulgating the idea of intermarriage as a panacea, one minister said it "could be a wonderful thing in the world, making peace on these issues because the partners and their children know the integrity of both traditions."

Marrying out of the faith is seen as a threat to Jewish survival and continuity. The threat may be real. First, most surveys show that intermarried couples are likely to have fewer children than same-faith couples.[4] Also, data on the family patterns of the children of mixed—that is, nonconversionary—marriages show that a large majority will not raise their children as Jews. And, according to some demographers, since the children and grandchildren even of conversionary marriages are less and less likely to restrict their marriage choices to Jews,[5] there will be attrition of the Jewish population year by year as a result of intermarriage in general.[6] Some non-Jews interpret the data on intermarriage in a positive light, as a breaking down of old-fashioned sectarian barriers, but many Jews regard the barriers as at least assuring their continued survival as a distinct group.

Every Jew is affected in some way by intermarriage. The strictly Orthodox Jew fears that a child or grandchild will abandon tradition and succumb to the pluralism of American society by dating a Christian. The seemingly assimilated nonreligious Jew who has already married "out" wonders how to impart some sense of Jewish ethnocultural identity to his or her children—and may also wonder why it matters to do so. In between lies a whole range of concerns: Jews who fear that if they invite a mixed-marriage (unconverted) couple to share a Jewish holiday their own children might erroneously assume approval of such a union; single Jewish women and men who, while claiming to want to marry Jews, confess that they don't want to date them; "secular" Jews who find themselves embarrassed by their inability to field questions from their non-Jewish in-laws about Jewish theology or ritual.

In its Jewish interpretation an intermarriage is a union between a Jew and a non-Jew. Under Jewish law a convert (or a "Jew by choice," as many converts to Judaism prefer to call themselves) is considered a full Jew, and there is no special official category describing a marriage between a born Jew and someone who became a Jew at any time before the marriage.[7] In reality, however, since being Jewish entails more than just religion, there are many characteristics of an intermarriage—including attachment to a non-Jewish birth family—even in settings where the non-Jewish partner converts to Judaism. There *are* significant differences between a "conversionary" and a "mixed" marriage (in which each partner retains his or her own religious identity), but for our purposes here, unless specifically designated as a conversionary or a mixed marriage, the term *intermarriage* refers to a union between a Jew and someone not born Jewish.

Intermarriage has specific meanings in the context of modern Jews' struggle to live openly in the world. The conflict here is between synthesis and separateness, between blending in (melting down into the melting pot) or staying distinctive, as in a mosaic. For Jews, the cultural dynamic has always been one of moving outward to explore while simultaneously turning inward toward the group, of relating to the mainstream culture while maintaining strong loyalty to in-group customs.

Many aspects of Jewish law, for example, developed and changed over the centuries as Jews lived among other peoples.[8] Historically, to live as a Jew one had to live within walking distance of other Jews, since many prayers required the presence of at least nine other Jews. Yet, despite the theologically derived need for geographic closeness, we have the image from the Book of Genesis of God telling Abraham to "go forth" from his birthplace (*lech lecha*, it says in Hebrew). So the movement outward and the pull inward became incorporated into the Jewish dynamic. This dynamic—described by sociologists today as a struggle between integrationism (the tropism toward full assimilation into American society) and survivalism (the persistence of the Jews as a unique and distinctive group)[9]—is very much present in current interfaith marriages of Jews. Jews have always been attracted to the outside world, and have struggled to reconcile that attraction, and that movement outward, with the centripetal pulls of a Jewish community that requires one to draw close. Intermarriage of Jews with Christians has become a measure of how far Jews are willing to go as they move toward ever-greater acceptance by mainstream society.

Until the sharp rise in intermarriage beginning in the 1960s (up from 1 percent in the 1920s to a rate of nearly 60 percent in some cities in North America in the late 1980s), American Jews were "the classical illustration of voluntary group endogamy."[10] This means that most Jews freely chose to marry other Jews, even when their logical or random pool for mate selection obviously contains many more Gentiles than Jews.

Jewish women have played a shifting role in this process. First, as representatives of a tradition left behind when Jewish men married out—until the 1970s men married out far more often than women—they faced a reduced number of available Jewish mates. Perhaps because of this, Jewish women began marrying Christians in numbers that by the mid-1980s were just about equal to those for Jewish men. One sociologist calls these women "reluctant exogamists," believing that in general they would have married Jewish men had there been any among their suitors.[11]

Men and women differ not only in their historical patterns of intermarriage, but also in how they are viewed by their own communities. For example, a non-Jewish woman who does not convert to Judaism is more likely to be considered "selfish" by her Jewish husband's family, whereas a non-Jewish man in the same situation is judged to be acting out of his own strong religious convictions. Some of the disapproval in the first instance may derive from the fact that under most interpretations of Jewish law, a child born to a mother who was not Jewish at the time of the birth is not considered to be Jewish, whereas a child of a Jewish mother and a non-Jewish father is Jewish. This is one of the several intersections of fact and feeling with which the interfaith couple learns to cope.

In an endogamous or in-group marriage—with neither one fearful of exposing an unbridgeable gulf between them—each partner may simply view the other as "different" and make appropriate accommodations. No one needs to defend a liking for Tex-Mex cooking, baroque music, or old movies, but there is a big difference between individual tastes and an individual's identity. In intermarriages, partners face the risk of mislabeling normal differences as irresolvable conflicts stemming from the intermarriage itself. The couples may need to clarify which conflicts are "interethnic" or interreligious, and which are the individual differences all couples struggle with. All happily married couples experience differences; recent evidence suggests that the success of their marriages is due in part to an ability to put aside many differences and live with them.[12] Intermarried couples also need support to acknowledge and endure their very real differences, and to grow from them.

One of the difficulties, however, is that many Jews have a problem articulating and defining their feelings about being Jewish. It's hard to learn to live with differences when you are unclear about what those differences actually are. Inchoate, visceral sensations about what "is" and "is not" Jewish may be very hard to communicate intelligently to a partner who has never experienced them. How to explain something to a partner when one doesn't fully understand it oneself?

The paradoxical nature of Jewish acculturation to American life (or the Jews' assimilation into it, some would claim) can be very confusing to Jews and Christians alike. Because they have been a tiny minority of the population in almost every country in which they have lived except Israel, Jews have a great deal of ambivalence about their own religious and cultural heritage, exquisitely captured in the title of a magazine article by Amy Stone, "My Kid Turned Out Jewish—Where Did I Go Wrong?"[13]

Few Jews and fewer Christians can explain the pull of Jewish identity on interfaith couples, the phenomenon that has been called "the tenacity of Jewishness."[14] Especially for Jews who may have spent a good deal of their adult lives trying to distance themselves from what they perceived as enmeshing families—and who stirred Jewishness into the recipe of what felt stifling in their families of origin—it may be hard to explain why being Jewish suddenly seems to matter, especially at life-crisis moments or important transitions—for example, the birth of a child.

For the non-Jew, who perhaps has a clearer view of the boundaries between religious and secular identities, the mystery is why something that appears to have so little objective meaning to the Jew suddenly takes on so much importance. The Jewish partner has usually not been particularly religiously observant—most American Jews, for example, do not attend synagogue services more frequently than once or twice a year—and may even have spoken scornfully about Jewish connections or traditions in his or her past. The Jew is often mystified, too. One problem in this regard comes from a failure of learning and language; insufficient knowledge about one's own religious tradition makes it harder to think through and to understand and communicate why it feels so important. Especially in a secular age, even to confess having feelings about a "religious" identity in the first place may seem embarrassing. This ambivalence about one's own identity provides an unsteady foundation from which to negotiate with someone of a different background. One woman, a Jew, told of going to High Holiday services alone every fall, without the Catholic man she has been living with for ten years.

> I come home crying, every time. We're both aching, for different reasons. It's a time when I want him to be Jewish, in some way, and when he is outraged that I seem not to love him enough for who he is. Religion is the one issue that hurts, that separates us, the one issue that can drive a wedge between us. Even when we have other conflicts, it's our difference in religious identity that everything else gets mixed up with, as if it were an open file into which we can throw every other conflict we have.

The open-file-for-all-discontents approach is evident also in the relationship of a second couple: A Unitarian husband, initially enthralled by his Jewish wife's warm and close relationship with her family, begins to feel left out—not so much because of religious differences, but because his own cultural conditioning and expectations are so much at variance with hers. What she experiences as normal parent-child bonds he describes as "pathological dependency"; he supports his opinions in their disputes by citing as truth the negative stereotypes of Jewish families he's read about in novels; she counters by describing his family as cold and rejecting, even to him. He fears she's a closet hysteric who will turn on him one day because he's not Jewish; she fears he's a closet anti-Semite.

The world outside impinges as well, not just the family. An articulate and outspoken Jewish man is married to a Methodist woman who agrees with his strong support for Israel but responds to his suspicions of anti-Semitism in others as "looking for Nazis behind every lamppost." "People are basically good," she asserts. Although she is seriously considering converting to Judaism, their different political responses to "Jewish" issues (as opposed to theological differences) make them nervous about possible future schisms. Neither of these two couples has differences based on theology in any formal sense, yet each characterizes the differences they do experience as deriving from their dissimilar religious backgrounds. In fact, for some couples there is so much confusion, anger, sorrow, and pain that both a progressive, sympathetic male rabbi *and* a female Presbyterian minister (both of whom have had extensive experience counseling families touched by interfaith marriage) independently identified the common emotion of all parties as "anguish."

This book attempts to take the lid off some of these superheated issues for interfaith couples. The individual situations presented here, with the details altered for the sake of anonymity, come from open-ended interviews with Christian-Jewish couples across the United States and Canada—unmarried partners and couples in both two-faith and conversionary marriages. In addition to these in-depth, individual interviews, observations of several ongoing groups of interfaith couples provided important information and insights reflected in these pages. Leaders of intermarriage groups around the country contributed their views as well. One fairly uniform conclusion is that open discussion of each party's expectations and anxieties can often solve some of the pain individuals express in one-on-one talks with clergy.

The groups provide an opportunity for couples to express individual feelings and concerns in a safe and public context without threatening the couple relationship as it might be if they were talking at home alone. For example, one couple, married three years, had never discussed whether or not they would have children (a loaded issue for most interfaith couples) until they came to several sessions of a group. Alone, they had successfully avoided the subject as "too hot to handle." As with inmarried families, some of the processes interfaith couples go through in preparing for marriage need to be reenacted when children are planned. The arrival of a child, however joyously anticipated, unsettles the balance in every couple's life, and raises additional issues in an interfaith family. Because many of the groups meet for a period of months to years, an observer can see how people change over time and how they grow in their understanding of each other as they try to balance their own needs with the stability they want in their relationships.

Real life often intrudes on the idealized version of perfect harmony a couple believes they will attain automatically once the marriage vows are exchanged and the warring in-laws appeased or ignored. Life-cycle events provide an opportunity to clarify what is important to each partner; things get shaken up and sorted out during transitions that have been termed "hinges of time.''[15] The birth of a child or the death of a parent can be powerful generators of a certain kind of energy and anxiety, reminders of past senses of ourselves and of the range of possibilities that life holds, from which we must select certain goals and reject others. Not all decisions remain in place one's whole life long, and some couples successfully negotiate whole new arrangements about the religious focus of their lives in the face of altered family structure.

Just as, in the wake of the women's movement, many families renegotiated their articulated or covert compacts about who wielded what kind of power in the household, intermarried couples may find themselves renegotiating their original decisions about religion as they gain new understanding. These changes range from trying out new ways of celebrating holidays to recognizing and respecting the differences between the partners as well as acknowledging that their similarities may well transcend religious issues. But even when a couple achieves an accurate understanding of both partners' concerns and desires—acknowledging, say, that having a child highlights the importance of transmitting something of one's heritage to the next generation—the interfaith couple may still not be certain how precisely to raise that child. ''We're living on the frontier. There are no rules,'' declared one woman. ''We have to invent our own solutions.'' Most of the paradoxical and complex situations faced by these couples raise problems for which there are no simple solutions. But for some readers just understanding that their dilemmas are not unique or isolated events will be helpful, and other people's ''scripts'' or ways of dealing with conflict can be very useful as adaptable models.

This book is intended as a guide not only for Jews and Christians who are themselves intermarried or considering an interfaith marriage, but also for those who find themselves reacting to an intermarriage—parents, friends, clergy, community leaders. Perhaps the most significant contribution that an examination of the phenomenon of intermarriage can make is to provide the opportunity for both the individual and the community to struggle with (and perhaps define) what Judaism, Christianity, and religious and ethnic identity mean to each of us.

# 2

---

# *Who Marries Out— and Why*

If you are a Jew whose ancestors came to the New World three or four generations ago and if you are not religiously observant, are under thirty, live in an area where there are few other Jews, and your previous marriage ended in divorce, you are a likely candidate to marry someone who was not born Jewish. And these days, if you are a single Jewish woman over thirty your chances for intermarriage are even higher, because the pool of eligible Jewish men is even smaller, obviously, than the total number of eligible men for a woman of this age. If you were raised in a Catholic-Protestant or mixed-denomination Christian family, you too are a candidate for marriage to someone not of your own religion.

One of the reasons people's marriage choices are so interesting is that they are not entirely predictable. Yet, even given the workings of chance and the random selection of romantic partners, certain patterns emerge from interviews and statistical data suggesting reasons why intermarried couples chose each other. In a somewhat impressionistic way, we can get a picture of who marries out and thereby also see what some of the issues are likely to be as such couples live out their family life cycles.

Twenty-five years ago less than 10 percent of Jews married out of the faith; now the figure for some communities is as high as 60 percent, with the average intermarriage rate for American Jews generally considered to be between 25 and 30 percent.[1] (Data on Jews who intermarry are available because the small Jewish community—fewer than six million in the United States—is concerned about shifting population statistics and has therefore commissioned studies that yield this information. No comparable body of investigation has been done among contemporary Christians.) What this means is that out of every 100 Jews who marry, between 25 and 30 will marry non-Jews.

While intermarriage is certainly more common today than in the past, it is not new; Jewish-Christian marriages have a long and dappled past. Their current prevalence represents a dramatic shift from the ways in which they have been viewed throughout most of history. When Christians were less welcoming of Jews than they are today, there was little chance of the widespread intermarriage we see now, and it was less likely that the non-Jewish partner would convert to Judaism. Nonetheless, the phenomenon was not unknown, and from biblical times to the present, Jews and Christians have married people from tribes or faiths other than their own.

In the past, some Jews who married non-Jews may have done so purely out of love, as did the biblical Ruth when she married Naomi's son, and just as most people today choose a marriage partner. But even then, context was important; the story does not appear in the Bible merely as a touching example of romantic love and filial piety and loyalty. Ruth's marriage makes a political point. Ruth represented a transition in history. She tells Naomi, "Your people will be my people." She identifies as a Jew and is considered to be the shining example of a pure-hearted convert. Many plot twists follow, including the prediction that because of her great righteousness one of her descendants will be King David and that through this line of descent will ultimately come the Messiah of Judaism. This may be the first instance of the dictum heard frequently in the 1980s—that "converts make the best Jews."

Look also at the Book of Esther. Esther marries Ahasuerus, king of Persia, but she does not even reveal to him that she is Jewish until she asks him to intercede for her people to save them from annihilation. Jewish schoolchildren around the world can limn this tale, and nowhere are they taught that Esther's "intermarriage"—which is certainly never referred to by that term—is bad for the Jews. Intermarriage in this case was a political necessity. It was the good fortune of the Jews of Persia to have had a Jew as queen.

In postbiblical times, interfaith couples were often reviled, unacceptable to both communities. Approximately 400 years before

Christ (B.C.E.—before the common era is how Jews refer to it) Jews were called upon in the Book of Ezra to cast off their wives who were "foreign women" and any offspring of these marriages. A certain xenophobia is evident here, and a strong desire to keep the Jewish community closed. (Because the Book of Ruth presents such a positive view of intermarriage and conversion, some scholars believe that this text was deliberately inserted into the Jewish Scriptures to counter the strong position against intermarriage put forth by Ezra.)

Yet intermarriage must have been a very attractive possibility to women and men from both communities, because many harsh laws were enacted to discourage it. With the emergence of Christianity, Christians themselves passed much legislation against intermarriage. Jews were considered heathen and infidels, and a real threat to the growth of Christianity. In fourth-century Spain, for example, Jews and Christians were forbidden to marry one another; social exchange was also anathema, with severe punishment for violators, including death for intermarriers. In medieval times, laws forbidding marriages between Christians and Jews and imposing harsh penalties—sometimes including death—for their violation were passed by local authorities in various European cities. Jewishness was viewed as "a kind of contagion" that might infect Christians.[2]

At the very least, those who intermarried faced great odds, and—since conversion would almost invariably have had to precede marriage—Jewish parents feared losing their children forever to someone from a different culture. For example, until 1846 there was no civil marriage in Prussia; to marry a Christian one had to become a Christian. To prevent this from occurring, Jewish authorities in many locales also passed laws intended to inhibit contact with Gentiles. For example, the laws of *kashruth*, referring to the kinds and combinations of food that are permitted to religiously observant Jews, were supplemented among some Jews by regulations stipulating that, in order to be considered kosher, dairy products and bread had to be manufactured by and purchased from Jews. This effectively prohibited casual social contact with non-Jewish merchants, and persists today in the form of dairies serving certain segments of the Jewish population with *chalav Yisrael* dairy products—made by Jews alone.

A loosening of class boundaries generally, and increased exposure to one another, certainly contributed to the increase in the numbers of Jews and Christians who intermarried during the Enlightenment in Western Europe. This is a period worth examining because of the light it may cast on contemporary Jewish-Christian marriages, especially since at that time Jewish women were more likely to intermarry than Jewish men, and outmarriages were both attractive and anxiety provoking to many Jews. In the latter part of the eighteenth century, when European Jews began to move from pariah status into a more accepting world (at least on the surface), one way for Jews to prove that they were just like other people was to marry Christians. Urban European Jewish women, who had received better secular educations than men but little Jewish education, were uniquely positioned to take advantage of the new openness. Known as "salon Jewesses" for the style of domestic entertaining they practiced, many of these economically advantaged women converted to Christianity in order to marry non-Jews they met in their social circles.

However, at that time one could not intermarry and easily retain one's Jewishness. The Christian men (often of the nobility) in these marriages were not marrying Jews so that they themselves could convert, or to have "mixed" households. The very "Jewishness" (including exotic good looks) that made these women attractive to Christian men was an impediment to marriage—not only for legal reasons, but also because of prejudice on the part of the social circles in which the Christians usually moved. Only three of the twenty or so "salon Jewesses" in Berlin at the end of the eighteenth century and beginning of the nineteenth died in the religion into which they had been born. Whereas Jewish men of this period who converted to Christianity appear to have done so in order to further their careers or for economic advancement, women converted in order to marry. And those who did seem to have considered their intermarriages as "the achievements of an often painful fight for personal freedom."[3] For most women, marriage was the only route to cultural mobility.

Many of these marriages were "an exchange of status for wealth."[4] Some brides married down, but by the beginning of the nineteenth century, Jewish women were marrying Christian men who were fairly close to them in age and social status. By contrast, the Jewish men who married Christian women at that time as a rule "married down socially when they married out religiously.''[5] The same differential in economic and social status between Jewish women and their Christian husbands and Jewish men and their Christian wives has held almost until the present day.

The same openness to diversity that is so often today seen as the hallmark of the Enlightenment (which was supposed to be so good for the Jews) also provided the backdrop against which Jews could marry out and swim into the mainstream of European life more quickly *if they gave up their Jewish faith.*

Social revolutions of various sorts caused the rate of intermarriage to rise. By contrast, in a more closed and stratified society, there is likely to be considerably less intermarriage. In Eastern Europe, Tevye in *Fiddler on the Roof* went into mourning when one of his daughters married a Russian non-Jew. Based on their history, Jews perceived Christians as the enemy, the inciters of pogroms, the attackers. Lines between Christians and Jews were only rarely breached, although the fact this occurred in the Tevye story meant that some marriages did indeed cross these lines. In a present-day highly stratified society, South Africa under apartheid, there is both little sanctioned intergroup mixing and a Jewish-Christian intermarriage rate considered the lowest in the world: for example, only 5 percent of Johannesburg's Jews marry non-Jews.[6]

In the United States, as elsewhere, opportunity often spurred interfaith marriages. In communities in the West, where few Jewish women ventured until the twentieth century, Jewish men—if they wanted to marry at all—often found themselves marrying Christian women. Similar to the loosening of internal and external strictures against intermarriage in Western Europe was the appeal of interfaith marriage in American life in the years after World War I. During the 1920s, upper-crust American Jews, largely those of German-Jewish and Sephardic descent, married non-Jews as a passport to the larger world—a world, they hoped, in which they would be free from a constricting anti-Semitism. Many of the men who married Christians changed their names to ''pass''; few of these couples gave any thought to maintaining Jewishness in their lives together. As part of the status exchange, the non-Jewish women the intermarrying Jewish men chose (and the intermarriers then were largely men) were not usually their equals in education or wealth. The men bought their way into

American society, as it were, by marrying beneath them. This "status exchange" is not uncommon when intermarriages take place in a society basically antipathetic to Jews.

By contrast, where once a Jew had to offer something special—an elevation in economic status, for example—in order to be found attractive by an American Christian, now, as Jews have become more accepted in American life, they are marrying their equals or their social "betters." (For example, in the 1980s, Caroline Kennedy, daughter of the late president, and Maria Cuomo, daughter of New York State governor Mario Cuomo, both married Jewish men.) The fact that the young partners in most Jewish-Christian marriages today have similar class and educational backgrounds makes their situations a little different from interfaith partners of previous generations.[7] Data from the mid-1970s suggest that there is also less negative feeling about intermarriage generally among younger Jews, in part at least because they don't see it as threatening to Jewish continuity.

Nevertheless, public uneasiness over intermarriage persists. The intermarriage television sitcom of the 1970s, "Bridget Loves Bernie," was taken off the air—perhaps partially because of viewer protests—and in 1986, when the television soap opera "Days of Our Lives" featured a romance between a Jewish doctor and her non-Jewish colleague, their love was doomed explicitly because they didn't share the same religious background. Prime-time television has presented viewers with the conflicts a mixed-faith couple experiences over conversion and a baby-naming ceremony ("Thirtysomething" and "A Year in the Life") and an extended family's ambivalence over intermarriage ("Cagney and Lacey"). Marriages between Christians and Jews—and the conflicts they trigger—are being served up as standard fare to Middle America, albeit usually in the older format of the Jewish man–Christian woman dyad. The networks believe that there is wide-enough viewers interest to warrant such coverage—interest piqued by the ways in which the interfaith couples resolve their conflicts as well as by the delineation of the struggles themselves.

In the 1980s, references to religious or ethnic identification in selecting a marriage partner can be made simply and directly as one would comment on being attracted to one physical type over another. Actor Michael J. Fox, whose parents are Anglican (the British and Canadian form of Episcopalianism) told a reporter from *People* magazine: "I'm going to marry a Jewish woman. I'm sure of it . . . I like women who are funny, independent, optimistic, hardworking and definitely the family type." Indeed, a couple of years after the comments by Fox appeared in the magazine, he did marry a Jewish woman in an "interfaith" ceremony which was also the subject of a *People* story (though no reporters were allowed into the event).

As more people intermarry, intermarriage itself obviously becomes less an expression of deviance (in the sense of a desire to flee from one's own community) and more a function of opportunity. A structuralist approach would predict that greater acceptance of Jews by non-Jews, plus wider exposure to people from other backgrounds and greater mixing with them at school, in the workplace, and socially, make intermarriage more common. This view is consistent with data that show that those who intermarry are likely to be older at the time of the marriage than their peers who married within their faith, and hence to have had more time to meet more diverse people.[8]

Many interfaith couples may be older when they finally marry because they have delayed marriage out of their uneasiness over the issue of their different religious or cultural backgrounds. Rather than deal with their differences while the relationship is developing, many couples prefer to let time test them and perhaps help build a trust that will ultimately work to mitigate those differences. When a Jewish man, about to be married to an Episcopalian, was asked how long they had been together, he replied, "A couple of years." His fiancée laughed and corrected him: "You always tell people that. It's been *seven* years. You just don't like to face up to that fact." By denying how long it had taken them to decide to marry, he was trying also to deny that there were any difficulties in the relationship. He admitted, "I guess I was hoping the problems would just go away."

Of course, the older a single person gets, the weaker the strictures against marrying someone of another faith. For many single adults, parents and other significant people—as well as the individual in question—are likely to feel most anxious over the possibility of no marriage at all. One woman said it very clearly: "My daughter is thirty-eight. If she were in her twenties I'd be very upset that she was marrying a Methodist and not another Jew. But let's face it, at this point, as long as she's happy . . . " For others, their parents have simply ceased to represent any form of social authority by the time they themselves contemplate marriage.

Every couple in love wants to believe that they have selected one another as an existential choice—that they are acting freely, writing their own script. But many people in interfaith relationships appear to share certain characteristics. In the past some analysts suggested that those who intermarry feel rejected by and hostile to their own group; according to this theory the intermarriers select mates from outside the group to express their hostility. They also tend to attract only the rebels from the group they marry into. Until the widespread increase in Jewish-Christian intermarriage in the 1960s and 1970s, the ''self-hatred'' or rebellion theory dominated the discussion of intermarriage.[9]

The profiles of those Jews who intermarried before the upsurge of the 1970s focused largely on psychological dynamics. One social observer stated that those who intermarry usually fell into one of four categories: emancipated, rebellious, detached, or adventurous.[10] The emancipated felt themselves to be beyond the narrow categories of religion or race; interracial marriages could fall into this category. (Many of these marriages in the 1960s involved Jews and blacks, usually Jewish women and black men.[11]) The rebellious would include the Jewish woman from Brooklyn and the Presbyterian from a farm in Iowa who fled their families and found each other in western Canada; each wanted something totally different from what they had known at home, and each was correct in surmising that both sets of parents would be considerably disturbed by the union. The detached couple could well be represented by Dave and Laurel, he a Jew and she a non-practicing Catholic. They met in the early 1960s in Oakland, California, where each had gone to escape any connection with the past; they weren't in rebellion against any particular tradition but just felt alienated both from religious roots and from their own families. The adventurous is typified by a Jewish anthropologist from Toronto who met and married a Catholic woman doctor from Argentina who was working in the African hospital where he was being treated for malaria. Not all adventurers go far away to meet their mates. Some people are simply attracted to those who are significantly different from themselves; one Nebraskan woman in her late teens, planning to marry a black West Indian Protestant, had always been drawn to people she thought of as exotic—her closest girlfriend throughout high school was Chinese.

Sociologist Egon Mayer, summarizing in *Love and Tradition* the data on how people choose their mates, reminds us that a couple relationship is forged over time. Underlying that developmental process is a key perspective, which all those who intermarry share: *Jew and Christian are able to see one another as potential marriage partners.* Their "field of eligibles" includes those people of another religious tradition or background. All other characteristics of their mate selections flow from this initial openness. About half the Christians who intermarry have dated Jews other than the one they marry.[12] Many Gentiles married to Jews reported having always found Jews attractive, as this Boston woman did: "I was always drawn to Jews and to Judaism—long before I met my husband. In fact, I had toyed with the idea of converting to Judaism as a teenager. And I always found Jewish men extremely attractive. They were always the ones who were so smart, so lively." (Her admiration for her husband's brainpower is interesting in light of her own—she is a Ph.D. with a senior government position.) Almost identical sentiments are expressed by a woman from a Baptist family in Nashville, who says that a rabbi in the small Southern town where she was raised taught her about Judaism; it was years later that she met the Jewish man she married, as if fulfilling part of something she had always desired. (Some mystical rabbis claim that every convert is really someone who lived as a Jew in a previous life.)

Direct observation, and a reading of the social science literature, suggest that at least part of the explanation of what leads a Jew to consider a non-Jew as a possible mate may be found in the family structure rather than in the community at large, and may involve not rebelliousness so much as a desire for both distance *and* closeness. This is not to say that the family is the cause of intermarriage, but that certain factors in the family may predispose a man or woman to intermarry. Freudian commentators talk about the incest taboo being violated when one marries a man or woman within one's own group. For example, young adults raised on a kibbutz in Israel seldom marry within their own kibbutz group—they see one another almost as siblings. The fact that the Jewish community as a whole sees itself as *mishpocha* ("family") may play a part in the desire of some people to distance themselves from anything Jewish—including potential mates. Unresolved feelings toward one's own parents would, according to this theory, prod women and men to seek mates who were unlike the members of the birth family. Black Christian–white Jewish intermarriages create unions with the most "unlikeness" from the original families, and are probably a very effective way for individuals to deal with both overly close and overly hostile families.[13]

For families that are exceptionally close, marriage of one of the children to a person from another faith may provide the only possible "circuit-breaker" in this system. A Jewish daughter who "adores" her parents and siblings and feels close to them, bound in a network of mutual caring, married a nonaffiliated Protestant man as a means of separating but staying close, it would appear. After her marriage she and her husband did not build any kind of religious or spiritual life together; she did not set up a "competing" household to that of her parents, but rather a satelite one. She never really left them entirely, remaining dependent on them for holiday celebrations and other occasions. Although they were not happy with her choice, and would have felt more warmly toward her husband if he were Jewish, ironically, interfaith marriage under these circumstances provided a way for her to stay close to her parents. Her intermarriage gave her parents a more active role in their daughter's life, as representatives of Judaism and the transmitters of Jewish tradition to her children, than they would have had if she had married a Jew.

A Jewish man married to a Christian woman who converted to Judaism but knows very little of the tradition admitted that he encourages his parents to have much greater access to his children (who call them by the Yiddish terms *bobbe* and *zayde*) than if he'd married someone born Jewish. Ties to his parents did not snap; they just slackenened a bit because of his wife's detachment. "I didn't marry Jenny because she wasn't Jewish," he commented, "but I couldn't have imagined marrying a Jewish woman—it would have felt too claustrophobic, as if I'd never left my parents' house."

In another vein, someone who marries a non-Jew as a means of *escaping* a tightly bound family may find it easier to relate comfortably and warmly to his or her own Jewish parents simply because the non-Jewish spouse provides the escape hatch. Some Jewish men interviewed expressed feelings of pleasure about the autonomy they experienced in choosing to marry a non-Jew: "I really felt my choice was my own. I was doing what I wanted to, not just getting married to a nice Jewish girl to please my parents." The theme of being "free to be oneself" comes up often with intermarrying Jews—as if to marry another Jew would be merely to live out someone else's expectations.

Not unexpectedly, this yearning for autonomy in marital choice is expressed much more strongly by the Jewish partners. Christians, living as members of the majority culture in the West, seem to feel freer to choose a mate according to their own desires, with less sense of having to check their own choices against parental or societal expectations. Marjorie Morningstar, the heroine of Herman Wouk's 1955 eponymous bestseller, was forced to ask herself "Is it good for the Jews?" when she made choices about love and marriage. Her non-Jewish cohorts, represented by the women in Mary McCarthy's 1963 novel *The Group* never needed to ask themselves, when considering the same issues Marjorie did, "Is this good for the WASPs?" Their choices—about careers, sex, marriage, family—were all individual ones, not influenced by the questions of group loyalty or group survival that Marjorie was routinely expected to consider.

Nowhere is the link between disloyalty and intermarriage worked out or lived out so intensely as it is in the infrequent instances when children of Holocaust survivors marry Christians. Children of survivors usually make the same in-group marriage choices as other first-generation Jews, rather than following the looser patterns more common to their American Jewish peers. But when survivors' children do marry Christians, the coupling has an electric charge all its own. The daughter of an Orthodox rabbi who had survived Nazi Germany married a South American Catholic but kept her marriage secret from her parents for years. She could relinquish neither her exogamous relationship nor her closeness to her parents, so she clung to both, living with a man who represented "the enemy," loving him, and presenting a duplicitous facade of singlehood to her beloved parents.

In other Jewish families the child who intermarries is the one the parents are most attuned to, the child whose behavior registers the family's emotional weather, or who is more important to the emotional balance of the parents' relationship.[14] Perhaps this child is the one who picks up more acutely on the parents' or his or her own ambivalence about being Jewish in the modern world.

Or, in an emotionally charged family environment, such children may confuse "feelings about their ethnicity with feelings about their family."[15] According to Edwin Friedman, an expert on Jewish family systems, "No Jew today can distinguish what is Jewish about his family and what is family about his family."[16]

The dynamic of simultaneously wanting intimacy and distance may be the motivation for some Jews who are drawn to intermarriage. Living as a partner in an interfaith family can allow the Jew to identify as a Jew as strongly as he or she wants while at the same time affirming a sense of universality or asserting membership in a larger humanity, a larger "family," thus relieving some of the pressure in the relationship with the birth family.

While the dynamic for the Jewish partner in an interfaith relationship involves some tension between moving "out" and staying "in," the majority of the Christian partners interviewed had some doubleness in their own lives—their own parents had often been intermarried, though usually within the Christian fold: Lutherans had married Episcopalians, Polish Catholics had married French-Canadian Catholics, Baptists had married Unitarians, Catholics had married Methodists. Although the general religious heterogeneity of Christendom had made these marriages possible, most had certainly involved the resolution of certain religious differences—or, in many cases, had required a resolve to live with the differences unmitigated by compromise. Perhaps today's Christian partners in Christian-Jewish marriages are just looking farther afield to replicate something of their own parents' marital situations.

For whatever reasons, the Christians who marry Jews "seem most often to be individuals who are generally uncommitted to and uninvolved with their own religious backgrounds."[17] In addition to not having strong positive feelings toward their own religion, Christian partners do not have the strong negative feelings toward Jews that might, in another time, have made them averse to marrying a Jew. The anti-Semitism that was a factor in keeping Jews out of mainstream Western society until the Enlightenment has been replaced in some circles by a philo-Semitism.[18] In part, the reasons for this shift can be laid at the feet of theology itself, and in part they stem from a rising interest in ethnicity in general. When Vatican II declared in the 1960s that Jews were not to be held responsible for the death of Christ, this paved the way for a reevaluation of Catholic-Jewish relations and opened the possibil-

tions for their own careers than do males.[26] Thus there is likely to be less opprobrium cast on an underachieving Jewish woman (entailing less lowering of her self-esteem), and therefore less likelihood that she will marry out because of feelings of alienation and deviance brought on by not having a college or graduate degree.

Being a functioning male in a Jewish context must feel a burden to those who are uneducated or, in some communities, religiously naive. Judaism is a culture which traditionally has emphasized learning, particularly for men. A religion that has located much ritual in the home requires its lay practitioners (traditionally men) to be fairly expert, or at least competent. Unlike Catholicism, for example, in which religious leaders or specially trained laity perform the religious rituals, Judaism requires a degree of active participation from all—at a minimum, leading a Passover seder and saying Sabbath blessings. One needs to be familiar enough, competent enough, and confident enough to perform these blessings or rituals in front of others. For Jews who feel uneasy about their skills it may be easier to opt out and not have to be the competent male in a Jewish household. Not all men who have these anxieties choose to intermarry—some just sit back and have other family members do the tasks. But there is an additional burden on underachieving Jewish men that isn't there for their Christian counterparts for whom, if any religious expression is required of them at all, might be no more than saying a grace before meals (and in their own language, too).

As the American Jewish community changes, and as "normative" Jewish life changes—for example, it is now "normative" for American Jews to have graduate degrees—so, too, will the explanations of what "causes" intermarriage. But what does seem clear is that Jews with low self-esteem may not feel entitled to marry another Jew. "The concentration of young Jews in high educational levels places the least educated in a smaller marriage market. . . . Hence, the choice among the least educated is to face a very limited Jewish marriage market of equal educational level, not to marry, or to marry out. In this context, it is not surprising that the least educated have the most accepting attitudes toward intermarriage."[27] In some communities they may find more easy acceptance by non-Jews of the opposite sex. Inverting the common remarriage pattern, for these people a first marriage may be to a non-Jew; later, with more confidence and maturity, they may

27

marry Jews. A Florida woman who has observed this phenomenon in several families said that her own daughter was first married to a "blue-collar non-Jewish motorcyclist. Her second marriage was to a Jewish attorney. She felt more self-confident by that time, and then she could marry a Jew."

Whether we are talking about a Jewish man who felt as a child that he didn't belong because his parents belonged to no synagogue in a town where every other Jew was affiliated, or whether we are looking at a Jewish woman who feels marginal because at the age of thirty-nine she is still single in a community that trumpets marriage and child rearing as paramount values, we are seeing people who are readier to consider including non-Jews in their field of eligibles because they may not feel totally accepted or acceptable by whatever passes for "the" Jewish community. (Parallel findings come from Rabbi Elyse Goldstein, who has worked with deaf congregants, and who states that because of their alienation from a Jewish community that has largely ignored their needs, "intermarriage runs excessively high" among deaf Jews.[28]) "Deviance tends to come in clusters," says Rabbi Mark Winer, so that if someone feels unlike the norm because of one characteristic—deafness or prolonged singlehood, for example—that person is more likely to consider other forms of deviant behavior, such as intermarriage.[29]

The question of why someone chooses as a mate a person of different background or culture pertains not only to intermarriage, but to marital choices in general. A European-born child of Holocaust survivors married an American Jew from the Far West. This, too, is an intermarriage of sorts. A Canadian Jew raised in a WASP-like, Anglophile home married a Brooklyn-born Jew whose style is quintessentially "ethnic New York." For each of these couples there was a draw, an appeal that came from the sweet combination of flavors—like and unlike all at once. Some of the same dynamic is at work in an interfaith marriage, with attraction based in part on similarities, with the added seasoning of differences. People who choose marital partners not of their own religious or ethnic backgrounds must have a high tolerance for diversity, believing, as the mother of one intermarried woman put it, "Just because it's different doesn't mean it has to be wrong." In the light of today's evidence that intermarrieds had friendship and dating circles that often included members of other religious groups, and that they moved in professional and academic circles that were not restricted to members of their own group, the earlier explanation for intermarriage based on Jews' desire to pass into the larger world is outdated. Most Jews are already in that larger world. Their acculturation may provide the opportunity to meet and mate with non-Jews, making it a cause rather than an effect of intermarriage. Thus, intermarriage today results from both the individual's willingness and the larger society's acceptance.

## 3

# Jewish Women and Jewish Men: What's Going On?

All Jewish men are on such a head trip. I want somebody who's not afraid that there are bones in the fish, and who's not going to make a rag out of me with his demands that I take care of him.

*—Forty-year-old Jewish woman, recently divorced from her Jewish husband*

A Jewish couple goes out on a dinner date. He looks at the menu and says, "I'm not sure I know what I'll order." She: "Why don't you order the chicken?" He: "What right have you got telling me what I should be eating for dinner? You want to control everything in my entire life, don't you?"

*—Couple recreating a scene demonstrating "how awful" Jewish partners are*

If I'm at a party for Jewish singles and some guy asks me where I live, or what I do, I tell him he's really out of place to be asking those kinds of questions at this stage. Let him chat with me and get to know me and then he'll come to my house and see for himself. Jewish men have such high expectations of what other Jews should be doing for a living that everybody who isn't a professional feels like a freak. I feel much more comfortable with some of the plain working-class non-Jewish guys I know than with Jews, but I keep going to these things anyway because I always assumed I'd marry a Jewish man.

*—Woman at a workshop for Jewish singles at a Brooklyn YM/YWHA*

While no one would cite the negative views some Jewish women and men have of one another as the only explanation for the increasing incidence of interfaith marriages among Jews, there is some connection. The fact that Jewish women and men often see one another in limiting, stereotypical ways certainly gets in the way of their forming romantic relationships within their own group, and may foster their attraction toward non-Jews. At the very least, the stereotypes prevent many Jewish women and men from including Jews in their "field of eligibles." The Jewish college students who claim that they want to marry Jews but don't want to date Jews are effectively limiting their potential marriage partners because of prejudice against their own group and a concomitant inability to see other Jews as individuals rather than as "types." The diversity of the human experience gets lost in the stereotyping. In some sense this parallels the stereotyped views Jews had of Christians and vice versa—stereotypes that limited intermarriage in earlier generations. Now, ironically, the stereotypes are more solidly entrenched within the group, and may act as a spur rather than an impediment to intermarriage. Understanding how the stereotypes of Jewish women and men arose can give us a sense of the forces that have shaped Jews' views of themselves (as well as of other Jews). Examining the ways Jewish men and women see each other helps clarify some of the dynamics between the partners in an interfaith couple as well, because—ironically—the characteristics that Jewish men decry in Jewish women are the very ones Christian men often say they find appealing.

Few Jews marry out today because they want to reject entirely the fact that they're Jewish; nevertheless, certain traces of Jewish self-hatred or discomfort remain. What has changed is that Jewish men no longer say that they want to reject Judaism's institutions and practices. (Some Jews actually become more religious when married to a Christian than they would have been had they married a nonreligious or turned-off Jew). Rather, Jewish men are claiming—with the assistance of the stereotypes—that it's Jewish women who turn them off, not Judaism itself.

In fact, Jewish women and men both report seeing each other as pursued by their own special, stereotypical demons—Jewish men preoccupied with their drive to achieve while being haunted by a corrosive fear of failure, their legacy from a historical past that for centuries closed off many avenues to "success"[1]; Jewish women walking a tightrope between making something of themselves as individuals while trying to live up to expectations that they'll be nothing less than perfect wives and mothers as well. Their absorption with these personal struggles gets translated into Jewish American prince and princess stereotypes—or worse.

Surveys of Jewish high school and college students give evidence of an increasingly open attitude toward intermarriage, though accompanied by guarded, ambivalent, and downright negative feelings about Jewish partners.[2] Most of the students questioned expect to marry and raise Jewish families, yet 85 percent of them consider interfaith dating perfectly acceptable. Some of them say that while maintaining a Jewish identity is important and so is their desire to marry, these factors don't necessarily mean marrying a Jew. Several who said that they would consider an interfaith marriage invoked the stereotype of the "Jewish prince" or "Jewish princess" in defending the acceptability of non-Jewish marriage partners. Demonstrating his own fears of encountering a woman whose needs he might not be able to meet, one young man commented, "Finding a 'nice Jewish girl' is a good idea, if you can find one who will settle for someone who is *not* a doctor, lawyer, dentist, etc. If you can find a mate who understands that a relationship between two human beings who love each other is more important than money or social status, you have a rare person. Far too many JAPs want beautiful homes instead of loving mates."[3] And a middle-aged woman asked, at a discussion group on women's issues in Jewish life, "What can I do? My daughter is twenty-nine and doing fabulously in her law firm. She's bright and nice and attractive. So where are all the nice Jewish men who are her peers and who should be pursuing her? Are they so threatened by the idea of an intelligent, independent woman?" In the same audience another woman got up to announce that her teenage son "refuses to take out Jewish girls. He says 'They're all a bunch of demanding princesses.' " What *is* going on? *Are* Jewish women and men substantially different from their non-Jewish counterparts?

In some respects, they are. While Jewish women, particularly those active in the contemporary women's movement, would be quick to point out that they make common cause with all women on a whole range of issues loosely constituting the "women's agenda," it is also true that Jewish women have grown up in North America today with a confusion and stress peculiar to their

own cultural and religious backgrounds. Along with their brothers they receive the conditioning associated with Jewish upward
mobility and success—with "making something" of themselves,
with striving for excellence in whatever they set out to do. As the
daughters of the "People of the Book," they are the best-
educated women in America today, attending college and graduate school at a rate that far exceeds their presence in the general
population. But they also receive a unique and sometimes crippling double message along with the achievement-oriented conditioning. This message reads: "Be smart, but not too smart.
Don't educate yourself out of the marriage market"—as if marriage were a job for which one could ever be overqualified!

The career aspirations of many Jewish women are seen by even
the proudest parents as potentially imperiling their chances for
marital bliss. Judaism typically has had no place for the single
woman. There is no religious counterpart to the Catholic nun's
state of "single blessedness," celibate and spiritually elevated,
or any social counterpart to the Protestant bluestocking spinster,
solitary and intellectual. Judaism, as both religion and culture,
has a strong tropism toward marriage as the appropriate state of
completeness for women and men. (There is also no tradition of
swinging male singlehood.) And while males typically become
more marriageable with increasing age and education, women
close out some of their marriage options with each passing year,
at least as long as men tend to marry women who are younger
and less well educated than they are. Anything that challenges a
woman's chances for marriage and motherhood—such as years of
higher education or career preparation—is seen, even by Jewish
parents who are themselves well educated, as a danger they want
to help their daughters avoid.

This means that Jewish women, strongly encouraged both to
achieve *and* to marry, have profoundly ambivalent feelings
toward their own bifurcated goals. The dichotomy may be a false
one, but many women experience it as their reality. In a startling
cross-cultural study of Italian American, Slavic American, and
Jewish American women, the Jewish women came out more
strongly than the other women in favor of being married, having
children, and staying home with those children in their preschool
years—a fairly old-fashioned women's agenda.[4] Paradoxically, the
Jewish women in this study also came out most strongly in favor
of what might be termed a feminist agenda—that women should

be able to achieve whatever they desire professionally and have no barriers to their education or career advancement. Many Jewish women believe they should be "having it all."

We also know, from another study comparing them to non-Jewish women, that Jewish women are significantly less likely to believe that women are happiest when making a home and caring for children.[5] Wanting "it all" doesn't necessarily mean liking it all equally well, and some of the conflicts Jewish women express (and Jewish men are aware of) surely come from the unresolved tensions between the yearning to take off on a career trajectory and the nagging feeling that life will be incomplete if that career path bypasses family life. One woman reacted this way:

> Twenty years ago, when my husband—who's Jewish—would discuss the claims some of his Jewish college friends made that the Jewish women they were dating were "more complicated" and "more trouble" than non-Jewish women, I told him that this was just another way of stereotyping Jewish women. Now that I've seen the emerging social-scientific data comparing the two groups, I'm beginning to see the truth behind some of the reactions of those college men. We really *do* seem to have more to deal with, and unrealistic expectations of how we'll deal with it.

The double message Jewish females receive does cause them greater conflict and inner turmoil. A radio broadcaster, a woman raised in an Italian Catholic family, referred to this difference when, in an on-the-air discussion of this issue, she compared the mothers of her Jewish and Gentile college classmates: "When I was in college in the seventies, my mother and the mothers of my non-Jewish friends would call up and ask, 'How are your classes? Are you getting good grades? Are the courses hard?' The mothers of my *Jewish* friends would call and ask, 'How's your social life? Have you met any nice Jewish boys yet?'" The college experience for non-Jewish women seems to be accepted on its own terms—as an educational venture—by their mothers, while the Jewish mothers strongly suggest that their daughters need to balance their learning with "social life." Perhaps each mother inquires about the area causing her the greatest anxiety.

And what about Jewish men? The strong message that young Jewish men receive—that their personal worth will be measured only by what they achieve in academic or professional life—often causes them to be career-focused and achievement-oriented to the exclusion of qualities of loving expansiveness and thoughtful concern for those around them that facilitate successful relationships. A series of programs for single Jewish women and men at New York City's Lincoln Square Synagogue, an institution known for its matchmaking efforts among Jews, actually offers instruction on "intimacy." Although Jewish men are not necessarily so different from Christian men in their devotion to professional or business goals (sometimes at the expense of their relationships), as members of a minority group who have learned since childhood that the only reliable way to succeed in the outside world is through visible achievement, their anxieties over not succeeding may be substantially greater than those of Christians.

One woman said that if "Jewish men could only get beyond their own needs" they would be more appealing as true marriage partners rather than merely as providers of income or status (what the male Jewish college student complained was all Jewish women seemed to care about in a mate). The downside risk of this success orientation is, of course, a crippling fear of failure. An exhilarating striving to perform well in one's work can degenerate (as in sexual "performance anxiety") into a lifelong struggle against the fear of failure. Not only is this fear read by Jewish women as a sign of weakness, but also chronic anxiety is not noted for its appeal or charm.

A Jewish woman in her middle thirties, divorced from a Jewish man and now living with a non-Jew, put it this way:

> My husband always made me more anxious in every situation than I needed to be. I'll never forget losing my pocketbook once. Instead of comforting me as I was frantically trying to put my life together again, replacing credit cards, cancelling bank accounts, replacing locks on the doors, and all of that, he just kept making me feel worse, telling me what a fool I was not to have been more careful and harping on how much he'd had to suffer as a result of my disaster.
>
> In comparison, my non-Jewish boyfriend, even if there's bad news to impart, or we're dealing with a crisis of some sort, always takes into account how I'll feel and tries to make things easier on me, not harder. My nervousness or worries seem to be the trigger for him to take on a nurturing role. It's

funny—I sometimes think that my boyfriend takes the same role with me—trying to keep me less anxious, for example— that I took with my ex-husband. My husband was so insecure—like many overprotected Jewish men, I think—that he was terribly threatened if something went wrong or if I showed any weakness or needed emotional support. Any dependency on my part made him angry, but he didn't want me too independent either.

Jewish men *have* been insecure throughout history, for obvious reasons. Even in the twentieth century, minority status still has a residual effect, and they may be more easily thrown into a state of disequilibrium than other men. Because of these historical realities, Jewish men may have lost a sense of responsibility for their own lives, their own fates. Maintaining equilibrium may indeed be outside their own control—which may explain the higher anxiety levels reported by Jewish men. This is added to the verbal expressiveness of Jews as a whole. Not only do they often feel more anxious, but they also talk about it more.

In popular American culture, nervous anxiety or an uneasiness about one's own worth gets translated not into the fascinating and attractive *Weltschmerz* of nineteenth-century Vienna (for example), but into a nebbishy Woody Allen–like neurotic dependency or helplessness—which is not particularly erotic or attractive except to those with overdeveloped maternal instincts. But perhaps that is part of what is going wrong with Jewish women and men, say the pop psychologists: Jewish women baby their men— husbands or sons—thinking them too weak to make it in the adult world of reality. While this approach sounds like another way of blaming women (this time the Jewish mother) for the inadequacies of men, it probably derives from the fact that historically— certainly in the small villages of Eastern Europe from which came the ancestors of most North American Jews—Jewish women were the active partners in the marriage, often earning money and seeing to all the material needs of the family while the Jewish men studied holy texts.

The daughters of strong, articulate working mothers of the immigrant generation were expected to conform to a Victorian-lady model of behavior quite unlike that of any of their role models. Especially after prosperity came to many American Jewish men, they wanted their wives out of the work force and in their new suburban homes. A similar change took place in the lives of non-Jewish women, but no other group suffered so great a discontinuity between past realities (woman as chief breadwinner, as emotional pillar of the household, as the strong parent) and current expectations (passivity, silence, "femininity," and of course being "emotionally appropriate"). Black women, for example, have had strong role models in working women and see themselves as having strength, despite the fact that they are often derogated by black men using the term "sapphires"—connoting a woman who isn't supportive "enough" of her man. (It's never "enough"—in any culture!)

Jewish women suffered a peculiar confusion because of this change. Though many adapted successfully to new realities, it must have been difficult for women whose mothers and grandmothers had seen themselves as powerful, instrumental figures to find themselves suddenly making decisions of no more consequence that what shade of carpeting to order for the family dwelling. As a result, many middle-class Jewish women, for whom paid work would have been considered an insult to their husbands' God-given right to supremacy as breadwinners, threw themselves into family life with all the energy that previous generations of women had divided among paid work, social activism, *and* family responsibilities. And while Sophie Portnoy's concern for her son might be viewed as extreme, it is different only in degree from the concern for which generations of Jewish mothers had been *praised* rather than denounced—namely, that of protecting their children from harm and trying to ensure for them a safe and healthy future. Characteristics that in the past were valued are suddenly, in the space of a single generation, denigrated. Similarly, in a world increasingly populated by jocks and joggers, Jewish men's traditionally cerebral qualities are vulnerable to attack as "head trips."

Despite the stereotyping, however, Jewish women probably had an easier time making the transition to life in America than did Jewish men. They had had multiple roles in the Old World (workers, parents, participants in extended family and community networks), and they had really experienced some sense of instrumentality and power in these situations. Only the synagogue was exclusively male turf. Many of these women operated more successfully in the real world than did their husbands, fathers, or brothers—prompting a whole spate of images in Jewish children's literature of the grandfather as the impractical dreamer and the grandmother as the hardheaded down-to-earth figure.[6]

Perhaps the current baiting of, and expressions of unhappiness with, one another (and the projection of a person's own negative feelings about Jewishness onto Jewish members of the opposite sex) are some of the penalties of Jews' hard-won mainstreaming into American life. The toll of decades of oppression and minority-group uncertainties in the Old World and the New has meant that Jewish women and men may not even see each other as sexually attractive. (For verification, we need look only to such films as *The Heartbreak Kid,* in which Brooklyn male abandons Brooklyn female on their honeymoon in Miami in order to run off with leggy Minnesota blond female, or *Over the Brooklyn Bridge,* in which Brooklyn Jewish male rejects ludicrous and comically exaggerated Brooklyn Jewish female to enter the shower stall and propose marriage to Manhattan blond Protestant female.) Jews think uneasy things about themselves as Jews, likely to see themselves as weak and ineffectual if they are male or as brash, pushy, intrusive, and too outspoken if they are female.

Jewish women seem to deal with feelings of uneasiness or insecurity—about appearing shorter or fatter or darker or hairier or clumsier than the general image of American female pulchritude—not by retreating or by dependency but by self-aggrandizement and self-adornment. The "princess" mystique suggests that the true prototypical Jewish American princess won't even go to the supermarket without diamond earrings and designer handbag. Why? Because in a certain bourgeois social stratum, American Jewish women learned to feel better about themselves by dressing up or tried to feel better about themselves by striving for perfection in self-presentation, which extended to the presentation of house and children as well.

When the majority culture strongly suggests that "attractive" means being a tall, slender blond or a Redford clone, women and men who do not fit this image (as most Jews—like most people in general—do not) may doubt their own attractiveness. In *Parachutes and Kisses,* Erica Jong fantasizes about a TV game show she calls "Shiksamania . . . in which Jewish guys had to vie . . . in singing the praises of their resident *shiksas* . . . competing in describing their ladyloves' excellent *shiksa*-like qualities—ski jump Draw-Me-girl noses, perfectly conical breasts, small waists, high, firm asses. The mirror image of this show would be called

Shaygets-o-Rama, in which two Jewish girls would appear with their *shkotzim.*"[7]

Interestingly, the selfsame qualities that many Jewish men say they find unappealing in their Jewish female cohorts—that they express their complicated feelings openly, become directly involved in the lives of those around them, and feel the need to operate in arenas beyond the household and family—are often considered attractive by non-Jewish men. One Jewish man accused the Jewish women he dates of "mother fixation, bossiness, telephone abuse, and overindulgence of children." Referring to the same behavior, a non-Jew married to a Jewish women said, "My family really appreciates her constant communication, her warmth, the fact that she expresses herself so openly." The independence that non-Jewish men value in their Jewish wives is the opposite of the stereotype of the "good" Christian wife, passive and deferential to her husband in every respect. Perhaps, in fact, it is this deference that Jewish men miss. Whether they'll get it from non-Jewish women is, of course, not certain; but one Jewish man claimed that "shiksas look up to their men." In a parallel development, what Jewish women see as weakness or self-absorption in Jewish men is what many non-Jewish women admire as openness and a willingness to expose their feelings to scrutiny.

Historically, oppressed groups turn violence, even verbal violence, inward. And since words are the weapons of the Jews, strong feelings get expressed in even stronger words. An Irish American psychotherapist confessed that she was terrified, early in her practice, by the overt and expressive sexual warfare—in which stereotyping is certainly a weapon—between Jewish spouses who came to her for treatment. Materialistic and self-centered people exist in every religious and ethnic group, but Jews have made a fine art of criticizing and excoriating Jewish women on these grounds—a further manifestation of the problem of being a minority in a culture that has often scorned them. For example, a poster popular in the late 1970s entitled "The JAP" showed a woman in designer jeans, credit cards spilling out of her pockets. She was wearing diamond earrings and smoking a long cigarette. Beside the earrings appeared the line, "These were a present from Daddy when I stopped smoking." Next to the cigarette: "Don't tell Daddy. . . . " If the same characteristics had been used to describe all Jews, the duplicity, manipulation, and rampant acquisitiveness implied by the poster would be reminiscent of the notorious *Protocols of the Elders of Zion* or the more current paranoid delusions that Jews control the economy and the press. But maligning Jewish *women* has become a convenient smokescreen for masking the self-hatred of Jews themselves, matching a more generalized anti-Semitism.

Incidents of harassment of Jewish women on college campuses in the mid- and late 1980s demonstrated that popular attitudes toward Jewish women have grown nastier. On one campus, any well-dressed woman standing up at her seat during a sports event could be fingered by the official cheering squad, which would then point up at her and start chanting "JAP, JAP, JAP"—a cry then picked up by the whole stadium. At another college, Jewish fraternities sold "slap-a-JAP" T-shirts and built cardboard caricatures of Jewish women for passers-by to hurl sponges at. Documentation of library and dormitory graffiti made the pattern clear: from "all Jewish girls are JAPS," to sexually aggressive and violent comments about Jewish women, to "Hitler didn't do enough."[8] The connection had been made in the minds of many non-Jewish students: Jewish women are fair game for Jewish men to deride, therefore they are fair game for non-Jews. The stereotyping of Jewish women by Jewish men gives non-Jews permission to express both the stereotypes and any latent anti-Semitism they may feel.

The fallout for relations between Jewish women and Jewish men was clear. Jewish men, who should have been the women's natural allies in protesting essentially anti-Semitic and misogynistic images in the media and in social situations were, in fact, part of the enemy camp. As a way of distancing themselves from characteristics that non-Jews used to think described all Jews (aggressive, acquisitive, self-serving), Jewish men have often projected these same characteristics onto Jewish women—and then walked away from them.

A question frequently asked about this stereotyping has to do with the "kernel of truth" theory. The best reply to the question, "Aren't there really Jewish women like that?" is, "Jewish women alone do not keep Bloomingdale's in business." Jewish women—whether as "Jewish mothers" concerned with their children's well-being or as "princesses" who want "the best" for themselves—are only doing what all American women are told to do. A line of greeting cards featuring an unattractive, caricatured

Jewish woman—fat lips, buggy eyes, kinky hair, ill-fitting clothes, and a Jewish star around her neck—has almost the identical punch line as a parallel card featuring an understated and highly attractive Yuppie female. The line inside the card is, "Shop the clearance sales." The point is that all women get the message that they should look good, be smart, have it all. Only Jewish women are mocked and derided and caricatured for living this out. The stereotype (originated by Jewish men but picked up by the culture as a whole) diminishes Jewish women's self-esteem, affects their willingness to identify as Jews (who wants to be part of a group seen in such a negative light?), and affects relationships between Jewish women and Jewish men.

The sex jokes about Jewish women accuse them of promiscuity before marriage and frigidity after ("How to get a Jewish women to stop screwing? Marry her?"). Their selfishness and lack of sexual responsiveness are so much a part of Jewish men's sexual references ("Why does a Jewish woman make love with her eyes closed? Because she can't stand to see anyone else having a good time"; "In a *coma*? I thought she was Jewish!") that *Playboy* can (and did) run a cartoon showing three sexes: male, female, and Jewish woman. This view is an odd distortion of the anti-Semitic perception that Jews (women included) possess a "special" sexuality—a projection often made onto people viewed as inferior.[9]

Why, then, despite the facts, do Jewish men persist in claiming that Jewish women are sluts until marriage and prudes afterwards? First, to "excuse" male interfaith dating and marriage. Second, because stereotypes and myths of this sort serve a very useful purpose in keeping people in line. In this case the object is to "correct" Jewish women in an orthodontic sort of way so that they will gradually transform themselves into quintessentially "American" females—"cooled out" mirrors for male narcissism.

Christian women who convert to Judaism are not immune from the stereotyping either; they, too, are painted with this very broad brush. A woman in Hawaii said, "I'm a fairly new—two and a half years—Jew by choice and had to put up with JAP jokes and veiled anti-Semitism from the time I made my choice public. One 'friend' even gifted me with a 'JAP' tape—the life of little Judy-Ann Perlman, whose first words were 'goo-goo ga-ga Master Card.'"

While Jewish men often insult or at least diminish Jewish

women (even in public, even on late-night television), Jewish women are heard to declare that Jewish men all want to be coddled as their mothers coddled them. One woman, a professor, single and in her thirties, shouted, "Don't ever talk to me about the Jewish princess. What about the Jewish *prince?* I should know—I've been fixed up with him about twenty times!" The image here is that the Jewish man is likely to be more demanding and less accepting of a prospective spouse's career goals (perhaps because he wants her around the house to meet *his* needs).

Jewish men, too, are burdened by American society's ideals of what constitutes the desirable man. A checklist in a popular women's magazine on "What makes a man attractive?" listed certain qualities definitely *not* in the arsenal of the prototypical American Jewish male, among them: handy around the house, independent, emotionally unflappable. Among Jews, intelligence was traditionally the key factor in men; competence, practicality, a certain skill in negotiating the real world, was supposed to be alluring in women. (See, for example, the exemplary qualities in the verse from Proverbs 31:10-31 for which a Jewish man is supposed to praise his wife every Sabbath eve: she gives charity, deals in real estate, knows how to manage her affairs.) As Jews assimilated into American life, Jewish men and women had opportunities to reevaluate what they found attractive in dates or mates, finding desirable only the latest models of male or female. Given the sexual hostilities between Jewish men and Jewish women, the increasing acceptability of involvements with men or women of another faith, and the unattractive media images of Jews, the question may be not why there are so many intermarriages, but rather why there are so few.

Why has the rate of *in*marriage remained as high as it is? When virtually any Jew who chooses to can marry a non-Jew, why do about three in five Jews still marry other Jews? Considering demographics in isolation, one might conclude that, once the field of prospective spouses has widened as much as it has, in time all Jews will marry out. The in-group attraction of the past (the centripetal force) is then explained as simple self-delusion: Both male and female Jews, having no other choices, convinced themselves that they were satisfied with the only mates available to them. The trouble with this explanation is that it fails to account for the powerful attraction of familiarity and solidarity for some women and men. There are Jews, both female and male, who say that they have never been attracted to non-Jewish partners. One woman likened it to eating nonkosher food. "I am not the slightest bit religious now, but I feel about interdating and intermarriage the same way I would about eating shrimp. I know it's probably irrational, but I was brought up believing that shrimp is yucky and disgusting, and no force on earth can now change my mind. It's not that I find my friendships with non-Jews unpleasant, but the idea of marrying one is just totally alien to me on some visceral level."

The early psychoanalytic explanations of intermarriage hypothesized that people marry out because marriage to someone of their own group would feel too much like incest. Some Jews, like the woman just quoted, find the instant intimacy of "like" more appealing than the differences she might experience with a non-Jewish man she would characterize as "other." Jewish partners would usually be more familiar with one another's cultural matrix, and that can have its own allure—making some relationships within the group even more appealing simply because they do represent the known, the warmth, the unconditional acceptance that many Jewish children recall from their own families. Yet, by the same token, the familial resonance in a couple in which both partners are Jewish can call forth a replaying of the "boundary disputes" all too familiar from childhood. The male claims his date or spouse is too intrusive (like the stereotypical Jewish mother), while the female says that he, like "all" Jewish men, is trying to keep her dependent the way Daddy wanted to. All potential Jewish partners become identified with Mommy or Daddy, and while it can be complicated and painful to move away from Mommy and Daddy, it is not so hard to reject their substitutes.

As we examine a rejectionist explanation for intermarriage, we have to understand that Jewish women have had different familial experiences from Jewish men and therefore have different familial emotions as adults. Since Jewish men have usually had more unconditionally loving and supportive childhood experiences at home than Jewish women, the women may be more prone to marrying out in the long run, once other social inhibitors disappear. Girls growing up in Jewish families report conflict with their parents over every issue from career goals to choice of friends, whereas Jewish men often confess, as a forty-year-old doctor did, "The worst thing my mother ever did to me was that she never told me the rest of the world wouldn't treat me as well as she had!'' According to a stereotypical joke on this subject, a man walks for blocks in a raging blizzard to buy two rolls at a distant bakery. The baker asks: ''Did your *wife* send you out on a night like this?'' The man replies: ''Would my *mother* send me out on a night like this?' ''

Although they may sometimes seek one another out as representatives of a remembered warm and happy past, Jewish women and men must also reckon with the fact that each may find the other spoiled and demanding. Since Jewish families have always had fewer children than the national norm (in every country, in every time), most contemporary Jews were raised with only one sibling, two at most. Jewish parents have thus had more time, energy, and money to devote to the children that they do have. Couple this with the Jewish family's tendency toward liberal child-rearing practices and strong child-centrism, and we see why Jewish women and men accuse each other of ''prince-'' or ''princesslike'' behavior, and why each may at some stage find non-Jews less demanding as partners and such partnerships hence less stressful than relationships with other Jews.

A further source of stress between Jewish women and men may derive from the misleading notion (among Jews and some Christians) that Jewish men make the best husbands. The implication for Jewish women is that they are lucky to have a chance at this magnificent marriage material. (Even non-Jewish women have accepted this image, giving rise to books with such titles as *The Shiksa's Guide to Jewish Men.*) In fact, non-Jewish men are just as likely to turn out to be loving, egalitarian spouses—or utter cads—as their Jewish peers, but the existence of this image of perfection puts Jewish women at a distinct disadvantage.

Also pertinent to the Jewish battle of the sexes may be the resentment some women express about growing up in families in which a brother's birth is marked by a *brith* (ritual circumcision) and his coming of age by a bar mitzvah, while any signs of his intellectual prowess are greeted with general and unambivalent rejoicing. Until ten or fifteen years ago, parallel ritual and emotional validation for females was not automatically provided.

All these features of family background and adult conflict provide the backdrop against which Jewish women and men can and do act out the negative feelings they have about one another. We see that for some exogamous or prospectively exogamous Jews

45

the choice of a non-Jewish mate is not neutral. It is, in fact, often fueled by overt or unconscious feelings of anger, hostility, or uneasiness toward Jews of the opposite sex. Indeed, there appear to be built-in conflicts between Jewish women and Jewish men that drive them away from one another as prospective marriage partners. A thirty-year-old Jewish doctor, describing his ideal date, said: "My mother is so emotional and irrational that she makes me crazy. I really want a woman who's going to be emotionally appropriate. I guess in my case this excludes Jewish women." In three sentences this man blamed his mother for his consistent attraction to non-Jewish women (not for the usual oedipal reasons, either) and generalized that *all* Jewish women would fail to be emotionally "appropriate."

The term *neurotic exogamy*—marrying out for neurotic reasons—was first coined in 1913 to describe a phenomenon in which "a man experiences an insuperable aversion to any close relationship with a woman of his own people or nation. Or, to put it more correctly, of his mother's people."[10] The unmarried Jewish doctor said that he disliked the emotional dependency of the Jewish women he met. In addition to his own projections, he may have been responding to the women's "messages" about the emotional closeness and rapport that many Jewish women say they expect in a husband or future mate.

Jewish couples have historically followed more of a partnership model than other couples. (As basic a document as the Talmud enjoins wife and husband to talk to one another.) A 1969 collection of interviews entitled *The Jewish Wife*[11] noted that Jewish husbands talked more and shared more of their work lives with their wives than did non-Jewish men. More recently, a cross-cultural study of women of diverse ethnic backgrounds concluded that Jewish women *do* have different expectations of their husbands; while most non-Jewish women said, "My best friend is my best friend," the Jewish women were more likely to respond, "My husband is my best friend."[12]

Perhaps that young single doctor looking for someone "emotionally appropriate" wanted more distance from his ideal marriage partner than he felt he would be likely to get with a Jewish woman. Perhaps he was already so absorbed in his work and its goals that he avoided relationships that might make their own set of demands on him. This consequence of careerism doesn't belong exclusively to Jewish males but to high-achieving men in general, in whose ranks Jewish men are overrepresented. What does appear to be peculiar to Jewish men is their readiness to condemn their own mothers and, through a guilt-by-association maneuver, all Jewish women. There's no parallel body of writing or joking about, for example, Italian mothers. Even on TV commercials the Italian mother is a benign stock character, at worst, never tinged with the malign intentions ascribed to so many Jewish mothers. She may appear to be a bit old-fashioned, but her children really do appear to love her spaghetti sauce and, by extension, her. The Jewish mother has not fared so well. Another man (this time a lawyer), told his date when they were planning an afternoon drive, "Why did you suggest packing a lunch for us? You're like my neurotic Jewish mother—always worried that we won't eat." The man interpreted his date's friendly offer to prepare a picnic as a device for control that reminded him of his mother—and which was too close for comfort. Ethnotherapist Judith Weinstein Klein has conducted pioneering work on the negative qualities Jewish women and men project onto one another because of their own uneasiness with being Jewish.[13] About disputes like this one she says, "There's confusion where the line is so thin between *caring* and *controlling*. Jewish women have to be *so* careful."

Ironically, the Jewish mothers who are often cited by their sons as a powerful factor in choosing *not* to marry Jewish women are the ones most sensitive to the emotional issues they and their children face in an interfaith marriage. Social workers who lead groups for the parents of intermarried Jews point out that the mothers are usually the ones who have to deal with the emotional storms the other family members experience, because they are more tuned in to, and comfortable talking about, people's feelings.

Not only Jewish mothers but Jewish women in general are blamed for the defection of Jewish men through intermarriage. The women's liberation movement is sometimes cited as having made Jewish women too outspoken, hence less desirable as mates for Jewish men than are less assertive women. Jewish-Christian intermarriage can be seen as a women's issue in many ways. All Jewish women are held responsible when Jewish men intermarry, their "movement" is at least indirectly to blame when women do, and when a child of either sex marries out it's the Jewish mother who must sort out her own feelings of guilt and responsibility (for being "too controlling" or for "not making the house Jewish enough") and who is left to pick up the family's emotional pieces and fit them together again. Meanwhile, the younger, not-yet-marriageable generation of Jews is picking up on the anti-Semitic and misogynistic "Jewish American princess" stereotype (perhaps because we are in an era that is more materialistic than early 1970s, when journalists and others first tried to eradicate this particular image) and hurling the epithet around with great vigor and relish. This helps to establish an environment in which romantic and marital choices are not made freely but in reaction to hostile feelings about one's own group. Judith Weinstein Klein sounded a warning about these hostilities when she noted that for minority-group members, self-esteem and group pride are inextricable.[14] Those who feel uncomfortable or embarrassed about their ethnic group will of course have these feelings not only about themselves but also—perhaps especially— about group members of the opposite sex.

Calling a cease-fire in the hostilities between Jewish men and women might not have direct bearing on rates of intermarriage, but discussing the problem helps ensure that the mate selection process will not be overdetermined by negative traits Jewish men and women project onto one another. In addition, both partners in an interfaith relationship will benefit from exploring and understanding what qualities each is seeking—or avoiding—and the past experiences that have influenced those choices, for all of these concerns and experiences will play a part in their future relationship.

## 4

*Trying to Say . . .*

Consider for a moment the concept of religion as a language. Each of us was born of parents who spoke a particular language and passed this on. . . . So, too, many of us learned a religious language. I like this analogy because there is no judgment in the concept of language as a tool for communication. Those who have acquired several languages can converse with those who do not share their native speech. Also, there is a development in language just as in one's religious beliefs. For example, a preschooler has more limitations in language mastery than a college graduate, yet they speak the same language.

—*Nancy Kelly Kleiman in* Times and Seasons: A Jewish Perspective for Intermarried Couples

This statement was made by an ex-nun raising two Jewish sons with her husband, a Reform Jew. She is very clear about articulating her religious feelings, clear about their spiritual basis, clear about how she is able to transfer her specifically Catholic "language" into other terms. Most contemporary Jews lack this clarity.

A dialogue overheard between two Jewish women illustrates the difficult time so many Jews have in articulating even to themselves what Jewish identity means, never mind trying to relate it to a non-Jewish spouse or partner:

LEORA: What is it about being Jewish that matters to you, anyway?

DIANE: Well, I like the ritual, the music, the sense of social concern.

LEORA: Really? Boy, for music and ritual I'd much rather sit in a cathedral service any day. And I don't think the Jews have cornered the market on social justice.

DIANE: Maybe you're right. So then I can't really explain what I feel attached to in Judaism.

For a number of reasons, Jews, especially those in an interfaith marriage, have a very hard time both conceptualizing and expressing what Jewishness and Judaism mean to them, and why it is important to many of them that something of both be lived out in their homes and transmitted to their children. The difficulty is twofold, based partly on very real impediments Jews encounter when they seek to define themselves Jewishly, and partly on a reluctance to introduce a subject that might highlight differences between the partners and thus create conflict. But when someone who professes to be a Christian, or who identifies as a Christian, is asked what that identity or allegiance means, the answer is typically belief in "Christ as the Son of God." A one-time Christian who does not believe is unlikely to say "I am a Christian." A "lapsed Christian," a "nonbelieving Christian," perhaps. For Jews the explanations are more complex, more tortuous, more uncertain. The difficulty in giving a clear definition of what "Jewishness" is stems from many things, but the difficulty itself highlights the difference between a *belief*—for example, in Jesus Christ—and a sense of peoplehood with many varied *associations* that include culture, languages, religion, ethnicity, family, and more.

Some Jews, like some Christians, are uneasy about religion altogether. Pure rejection is one thing, but ambivalence is much harder for a spouse to deal with. Jews who are not themselves religiously observant may comment on religion only to say how atheistic they are or how little use they have for organized religion. Yet they often also want to maintain a connection to their own backgrounds. A woman bringing her concerns to a group of interfaith couples asked, "What do you do when the religious problem between you is not your religion versus his, but basically a person who is not a believer at all marrying someone who is?" This is a common issue, expressed most often by the Christian partner about the Jewish one; the Jew is sometimes reluctant to engage in any formal Jewish religious discussion or activity, but is even more reluctant when the Christian spouse wants the family to participate in Christian services.

"People think religion is a 'hot potato,'" said Reverend Richard Spalding, a Presbyterian minister at Boston's Church of the Covenant. "They believe you're safer if you stay away from it. Interfaith couples I've known who wanted to deal with it did it intellectually. But they shy away from any kind of practice." A Protestant woman whose Jewish husband always had nagging doubts about having committed some indefinable act of treason when he accompanied his wife to church said, "I have to remind my husband that he married a person, not an idea."

Many Jews stutter and stumble as they try to explain—to others and most of all to themselves—what it means to them to be Jewish in part because they may be ignorant about their own culture, since the majority culture teaches Christianity as the norm. For example, one Jewish woman interviewed had learned in high school all the fine distinctions between Martin Luther and John Calvin as shapers of early Protestantism, yet had no idea at all what Hasidism was, although she encountered members of this ultra-Orthodox sect each day in her own neighborhood. One has to go out of one's way to learn about Judaism—a hard task not only for non-Jews but also for those Jews whose own families were assimilated, ambivalent, or ignorant about religion.

Precisely because being Jewish is both a biological fact (for many born Jews, at least) *and* a way of life that can be chosen, by Jews and non-Jews, its meanings for—and pull on—the individuals involved need to be articulated, not merely assumed. Especially in determining which will be the dominant culture in an interfaith household, or which aspects of Jewishness will be retained in a bicultural, bireligious household, the Jewish partner needs to be able to be as explicit as his or her Christian counterpart. This is often difficult for the Jew because Judaism encompasses more diverse facets of experience than Christianity. It is an ethnic identity and a shared history, as well as a religion to be practiced and a theology to be studied.

Most Jews in North America are very well educated in secular realms. Yet for most, Jewish education stopped in early adolescence (at about thirteen, or the time of bar or bat mitzvah). Their talent in secular discourse (because Jews are among the best-educated people in the country today[1]) casts into sharp relief individuals' lack of knowledge on Jewish subjects and their inability to think through in a mature fashion what being Jewish means to them. They often lack the facts, the concepts, or the words, because Jewish learning has been absent during an important time for identity formation—adolescence. Millennia of anti-Semitism have contributed an added dimension to the Jew's difficulties in speaking about Jewishness. There is a layer of guilt—both existential and externally generated—that an oppressed minority feels when that minority identity won't conveniently disappear. Some people may actually feel guilty about still existing as Jews. Many Jews feel an uneasiness at some level about their minority status at the same time that they feel a pride in belonging to a people that has survived oppression and dispersion for so long.

Due to the legacy of the immigrant experience—namely that "too much" Jewishness would get in one's way in the New World (see Joan Micklin Silver's 1974 film *Hester Street* for a depiction)—many Jews alive today had parents who were profoundly uneasy about and even ashamed of being Jews. And many had themselves explicitly negative experiences with being Jewish. Some were beaten up or physically harassed or verbally abused by others. Some (especially boys) experienced acute discomfort around public rites of passage, notably bar mitzvah, where small, embarrassing lapses became magnified by memory or by others into large humiliations. Some encountered polite but pervasive anti-Semitism at elite educational institutions.[2] Thus pride and the shame of the oppressed are intermingled, creating a painful ambivalence: On the one hand many Jews would perhaps like to blend into the larger society, yet on a deeper level they want their distinctiveness recognized and maintained. To be Jewish indeed means on some level to be different. The *Aleinu* prayer, among other liturgical statements, chanted by religious Jews three times a day, gives thanks for that distinctiveness. According to the translation in the Conservative movement's daily prayerbook: "He made our lot unlike that of other peoples; /He assigned to us a unique destiny." Jews want to retain their identities yet be a part of the larger world, and for some an interfaith marriage provides the perfect opportunity to do so.

But Jews also want to be able to say what they are retaining and why. Even those who have had negative experiences *as Jews* see surfacing in themselves a desire to express at least some part of their Jewish identity. Interfaith couples report trying to come to grips with a paradox. Once Jews have asserted their separateness from the group (often via an interfaith relationship), they are able to explore more safely what their Jewish connections are.

The very common inability to say something clear about being Jewish is demonstrated in groups of interfaith couples where a discussion of these issues *is* the agenda. In just such a group in Brooklyn, one man, married to a non-Jew who is dedicated to raising their children as Jews, spoke for many when he said, "I don't see where I get the Jewishness from, although I do remember my grandmother kept a kosher corner in my parents' kitchen." Another Jewish man, married to a Catholic woman from the Philippines, mentioned with real puzzlement that being born Jewish meant little to him but that "having a child changes the equation. I want the child raised Jewish." He believes that "each of us has a right to be who we are" and at the same time expressed a desire "to belong, to identify with, something Jewish." He cast these two aspects of himself—being an individual and being a part of something larger—as if they were mutually exclusive, which of course they are not. Yet to him identifying as a Jew smacks of capitulating to something inauthentic. His reluctance to identify formally is so great that, although he went out of his way to make a financial contribution to a synagogue that was the equivalent of their membership fee, he would not "join." His ambivalence is not uncommon. Many Jewish partners in interfaith relationships say that they do not want any Jewish affiliation, they want to be individuals, they want, as one woman put it, "to get the community out of my bedroom," and yet they draw near to a Jewish context—often via intermarriage groups based in a synagogue or Jewish community center.

Intimacy in marriage (or in any relationship) depends in large measure on being known to and by one's partner. There is an exciting tension between unknown and known (popular sayings like "opposites attract"—reflect this assumption). Yet, while distance and difference have their dramatic appeal, in the end one also yearns for a degree of closeness. Not to be exactly *like* one's partner, but to have one's own self known and understood by him or her. One man interviewed reported an exchange with his wife: "How could you have bought me this gift?" he asked. In reply to her comment, "It's the thought that counts," he said. "That's precisely what I mean. How could you have thought that I would ever like something like this? I'm so hurt because of the thought, not because of the gift." This exchange tells us a lot about the nature of intimacy. He wanted to be *known* by his wife. Not that her tastes should match his, but that she should at least know them and respond to them.

Overcoming differences and creating intimacy in a marriage between any two people requires sharing information about feelings, past experiences, likes and dislikes. In an intermarriage, there is likely to be less common language, fewer common experiences and shared assumptions; therefore the partners have a greater need to be explicit in telling each other who they are. This may be difficult for people whose sense of themselves, especially along the religious axis, may be blurred or fraught with so much ambivalence as to make the telling especially hard. For example, when asked, "How did you know you were Jewish?" a Brooklyn-born Jewish woman married to a Presbyterian from Nebraska replied, "It's very hard to articulate. The only stuff my mother ever made explicit was 'Jewish girls don't. . . .' But every word she said to me meant 'You are a Jew.'" Psychotherapist Esther Perel commented that "much of it is passed on unspoken and that's why we don't know what it's about." It's not just that many modern Jews are undereducated Jewishly, but also that in the context of their own families, especially if their parents were not traditionally observant, messages about being Jewish were muted or garbled.

Trying to talk about identity and interfaith issues can be a struggle between the couple and their own parents. Parents "may become so angry with their son or daughter that they are unable to express themselves adequately. Concurrently, when sons and daughters are faced with their parents' rage, they feel so alienated from their parents that communication may cease completely."[3] To ease the dialogue between the interfaith couple and their parents, a synagogue in Pennsylvania struck upon the idea of linking couples to older adults who had been affected by interfaith marriages, but who were not their own parents. Communication between the generations, and even between the interfaith partners themselves, was considerably easier, as it turned out, when the issues could be brought to the fore in a context one step removed from the participants' own family ties, providing "a unique forum for parents to relate to a youthful interfaith couple and particularly to a Jewish adult who is 'someone else's child.'"[4]

A generation ago, most intermarried Jews would have fallen into one of two categories—those who rejected utterly a connection with their Jewish background, or those who insisted that their non-Jewish spouses convert and bury their own pasts as a precondition to the marriage. Today, as the ex-nun's comments at the beginning of this chapter demonstrate, there is a climate of religious relativism surrounding intermarriage, with more compromise, attempts to yoke disparate traditions, and the possibility for more open negotiation over what each partner wants to retain of his or her own tradition.

It is the negotiation process, however, that is painfully difficult for many Jews. They are handicapped in not having the language in which to say that being Jewish matters. Some Jews feel embarrassment at their own specificity. They think that these differences really "shouldn't" matter. Perhaps some of these feelings are expressions of the conflict between two images of acculturation: the more assimilationist "melting-pot" model and the "mosaic" one, in which each group maintains its separate identity as part of the whole. While the United States has been experiencing a new respect for group differences since the "new ethnicity" got its name in the late 1960s, Jews still aren't sure where they fit in as a minority group with a distinct ethnic heritage, though they are not now suffering in the same overt way as, say, blacks or Hispanics.

They cannot find the words partly because they're embarrassed at wanting to stay attached to a particularistic culture while living in a larger society that, at least when they were growing up, claimed allegiance to a "melting pot" theory that would obliterate distinctions among peoples. Jews trying to remain loyal to their own identity found themselves bucking this flattening trend in American society, sometimes lacking the conviction that as a small minority group—less than 3 percent of the population of the United States—they were entitled to have those feelings of distinctiveness in the first place. One woman placed this struggle succinctly in context as "a critical tension between we-are-the-world view and we-are-the-Jewish-people view."[5] One aspect of the difficulty in finding an expressive language for Jewishness is that many well-educated Jews sense coercion in the very idea of marrying another Jew. They don't want to see themselves as sectarian or discriminatory—and inmarriage means doing this with the most intimate aspect of life. Pressure to marry within the group is a big issue for modern people—"as if you can choose your career freely but not your partner," noted Esther Perel.

The ambivalence and confusion over how much fuss to make in defending differences is evident in the relationship of Robert and Joann. They are both architects in Boston with shared, broad-ranging interests and similar expectations for how their two children will be reared. He is Jewish and she is a nonpracticing Catholic (interesting that one rarely says "nonpracticing Jew"). Despite their harmony in many areas, conflicts over their religious differences surfaced in conversation, which began with talk of travel. Robert commented that he wanted to go to Israel and was planning to go for the first time in a few months. "I've already told Joann I'm going alone, without her. Why? Because it's a kind of pilgrimage. I've always wanted to go. And I don't feel like taking her and having to explain everything." He clearly meant the need to explain—or defend—his own feelings and reactions, not just the history or the politics of the country.

"My feelings about Israel and about Jewishness weren't ever a conflict for me until very recently. I think it's a post-forty thing. My son turned thirteen this year, and frankly it really bothered me. When he was about twelve his friends started to have bar mitzvahs, and we talked about my bar mitzvah and what went into it. He decided in the end that it wasn't for him—it seemed like too much work. Of course that was with a twelve-year-old's consciousness. I tried not to let my feelings show."

The boy in question is a talented musician, a competitive athlete, and a bright, hardworking student, yet his father thought that studying for a bar mitzvah would have been too formidable a challenge. In other areas, neither Robert nor Joann had ever felt uncomfortable about guiding the children's choices and behavior firmly, articulating unambivalently their expectations about deportment, bedtime, entertainment, and so on. Robert had not often given the boy the same freedom to act without guidance in making choices about important matters in his life as had on the matter of a bar mitzvah. "It was his decision. I guess I'm just too democratic. And frankly I think that if he had gone ahead with it, Joann would have been very angry. I know that when our daughter—who likes to sing—sings with the Christmas choir in her school it makes me uneasy. She loves pomp and ritual, so I'm always a little nervous around the holidays; and if she got involved with anything Catholic *I* would be unhappy."

It turned out that Joann was very nervous about expressing any negative feelings about Jews, afraid that Robert would interpret any criticism of him as anti-Semitism. Robert, a talkative man who discussed a wide range of subjects most engagingly, did not have the words with which to express his feelings about Jewishness. Why couldn't he find them? First, he had never spoken about them before. Imagine a person, for example, in his or her first-ever discussion about politics, or poetry, or skiing, and you can grasp some of the language deficit that comes into play when an otherwise well-spoken individual is trying to express complicated feelings in a vocabulary that probably hasn't had an infusion of new concepts since childhood. Religion is not a subject that many mid-twentieth-century liberal intellectuals take very seriously. "You're just using religion as a crutch!" was the accusation one participant in an intermarriage group leveled at those of her coparticipants who wanted to talk about religious differences. It was a shock to her, as it was to Robert, to discover that religion, or the consequences of religious identity, does have implications in the lives of "nonreligious" people.

Second, the covert bargain that Joann and Robert struck in their unstated marriage contract was that neither would push much for religious expression of any sort, and Robert felt that disturbing the status quo after so many years of marriage would be to challenge the relationship. Since their marriage hadn't broken up after all those years, he figured, why rock the boat by raising the issue of the children's religious identity "at this late date"? It frightened him to raise the possibility of conflict within a marriage that he cared a great deal about. Like partners in many other interfaith couples, Robert refused to deal openly with the differences between him and his spouse. But they don't disappear, and crisis points, turning points, life-cycle marker events, or just plain daily life can cause the differences to surface suddenly and unexpectedly, increasing the partners' fear or anxiety.

Some Jews' inability to communicate their thoughts and feelings about being Jewish can have more pernicious consequences. Their non-Jewish partners sometimes interpret the silence as further evidence that the Jews are "stiff-necked" and don't want to admit others into their inner sanctum—not even husbands or wives. The explanation may be less arcane but harder to counter: namely that modern-day Jews, those masters of the word, may be *unable* to talk about Jewishness and Judaism, reluctant to confess to any Jewish specificity that might pull them out of the American mainstream. (Some people do need the distance that intermarriage provides, don't want closeness and communication, and therefore choose a partner with whom some barriers will already be in place because of their personal and psychological history, but this is not the norm among the intermarried couples discussed here.)

Some Jews are reluctant to confess that Jewishness matters because they are anxious not to threaten the relationship. Others find it too painful to confess that they would prefer to *avoid* dealing with their Jewish identity at all, so they blame their partners' needs for their own lack of Jewish identification.

"How can I get my WASP to be part of a *Shabbat* celebration?" asked a Jewish woman who said that her own family had been very "hypocritical" about Jewish observance. "I don't want to *force* him." By projecting her own uneasiness onto her husband, and by saying "I'd do more Jewish stuff at home but I don't want him to feel excluded," she excused her avoidance as a favor to him. She had mixed feelings of pride and anger at her own Jewish background and yet laid most of the responsibility for the family's lack of observance at her husband's feet. She projected her feelings onto her Christian husband and then went out of her way to "protect" him.

It is often easier to deal with a painful and complicated situation if one does not "own" the feelings oneself, but can ascribe them to someone else. Of course, this is a ploy not used exclusively by interfaith couples. In many families one partner avoids a painful situation—say, a long visit with estranged parents—by declaring that the reason not to do it is because the *spouse* "gets up tight."

Ambivalent people often project onto a partner of another faith their own feelings about religion. An Italian American woman marrying a Jew decided to convert to Judaism just before their marriage. "It's her *own* idea," her fiancé commented. But for the year and a half that they were dating he refused to have his parents meet her. "I wouldn't subject you to them," is how he explained it, projecting all of his nervousness about subjecting *them* to *her* onto them. She understood that she would estrange him from his parents completely if they married with this tension unresolved and without even attempting to draw his family closer. She felt that an estrangement between her fiancé and his parents would be blamed on her and the new marriage would likely be stressed by this. So the conversion really took place for *his* sake and for the sake of his relationship to his parents, although officially, yes, it was "her own idea."

The implication here is that the Jewish partner is helpless and reliant on someone else to notice something very important about his or her own needs and identity. In contrast, Scott—a young Jewish man in a group of interfaith couples, after several weeks of discussing his family's response to his Catholic girlfriend—stood up and shouted, "*Screw the family!* It matters to *me* that we have a Jewish household and that our kids be raised Jewish." He was finally able to say what *he* wanted, not what his parents did.

Barry, a Jew in his early forties, is married to Lorette, an Asian Catholic (after years of dating and courting only black women, saying that he found their families so warm). Barry could only communicate his somewhat unexpected desire to raise his baby daughter Jewish by drawing analogies to lost cultures. "I wouldn't want to see the Jews disappear, the way the Phoenicians did," he said several times. He could not say that it mattered to him for more personal reasons that the Jews not disappear; he had to cast the sense of loss in anthropological terms. Then he added: "Why does it matter to me so much? It's not the nuts and bolts of Judaism I want to find out about—like the prayers for lighting the candles—I could get a manual for that. My parents couldn't answer my 'whys,' but I want to know for *my* kids." When he was finally able to say that his Jewish identity did mean more than simply an abstract concern over an ancient culture fading away, he declared that it mattered only because of his daughter.

For many intermarried Jews, the easiest way to avoid having to speak up about their own yearning for some manifestation of Jewish identity is to displace all the need not onto the partner but onto the children, as reflected in "I want my kid to have this connection to the Jewish people." Indeed, this future orientation is important for Jews and Christians alike, but only if it is acknowledged that it matters to the parents also. If it matters enough to warrant passing on, the parents need to realize that what they are doing is important for themselves, not only for their parents, grandparents, or children. This frees the young child from carrying the full burden for the parent and allows the parents to connect more directly with their own faith—which is what, in the end, most want to do. The confusion and ambivalence expressed by many intermarried Jews—like Barry, who knew a great deal about Asian religions and very little about Judaism—is frequently related to lack of knowledge. Rabbi Irving "Yitz" Greenberg tells people that one reason they should encourage their children in Jewish studies is that unless they do, the children's secular intellectual growth will continue, but their perceptions about Judaism "will be stuck at the eighth-grade level forever." Greenberg says that these Jews will always relate to Judaism in a childish, nostalgic way, and this prediction seems borne out in the way many Jews respond to Jewish ritual.

Here is a telling example. At a Rosh Hashanah (Jewish New Year) dinner, a group of Jews in their twenties and thirties were celebrating the holiday with the traditional *challah*. They all knew that there was a blessing to be said over the bread, and they all knew the Hebrew words, yet not one of them would pick up the knife, cut a piece, and say the appropriate blessing so that the festive meal could begin! They had all come to celebrate, yet not one of them could take the celebration seriously. They were embarrassed, they wanted to keep religion out of their identity as Jews, and they made awkward jokes of protest about the rituals themselves. If this is the response in an all-Jewish gathering, imagine how difficult it would be for them to involve themselves in the genuine meaning of blessing the bread if they had to explain it to non-Jewish spouses or offspring.

Judaism for many people is not integrated into their whole selves. It becomes a remnant from childhood that is confusing to deal with as an adult—rather as if, as a grown-up, you found yourself yearning for childhood's tattered blanket or a favorite toy. It becomes very difficult, obviously, to explain the religious significance of something you relate to in an immature way.

The group of Jews at that holiday dinner, however, didn't need to explain much to one another. Because Jews have been bound together as a group in the United States—by many factors: education, geography, occupation, and, until recently, very high inmarriage rates compared to other ethnic and religious groups—they have not had to explain themselves much to non-Jews. There has been a sense of uneasy collusion over the vagueness of what constitutes Jewish meaning or identity. There has been no need to be explicit: "We all know what we mean, so we don't have to say it." The familiar trappings of Jewishness—ethnic foods, political views, styles of conversation, and so on—are disparaged as superficial, while deeper ideas about Jews and Judaism may be either unknown or avoided.

In fact, many contemporary, well-educated people are awkward in speaking about spiritual or religious matters. But the issue is more convoluted, because the majority of Jews now see Judaism not necessarily as a theological belief system but as an embodiment of the cultural assumptions of a people or a nation. Just what the Jews *are* is a subject that has been hotly debated for years by the Jewish community and by anti-Semites as well. Are they a people? A nation? A race? An ethnic group? There is no parallel ambiguity about how one would define a Lutheran or a Baptist or an Episcopalian, so it is sometimes difficult for non-Jews to understand that for Jews the "religious" definition may be only one aspect. Cultural or ethnic feelings provide other kinds of meaning. A Jewish woman looked at her Unitarian husband and said, "Christians think that religion, nationality, culture are all separate categories. For me the answer to all of these is 'Jewish.'"

It's never quite so simple for Jews, and that's why one of the dilemmas facing intermarried couples is the lack of a common vocabulary or a common experience even of what the options are with regard to religious or cultural identity. Most non-Jews are unfamiliar with the confusion some Jews feel: Where to place themselves along this continuum of belief and practice? Just as an Australian will always answer the question of nationality with, "I was born in Australia," whether he's been back there in fifty years or not, so for Jews there's the ineluctible, inescapable fact of having been born a Jew regardles of how infrequently he or she has "touched base" in any formal way with anything Jewish. A Jew ceases to be Jewish only after renouncing Judaism, and formally converting to another faith. No matter how much one may question or probe or make trouble by challenging Jewish practices or theology, one is nevertheless still a Jew.

These problems of definition are not unique to the intermarried, though intermarriage provides a window on them for all Jews. Probably every non-Orthodox Jew—and many an Orthodox Jew, too—has wrestled with defining where his or her personal boundaries as a Jew lie. The difference is that a Jew married to another Jew doesn't have to make all these uncertainties explicit. The questions of how Jewish to be, of precisely what one believes about God, death, afterlife, prayer, spiritual matters, all may puzzle people for whom the standard theological responses are unknown or carry little weight. The synagogue itself has been used less for strictly religious purposes by many American Jews, and more as a hub for social and political activities that afford the opportunity to connect with other Jews—Jews' actual rate of attendance at religious services is far below that of Protestants or Catholics.[6]

Religion for many Jews is a way of establishing a culture. Or as Mordecai M. Kaplan, the founder of Reconstructionist Judaism, phrased it, Judaism as civilization. A Jew can state, "I do not believe in God," and yet feel profoundly Jewish, with this Jewish identification providing a whole array of cultural values and attitudes. Rabbi Albert S. Axelrad says, "We are, in my view, not a church or an organized religion, but, with Mordecai Kaplan, a trans-national people, with a religious heritage as our single most central but not exclusive bond, and, with Martin Buber, a 'covenanted community.'"[7] Certain "religious" acts, then, such as holiday celebrations or life-cycle rituals, are observed as a way of connecting with, and being nourished by, Jewish history and Jewish culture. There's a confusion of meaning here—with religious activity performed not for spiritual reasons alone—which makes it difficult for a Jew to sort out and explain, especially to someone whose own religious experiences are more discrete and ongoing, less diffuse and sporadic.

Many Jews don't feel *entitled* to their feelings of being bound up with their own Jewish identity if it is not strictly (or even loosely) a *religious* identity. So Jews who feel "something" for their Jewishness but think "it's not really spiritual," become defensive toward their partners, and even angry, in part because they don't know how to express what it is about their being Jewish that does matter. Daria, a Catholic woman in her thirties, about to marry a Jewish man and becoming exasperated by the ambiguity of her fiancé's comments about Judaism, burst out with real pain and anger, "If you don't believe in God, don't call yourself a Jew. If you don't believe in Christ, don't call yourself a Christian." Her fiancé tried to explain to those who have overheard her that "Daria comes to a Passover seder, to a Jewish family that has been very upset at the idea of a priest at our wedding, and there's joking about the *Haggadah* [Passover text], and people say, 'Hurry up, let's have the soup,' and she thinks, 'These people aren't religious at all.' But for us, we're sitting around the table and we *know* we're Jews.''

With less anger, but considerable impatience, another Catholic woman turned to her Jewish husband and asked, ''If you don't believe in Christ, you're not a Christian. Why can't it be this simple for Jews, so that if you don't believe anymore you're just not Jewish?'' Her husband responded as an aside: ''My wife keeps wanting me to take the kids to synagogue. To me a lot of that is hokum. I'm no less a Jew because I don't go to temple regularly. But try to get *her* to understand this! She's so literal-minded. I think that Catholic girls' school must have wrecked any ability she'd ever had to think in abstractions. She's so concrete about all this!'' He can't say what he wants to, so he calls her obtuse!

The same uncertainty—coupled with a calibration of just ''how Jewish'' it is appropriate to be—comes across vividly in a film about different ethnic groups and their attitudes toward being parents.[8] The black parents interviewed are very clear that they want their children to grow up with a sense of black history and the black experience in Africa and America. The Irish Catholic mother in the film says, very clearly and firmly, that she wants to transmit to her children her strong feelings of religious faith. For the Italian parents it is their feeling of family connectedness; for the Hispanics it's the language. The Jewish parents (in a scene that has the ring of both familiarity and authenticity) say that they are just not sure what they want to pass along to their children. One woman says something like this, in a rapid-fire monologue that could be a street rap, ''Look, I want my son to grow up knowing he's a Jew. I mean, it's important. But I mean, I don't want him to turn into the kind of person who goes to synagogue every Saturday morning or anything like that. It's just important that he has something Jewish, though I'm not sure I'm the one who could really teach him anything about it.'' The Jewish responses to the interviewer's questions are awash in ambivalence. The Jews want ''something'' Jewish for their offspring but aren't sure what or how much. Some of the ambivalence gets transmitted to the children themselves; they also are ''trying to say'' what being Jewish is all about.

Those who are better able to communicate what is important to them are well-educated Jewishly (these are also—no surprise—the people most likely to request that a Christian spouse become

Jewish). For most Jewish partners, however, specific communication on this subject is garbled in transmission or avoided altogether, whether between parents and children or between spouses. Intuition, never 100 percent reliable, then replaces speech.

Sandy, the Protestant wife of a Jewish man, recounted that her husband, Lou, "didn't know when we were first married that anything about his being Jewish mattered to him at all. But *I* could sense that it was enormously important for him—maybe just because he couldn't or didn't talk about it—and he talked a lot about everything else in his life! He just had such strong feelings that he didn't even know about—I responded to his unknown factors. He just had this *thing* inside him." Sandy was not tempted to give up her own occasional attendance at church to try to convince her apparently disinterested husband to go to synagogue, but he didn't object to her insistence that their children should attend Hebrew school and that they have some Jewish observances in their home—the lighting of Hanukkah candles being the first.

Gradually, after twelve years of marriage, Lou became more comfortable not only with his own Jewishness but also with his parents and the experiences of his own childhood. He spoke with real delight and pride about the Passover seders that he and his wife have each year and to which her Episcopalian parents are invited along with his Jewish ones. But, he freely admitted, "It was Sandy who encouraged me in all this. I didn't care at all when we were first married." And it was Sandy who countered, "It mattered a whole lot to him, but he just didn't know it." Lou was taken aback by his wife's intuition that his Jewishness was an important part of his makeup. Another man, a Jew married to a nonpracticing Catholic, reported having been "really surprised at my own responses" when he felt saddened and a little repelled at the idea of decorating a Christmas tree in his own home, yet he offered nothing Jewish in response; he expected his wife to pick up on his "vibes," he said.

The non-Jewish partner has often been made responsible for *intuiting* the situation, for picking up on cues that the Jewish partner may not even be aware of, as Sandy did. Paul Cowan recounted that as one of her first gifts to him his then-Protestant wife, Rachel, bought a Passover *Haggadah*.[9] He was at that time a completely unaffiliated Jew, but she saw in him something quintessentially Jewish, which both attracted her and suggested that he would respond to having it brought out. Here is how she told it:

> Just after we were married, I bought the Ben Shahn *Hagada* for Paul, though neither of us knew anything about seders. I must have been looking forward to setting up a Jewish home. Though Paul was always consciously proud of being a Jew, he had given no thought to leading a Jewish life. My interest in introducing ceremony into our home life was an impetus for him. I was helping to make a connection between the fact of his birth status and the traditions of the Jewish people, helping him to feel part of his people in a new way.[10]

Leaving it to the spouse to pick up on unstated themes about Jewish identity might have worked better in the past than it does now, because until recently intermarrying Jews were largely men, and the intuitive non-Jewish partners were women. Men do not have to articulate their concerns as clearly when women are more acutely tuned in to perceiving and acting on the needs of others.[11] One suspects that the Jewish women now marrying Christians will have to find the words to make *overt* their spiritual or communal links to Jewishness, because their (male) partners will be less able to intuit them than the non-Jewish wives of Jewish men are.

The non-Jewish husbands are more likely to ask for specific information about Jews, Jewishness, and Judaism when they are expected to participate in households with at least some Jewish content. The desire for concrete statements comes from Christian husbands across the board, from "regular fellows" to eminent Protestant theologian Harvey Cox, who went to a rabbi to learn exactly how to help raise his son as a Jew, since he and his Jewish wife have agreed to do so. Jewish wives may be less able to provide the specifics than Jewish men who marry out, because until recently many Jewish girls did not receive the same quality of Jewish education that their brothers did—even today, boys outnumber girls in Jewish religious schools of all kinds.[12]

A practicing Catholic in his late twenties and his Jewish wife had begun to discuss how to raise their first child, who was a few months old at the time of the interview. Joseph, the husband, said very gently and sweetly and with genuine concern and confusion, "I've agreed to raise her Jewish—or rather to let my wife raise her Jewish. I know about the Holocaust, and Janie has told to me how much it means to her to have the child be a Jew after all those losses. But she can't seem to explain to me why the being Jewish part *itself* matters or exactly *what* we should be teaching our daughter. How do Jews justify raising kids Jewish? Why? Why is it important?" Janie replied, "I'm really not sure. I just know that it matters to me."

A historical problem that Janie and Joseph came up against is that many people know little but the "bad news" about Jews and Judaism: Since the immediate ancestors of most North American Jews came to these shores from 1880 to 1914 fleeing pogroms and other persecution in Eastern Europe, or in the traumatic years surrounding World War II, the associations of their children and grandchildren are that they should "raise Jewish children or [they'll] be defiling the memory of previous generations." The generation that fled to America often wanted to put formal study of Judaism behind them as old-fashioned, an impediment to getting ahead in America, so all many of them were able to pass on was the immediate history of Jewish persecution. As a result, one reason why so many Jews have trouble expressing why they want Jewish families, or how they want to infuse their lives with "some" Jewishness, is that for the post-Holocaust generation being Jewish has largely negative connotations. Elie Wiesel reported that some of his students know nothing else of Jewish history but the Holocaust experience. And a West Coast psychologist recounted that when she questions the Jews whom she sees in therapy groups focusing on self-esteem, they reply by repeating the negative Holocaust imagery, such as "they went like sheep to the slaughter."[13]

Robert's clearest Jewish recollections—aside from his still-present pride in his own bar mitzvah performance—were of these stories of persecution. His positive associations with anything Jewish were much harder to elicit. He talked about having lived and traveled in areas with few Jews, and of his delight now in finding at conventions or business gatherings other Jews with whom he can feel a sense of closeness. "Sometimes we talk about sports or our childhoods, but we're really just looking for ways to be Jewish together."

When Robert tried to define what it was that drew him to other Jews, he focused on a common bond against non-Jews, not in distaste but as a way of buttressing his own identification with things Jewish. One is tempted to ask if he feels this same sense of distance from his own Christian wife. How to relate, then, to a person who represents at the same time the most intimate relationship in one's life and the most threatening, the most "other"? Robert voiced the feelings of many other interfaith partners when he mentioned the kind of talk that does bring out hidden feelings, mostly negative ones. "In the end, you're 'a Jew.' The nastiness surfaces when you fight—the feelings about Jewishness that may have been hidden all along come out then." The fear, especially from the Jewish partner, is that in a time of acrimony, one will be accused of being "a dirty Jew" or "a Jewish bitch." The fear that the most dearly beloved will turn into the most deeply feared or hated "other" is one of the strong motivations for both partners to keep silent about their differences even when they may suspect that silence may do more harm than speech. The same feeling about the possibility of prejudice or negative stereotypes emerging is mentioned by Christians who feel a strong ethnic-group identity. Individuals with less impulse control are likely to speak such slurs in the heat of an argument—not necessarily out of deep-seated prejudice but because the negative images exist in the culture and can be called up at will.

With this background, some partners simply deny that the differences exist, and when they surface, claim that they are unimportant. Take Norm, a Jewish man married to Helene, a woman whose own background was a mixture of Polish and French-Canadian Catholic. When their oldest child reached the age of ten, the boy decided that since many of his friends were Jewish and were planning their bar mitzvah ceremonies, he wanted one too. To the suggestion that this would be possible in a Reform congregation (which recognizes the child of a Jewish father and a non-Jewish mother as being Jewish), Helene responded, "To tell you the truth, I'm not sure how I'm going to break the news to Norm that he's going to have to join a synagogue. He's going to be very upset." Norm was much happier when he could imagine that the religious differences in his and Helene's backgrounds would stay forever in the background; he had never imagined for a minute that either of his children would want anything more than the identity as cultured and intellectual citizens that he had so carefully forged in his household. In this case, his son forced his hand and chose an identity for himself, causing Norm to confront (or at least to move beyond) his own ambivalent feelings about Judaism.

Norm's refusal even to consider religious affiliation as an issue in his family is only one strategy of people who want to avoid conflict. A Jewish woman living in Brooklyn with her Protestant-born husband and their son claimed that the differences between people of different faiths were generated by narrow-minded people. She remarked, "If we brought up our kids in a vacuum, we'd be fine. The three of *us* have no problem." The "no problem" statement is very common at the outset of intermarriage discussion groups. The couples come together to discuss specific aspects of their lives as families—sometimes, in late November, "the December dilemma" of how to celebrate Hanukkah and Christmas in the same household. Yet the opening statement by one or more participants is likely to be, "We don't have any problems; the rest of the world sometimes has difficulty categorizing us, that's all."

A second-generation American Catholic told one group that although religious and ethnic differences mattered to his European-born father and others of an earlier generation, "These things have all been laid to rest. They have no meaning in our lives today." His Jewish girlfriend replied, with some astonishment, "How can you say that when we have so much pain at our differences, at Yom Kippur, at Christmas, at the bar mitzvah of my son?" For many partners in an interfaith relationship, even suggesting that there are differences to be discussed can be very threatening. The purpose of these groups, and of this chapter, is to describe the process and the interactions through which partners find a language to express and acknowledge, and search for ways to live with, differences.

First of all, it is necessary to detoxify the subject of religious or cultural differences. The sky will not fall in if people discuss the areas about which they agree to disagree. Again, women tend to be more accommodating than men, and sometimes more prone to avoid conflict. Men, more often raised to accept the scrappiness of the athletic field or the competitiveness of poker or business, may be more confrontational than their wives, or less frightened that conflict will spell doom for their marriages. Women who feel more economically or emotionally dependent than their husbands are less likely to precipitate a discussion that may undermine the couple's bonding.

When Margo, a New York Jewish woman, married Peter, a man from a Southern Baptist family, she put up a *mezuzah* on their apartment door (although she had never had one on the doors of the numerous apartments she had occupied when she was single) and frequently reached up to touch it when she came in. Peter was mystified, then angry. "What is all this mumbo jumbo?" he shouted at her. "Why are you touching a piece of silver every time you come in or go out?"

His own family had had a very judgmental attitude, as he perceived it, toward any behaviors that deviated from their religious beliefs—smoking, drinking, divorce—and he had experienced all of these. He saw his wife's growing identification with things Jewish as a reminder of the narrowness he had known as a young man in his parents' circle. He viewed her frequent suggestions that they attend services together as similarly coercive and judgmental. He certainly made no parallel requests of her, since he had long ago cut himself off from his family's beliefs and practices. Peter's reaction to Margo's religious observances came from his feelings toward his own family. His parents were dogmatic and cold people, he reported, and it seemed that religion was only one of many ways in which they had controlled him. Peter was responding to something in his own past—having nothing to do with religious belief—when he got angry with Margo. Peter continued to be annoyed with what he perceived as the irrationality of his wife's touching the *mezuzah*, angry because she had not demonstrated any such behaviors during their courtship, and threatened by what seemed to him her strong need to assert her Jewish identity in non-verbal ways. In fact, Margo couldn't say why the *mezuzah* was so comforting to her. She needed to explain the "irrational" pull, yet couldn't.

Despite his attempts at open-mindedness (he went because he genuinely cared for her), he found himself in synagogue having almost an allergic reaction to the references to Jews as the "chosen people." He admitted, after giving the matter a great deal of thought, that he felt he was being "condemned" for not being Jewish; any suggestions that he attend courses in Judaism to clarify for himself Jewish belief and how it differs from the fundamentalism he had been confusing it with just made him feel more alien and more in the wrong. And because Margo—an assured, confident, and well-educated woman—had not shared with him her deep sense of vulnerability about Jewish continuity (made even more real for her by her intermarriage), Peter viewed her simply as a hysteric, and Margo began to see him as "the enemy.'' She actually just wanted his understanding and support for her feelings as a Jew—for example, her sense of discomfort when the lobby of their apartment building sprouted Christmas decorations in December. And he wanted her to understand the loss he felt in giving up a Christmas tree in order to make their apartment ''Jewish.'' Each needed very much to feel understood by the other, yet neither had said enough for the understanding to take place before the shouting began.

Their initial attraction to each other may have been heightened by their differences, which made each seem exotic to the other. But now each wanted deeply to be understood and validated and *known* by the other. Greater than any potential discomfort or discord over religious differences was the feeling of not being understood completely by the other; this seemed to be what most upset them. He wanted her to understand that the closeness of her extended family made him claustrophobic, and she wanted him to understand that when his mother served meat in a cream sauce she found it offensive. (Even though Peter said he liked Margo's parents very much, the family closeness made him feel guilty that he did not see as much of his own family; even though Margo herself did not keep a kosher home, the fact that her mother-in-law would cook meat with dairy products reminded her of the gulf between the two families.) Each wanted the freedom to express the positive feelings they had about their own group, yet each was afraid of opening up a huge rift between them. Their uneasiness about these unspoken issues was transposed into a debate about religion itself and about his ''rigidity'' and her ''hysteria.''

Only after Margo's sister reminded her that she had never been particularly religiously observant and asked her bluntly, ''What the hell is all this about, suddenly?'' did Margo come to realize what most Jews in this situation discover—that precisely because she was married to a non-Jew she felt, more strongly than she would otherwise have acknowledged, that she had to have a ''Jewish'' home. Margo didn't feel it was enough that the ''mistress of the house,'' as she put it, was Jewish. It mattered that the house *itself* be so designated. But she couldn't say this directly, she discovered, partly for fear that her husband would say no. Normally an extremely verbal and analytical person, Margo had never been able to tell even herself what reasons lay behind what her husband termed her *mezuzah* ''fixation.''

This couple learned to communicate their feelings around religion partly because they were prodded to do so by family members and partly because, as their marriage ripened and they built some history together, they felt less frightened by their differences. As they talked more honestly they found the tension between them significantly reduced. What each had been imagining the other was feeling turned out to be much more radical than the reality itself. Peter had no strong religious feelings for his own tradition; instead, out of his past came a determination not to let other people make decisions for him. And it turned out that Margo's leanings had much less to do with religion than with a sense of Jewish history and community, which Peter could accept on an intellectual level. She wanted him to understand her gut feelings as a Jew, but did not need him to share any theological position. If such a distinction is possible, theirs turned out to be a problem of communication rather than a true incompatibility relating to their different religious backgrounds or convictions.

The situation that triggered Margo and Peter's negotiations had to do with religious ritual, although their differences were not over belief. Many interfaith couples wrestle with the *meaning* of these rituals in their lives, aside from their simple observances, asking: Is ritual observance hypocritical? A betrayal of rational thought? For many contemporary Americans, especially those of the third generation whose parents were born in the New World, the messages they got from their own families were confusing at best. One Jewish man recalls that his parents dressed up every year for the High Holidays and appeared to be going to synagogue, but after strolling in front of the synagogue long enough to be spotted by their neighbors they turned and went off to the theater instead. Others speak of their parents' hypocrisy or confusion over what to retain of Jewish customs and what to discard in the interest of becoming more thoroughly Americanized. For a Jew raised with such ambivalence, the specific rituals people perform seem unreliable indicators of their real feelings about religion. They do not necessarily provide the solution to questions of identity that one may be seeking. The outward manifestations of identity are only pathways, and they cannot be relied on by Jews trying to get at the core meaning of their own Jewishness.

Certain concrete observances are more routine for Christians, since they are commonly practiced in the prevailing culture. For Robert and Joann's family *not* to have a Christmas tree would have seemed strange to Joann, especially in light of the fact that theirs was not a self-declared "Jewish" family. In a blurring of religious distinctions that her husband has never contradicted, Joann is delighted that their family celebrates "all" the holidays. "It's kind of fun; it's the family value of the celebrations that's important, not exactly what the celebrations themselves are." Such reasoning is troubling or problematic to the Jewish spouse not merely because it negates Jewish specificity and means one is likely to celebrate more Christian than Jewish holidays. It is also troubling because for Jews to celebrate the birth or the resurrection of Jesus Christ runs directly counter to Jewish teachings; even if some Jews cannot be specific as to what these teachings are, most understand Christianity as essentially very distinct from Judaism. Celebrating Hanukkah or Passover does not contradict any Christian tenets, and these holidays can be celebrated by Christians as part of their own history too.

It is easier for some Jews to voice negative feelings about Christian holidays than to acknowledge the positive feelings they might have about Jewish ritual and to translate that into meaningful activity for themselves and the non-Jewish members of their families. Take Seymour and Karla. She's a devout Methodist, whose religious faith brought her through many terrible trials, including grave illness, in her life before she met Seymour. He is a self-confessed agnostic. Yet Karla said, "If you asked me 'Who are you?' I'd answer, 'A mother.' Seymour would answer 'a Jew.'" She's right. She has picked up very strongly on Seymour's Jewish identity, and yet she cannot get him to "use" it in raising their child; in this family, they have decided that their young daughter will be raised as a Christian. Why? Because Karla felt that faith—"a sense of rootedness"—had been so vital to her that she wanted some of the same for her daughter. She said it didn't matter to her what faith. "But Seymour was not about to take her to synagogue every Friday [sic], so I take her to church each week."

Seymour is still not at all sure of what he is passing on to his dearly beloved daughter, but a Jewish identity is not one of the items in the legacy. Yet this man, who grew up speaking Yiddish as his first language, said to Jewish guests when the baby cried one evening, "Maybe if we say *tehillim* (psalms) she'll stay in her crib." Even though they may have fond memories and proud associations regarding Judaism and their own Jewish identity, Jews like Seymour are unable to pass that legacy on to their children because some lack motivation, some lack information. For others the difficulty is compounded by conflict or fear of conflict over the religious differences between the partners.

Robert and Joann's approach in a situation that was not charged in the same way that their son's decision about his bar mitzvah was—that is, one that didn't hold any hidden fears for either partner—is a clue to how interreligious conflict could be managed. When choosing a school for their children, each mustered as much information as possible, and although their views differed, they approached the decision in a rational way. It is more difficult to engage in the same kind of rational, egalitarian decision making about religious identity, with its strong ties to childhood and earlier feelings about one's own past and parents, in part because both partners are unable to explain fully why they feel as they do. When Robert wanted to convince Joann that his first choice for their son's school was the right one, he had a great deal of information on his side and no difficulty putting it into words. In discussing or arguing his Jewishness, Robert did not have the same confidence even in the information he possessed, because he attributed all his Jewish feelings to the "irrational" side of the ledger. And as much as he thought he wanted to pass something Jewish along to his children, what he often came up against was his own censoring attitude—that he was "wrong" to want to do it, and that the "Jewish" feelings themselves were somehow unworthy of him.

What shines through Robert's situation and the comments of others is that the Jewish partner needs not only the courage or conviction to dare to say "being Jewish matters to me" but also the *content*. Conviction alone is not enough. One way to address the uncertainty is for both partners to study something of each other's religious tradition, through formal classes in churches or synagogues, in community centers, or sometimes privately with members of the clergy who are willing (in a nonproselytizing way, if that's what is desired) to set up individual programs. Even watching the PBS television series "Civilization and the Jews" can help answer both spouses' questions about Jewish culture. Attending classes together gives the couple a shared baseline of information, but as with any situation in which backgrounds differ, the partners are likely to uncover differences between them. These differences of belief and approach are not necessarily schismatic, but since Judaism and Christianity are not one faith the partners may feel sometimes as if they are players on the teams of friendly (or not so friendly) rivals. On the whole, though, the process of learning together has been reported by most couples to be an enriching and supportive experience. Sometimes the setting of an "intermarrieds" discussion and support group can provide both the permission to speak and the concepts themselves. Here is an example of the process at work:

A group of intermarried couples (in which no one had converted) had been meeting in a big-city suburb for about two years to discuss in a fairly casual way the solutions each family had found to their routine problems in celebrating holidays and marking other occasions. One day a Presbyterian woman, married for about fifteen years to a Jewish man, started to voice, hesitantly, her negative thoughts:

> I have a feeling you're all going to jump on me for saying it, and I feel really nervous about this, but I have to say that Jews all seem a little stiff-necked, as if they're better than everybody else, and it makes me very uneasy. I mean, I know that Jews never want to reach out and convert other people, and they make it very hard for others to get close to them or their religion, and it seems to me that there's almost a wall around Jews—they don't want other people in. Like the Jewish mother-in-law of a Protestant friend of mine who didn't invite her daughter-in-law to her Passover seder. She said her son was welcome but not his wife. Maybe she thought that this woman was a big threat to her Jewish celebration, but my friend just thought it was excluding her in a horribly rude way.

Some Jews do in fact think that non-Jews either cannot or should not share in what it means to be Jewish—for example, the grandparents who stubbornly refused to believe that their grandchildren, born to a Jewish man and a woman who underwent a strictly "kosher" conversion before their marriage, were really Jewish. Some Christian spouses also believe this. One woman said that she insisted, even though she was not ready to convert to Judaism, that her household and her children be Jewish because, she said, "I felt as if I had robbed the world of one Jew when I married my husband and I didn't want to do it again." The same woman declared that despite the conversion of her children to Judaism when they were very young, she isn't quite sure that they are "as Jewish as a born Jew." (One must ask if she really would prefer that they not be "as Jewish," or if she really believes in a biological component to Judaism. But in either case it is clear that she thinks Judaism is something special that only born Jews have complete access to.) The other members of the intermarriage group—Jews and non-Jews alike—listening to the woman who was critical of Jews all supported what she was saying. The Jews were not sure of what to make of the traditional bias against converting Gentiles to Judaism. But then a change took place in the group. After the woman expressed her negative feelings—and remember, she was initially afraid to speak out because she feared a powerful negative response—the whole group became freer to move on.

When Rabbi Melanie Aron, present at a meeting one of these groups of interfaith couples, explained that the historical refusal to convert non-Jews to Judaism evolved only in response to harsh Roman laws that punished any attempts at religious conversion by swift execution, the Jews themselves were astonished—at last they had a fact with which to refute a negative image of Jews. Equally unsettling was the image that all Jews "think they're better than other people." In response to this, the leader, Esther Perel, reminded the participants that "it's only the Jews about whom the prejudice states that they're 'better.' Some groups are denigrated for being inferior: shiftless, lazy, drunks, stupid. Only the Jews are hated for being superior." The nods of recognition made it clear that for the individual intermarried partners to communicate effectively with one another they had first to get through layers of misconceptions—not only the misconceptions of one group about another but those held within each group as well.

For it is not only the Christian spouses who bring negative associations about Judaism or Jews to these discussions. In one group, when the leader asked the participants to say the first words they associated with the word *Jew*, the initial responses were all negative. (Curiously, when she asked them to do the same thing for non-Jews, the uniform response was, "That's impossible, they're all different"—as if this wasn't also the case with all Jews!) Getting people to articulate any positive comments about Jews took a very, very long time. A core problem in finding a way to discuss Jewish identity had been that once they learned to talk there was, for many of them, very little positive they wanted to say. The "stiff-necked" and "think-they're-better" associations—plus much less pleasant ones—had to get out first. This confrontation-and-explication session marked a real turning point for the group, after which the participants decided to continue their meetings into the following year but to meet as a Jewish study group rather than to focus simply on the dilemmas facing them as intermarried couples.

There are consequences to communicating about these differences. A rabbi who often works with Jewish-Christian couples said, "It's ironic. They come looking for similarities and end up finding their own religions and the differences between the partners." A Unitarian woman in New York, after protesting how divisive and foolish it was for couples to discuss their religious differences, finally told the group she had been attending for a year, "My marriage is rocky enough as it is. If we add our religious differences I'm not sure we can withstand this." But they did and it did. It is true that people's fears that the worst will be spoken if the talk turns to differences fuel their reluctance to get those differences out into the open. Hidden anti-Christian and anti-Jewish feelings often do emerge, forcing partners to acknowledge them and to track them, sometimes back to their own parents' prejudices. This means that an honest discussion of these feelings can lead to a distancing from one's parents, or at least to seeing them in a new light. The discussion also may mean that the "simple" solutions a couple thought they had accepted before the fact—for example, deciding before children are born that they will be raised as "citizens of the world"—may need to be renegotiated if either partner becomes drawn (back) to his or her own religious tradition in an attempt to explain it to the other.

Acknowledging the differences allows each partner to grow—both in the religion of his or her choice and, importantly, as a couple. Keeping the differences under wraps means that one is always playing a defensive game. Exploring them both reveals a new dimension to one's partner and provides a new opportunity for self-definition as well.

————◆————

# Living with Differences

As I like to put it, although the gap between us remains immeasurably deep, it is not very wide. We can hold hands across it (and often do).
—*Stanley M. Rosenbaum, in* Christian Century *(October 28, 1981)*

Jewish and Christian partners in an interfaith marriage each face certain issues—some jointly (as in how to relate to clergy or parents) and some separately, for each religious tradition extracts its own toll or assigns its own psychological tasks to be performed and hurdles to be overcome. Some, of course, are unique to each couple. Other issues, more common, are brought up frequently by participants in mixed-marriage groups at community centers or synagogues and by couples in premarriage groups and in private interviews—so frequently, in fact, that they are presented here as paradigms of the normal challenges interfaith couples face. The differences themselves are not to be feared. They do not necessarily represent any level of pathology in a relationship; they are simply the most common issues that come up between two people of different traditions and cultures learning to live respectfully and creatively together.

A question that looms large as couples try to create their relationship happily is how to preserve those aspects of the two different religious and cultural traditions that have meaning to each partner without wounding the other. If the couple has decided on a single religious tradition for their home, there are alternative methods of respecting the memories and holiday celebrations of the other tradition. One analogy might be how people feel as they look at pictures of good times shared with family members who now live far away or who have died—the sense of pleasure recalled, of nostalgia, of delight at having had the happy experiences is still there, even though the "primary" experience is no longer available. Similarly with holiday times. For the Christian-born partners—even those who convert to Judaism or participate in the creation of a Jewish home—Christmas, for example, will always be a real part of their past experience. The traditions of the past, however alien from the household's current practice, need to be acknowledged. And for couples who have decided to "hold up both traditions," as a Protestant minister put it, both individuals certainly need to have an understanding and respect for one another's religious roots and practices. The very differences in the way the partners in an interfaith couple approach religious occasions can provide an opportunity for growth. Each can find a special impetus to learn more about his or her own faith out of the need to explain it more coherently to a partner.

Nevertheless there is an imbalance in the concerns expressed by Jews, a distinct minority in American life, and Christians, who are the majority culture. What they want may be different, and this is one of the critical issues that interfaith couples need to recognize. Jews often feel strongly that after an interfaith marriage they want to retain something of Jewishness in the fabric of their lives; Christians often express feelings of wanting to make the two traditions one, restoring them to what they think of as a primary unity. The Jews want to acknowledge their distinctiveness; the Christians are seeking to blend the traditions. Many Jews fear Christian symbols and celebrations, whereas Passover seders or Hanukkah rituals (the most commonly celebrated Jewish home holidays) are not taboo celebrations to the Christian. Since Christians have not historically feared Jews, Jewish symbols and liturgical objects don't have the same connotation for Christians that Christian ones do for Jews.

The Christian-born partners may find a Passover seder incomprehensible or alien (even if it is celebrated only as a festive meal) or may delight in it as a ritual connected to their memories of the Easter story, but they are not likely to find participating in such a seder an excruciating act of disloyalty to another religious tradition. Many Christians say that they see synagogue rituals or Passover home celebrations as a part of their Christian heritage, too, viewing Judaism as a precursor form of Christianity. "Hey—it's just like my Bible, only we take it a little further,'' said a Baptist about the synagogue services he attends with his Jewish wife. "Even Jesus Christ attended a seder," said a Catholic man whose Jewish wife was worried about how he'd react to their first Passover together.[1] Most Christian-Jewish couples today provide some acknowledgment of the Jewish elements within the household. And these elements are *not* viewed as "toxic" or especially threatening by the Christian partner.

A Jewish man, on the other hand, "allowed" his wife to have a Christmas tree in their house and then refused to hand anything on it himself and wouldn't approach it or touch it. The tree was a taboo object to him, and he wouldn't let his wife join in singing carols at holiday meals for the same reason that he avoided the tree. (Although some Jews claim that they do not want a tree "because of the children," the person who is often really being protected is the adult.)

Therefore, it is not surprising that recent research on interfaith couples demonstrates that the adjustments around religious issues usually favor the Jewish partner. Contrary to the assumption that the majority culture will always "win out" in the power dynamics of Christian-Jewish intermarriage, the foremost researcher in the field has announced: "We can state unequivocally that . . . the norms of marital power under which they usually work out their adjustments as a couple most often favor the resolution of . . . problems in the direction that is preferred by the Jewish spouse."[2]

One reason for the persistence of Jewishness in interfaith homes is the general concern of a minority group for its very survival. In some households, making the home "more" Jewish and engaging the non-Jewish partner in life-cycle and holiday events is a way of overcoming the Jewish partner's dimly perceived feelings of participating in a betrayal. If a non-Jew can be brought into the Jewish fold, this reasoning goes, the Jewish people is increased, however slightly. If there's any residual guilt or discomfort over the marriage itself, there's likely to be a stronger push to draw the non-Jewish partner more tightly into Jewishness. While there is evidence that some Christian partners are resentful or confused by this imbalance favoring Judaism, talking about "why it matters" (see Chapter 4) can at least rectify an impression that the Jewish partner is trying to steamroller his or her spouse just to control the situation.

When one woman insisted, as a precondition to her marriage, that her husband throw out his Christmas tree ornaments, his initial response was compliance, then anger, then a modicum of understanding. The Jewish-born partner may never feel comfortable with Christian celebrations because of the basic asymmetry of the Jewish and non-Jewish populations. Therefore, when Christmas or Easter rolls around, the Jewish partner may declare certain rituals or holiday celebrations off limits, at least to the new family as a whole. What does this do to the relationship?

When Stan, a mainstream Protestant, had literally thrown away his Christmas mementos before their marriage, Hannah, his Jewish wife, was furious at suggestions from her friends that such "clean breaks" from a complex past might extract their own high emotional toll later. In fact, in the first year of their marriage every argument was laced with his anger at having forfeited a part of his own cultural identity to please his wife:

> I felt cut off from my own past when I threw out those ornaments. I didn't care religiously at all, believe me. I haven't gone to church in years. But some of them had been mine from my family, since my first Christmas away from home, in college twenty years ago. I didn't realize when I said we'd have nothing of Christmas in our home just how wrenching this would be. I haven't really been able to tell my wife about it because she'd see even my *feelings* as going back on my promise that even though I'm not converting to Judaism we'd have a Jewish home together.

Should she *not* have extracted the promise of "a Jewish home" as the bride-price to assuage her own guilt at marrying a non-Jew? Should he have made a more realistic appraisal of his ability to keep this promise? If the rabbi who agreed to marry them had deliberately elicited information about how they were planning to handle their religious differences, they might have some answers. As it is, love is called upon to bind up the loyalties divided by these questions.

Because Christian celebrations have no place in some mixed-marriage households, the Christian partner is the one to feel a potentially profound sense of loss—loss of the holiday objects, often treasured reminders of his or her whole past family experience, not just of the religious celebrations but of the warm family times now, apparently, never to be recaptured.

Because many Jews associate Christmas and Easter wih persecution and oppression, they may have a hard time acknowledging that the non-Jewish partner remembers happy times around these (and other) holidays. There is a double burden here on the Christian partner—not to celebrate in traditional ways, and then not to express fully any feelings of loss at not being able to celebrate fully. The Jewish partner needs to be able to recognize this, and to try to make it possible for the other tradition to be respected and noted, whether it is by visiting others on Christian holidays so that the non-Jewish spouse can recapture some of that relinquished warmth, or by looking for other ways of marking the occasion in a "new" way that is acceptable to both partners. For example, in a Jewish household, both partners can give Christmas packages directly to the homeless or the poor. If the partners have decided on a Christian identity for the household and children, or in the case of a blended family that includes Christian-born children, Passover, for example, can still be celebrated as a holiday of liberation and Hanukkah as a victory over political persecution and oppression.

## If Judaism Means So Much to You, Then Why Didn't You Just Marry a Jew?

The central paradox of the conflicts in a relationship between people of different faiths, each of whom wants to hold on to something from that faith, is reduced to its simplest form in this typical question, asked by a Christian man of his Jewish wife. Sometimes it's asked in anger, sometimes in exasperation, sometimes out of curiosity, and sometimes to satisfy an uneasiness that the partner really would rather have married someone of his or her own faith. The question is asked in intermarriage groups, in family gatherings, and in the privacy of breakfast-table conversations, and it is posed more baldly by husbands than by wives. Perhaps husbands bring this up more because men ask questions in a more confrontational way in general or perhaps as a way of deflecting real conversation about differences, which would mean that changes might have to be proposed and considered. This man's confrontational "take me or leave me" attitude may also stem from the fact that men know they were free to choose a mate. If they perceive women's choices as more limited, they may fear that their Jewish spouses would have accepted the proposal of a Jewish man over their own if there had been such a rival.

The parallel question a non-Jewish woman might ask of her Jewish husband is, "If being Jewish means so much to you, why aren't you more involved [in synagogue attendance, Jewish community affairs, and so on]?" Once again, because Judaism (or, rather, Jewishness) represents more than simply a religious commitment involving a broader cultural and familial identification as well, the non-Jewish partner may be mystified by so strong an attachment that nevertheless often lacks any objective correlative. That is, a Jew may have strong feelings about being Jewish and identifying as a Jew—at its most superficial, for example, taking special note, as one man did, of "Jewish" names in good or bad news in the media—without ever doing much to *show* that he or she is a Jew. This is even different from the cultural component of the ethnic Catholic churches, for example, where religious participation is the key to the identification with the community.

The paradox arises again, powerfully, when conversion of a Christian partner to Judaism is discussed (and the other way around, too, although the percentage of interfaith couples in which the Jewish partner actually undergoes religious conversion to another faith is minuscule). "If you loved me enough to marry me, why do you want me to become something else? If I'm not good enough the way I am, why were you interested in me in the first place?"

The dilemma, especially for the Christian partner, is to reconcile the love bond (after all, this is the person he or she chose) with the fact that the Jewish partner wants the Christian to be or become something else (or to help the Jewish partner become something else—for example, more Jewish than he or she has been in the past). So the questions begin. A woman who was never a regular synagogue-goer when single now wants her non-Jewish husband to accompany her to the local temple every Friday night. She wants more holiday observances in her own home than she had growing up in her parents' home. A Jew who was always observant wants his non-Jewish wife to join him in more holiday rituals. The same issues arise here as when conversion is discussed, of course: "If you loved me enough to want to marry me, why do you want me to become something else now?"

The fact is that the partners did choose each other—whether because they had always been attracted to people of another group, because they felt themselves in some way marginal to their own group, or simply because of the serendipitous nature of human attraction and mate selection. Regardless, interfaith couples have in their religious differences a convenient file into which to toss every conflict. In one family, where the Catholic mother gave up practicing her own faith (without converting) and raised the children Jewish at the insistence of her Jewish husband, the resentments had been simmering for fifteen years. They had made their decisions and lived with them, but the woman had never made peace with the choices. She wanted recognition of her loss and made this the focal point of every single dispute with her husband. Even their rabbi finally announced to them, "Religion is your scapegoat for all the other issues between you." The interreligious differences loom large even when the disputes are ostensibly about behavioral or cultural disparities. ("Do you have to wear that 'uniform' to every dinner party?" "Why do you have to push food on all the guests? It's wasteful to put out a spread like that for only six people.") "If you don't like the way I dress or look," said a quintessentially WASP male stockbroker to his Jewish wife, "why not find yourself some Upper West Side New York Jewish shrink with curly hair and a black beard?"

Each partner presumably wants what she or he has (namely, one another) but is perceived by the other as longing for a mate who is more "like" (at least in cultural background). Each partner in a moment of conflict *imagines* that the other needs an opposite-sex counterpart from his or her own group—often pictured in a very stereotyped way ("the *shiksa* doll," "the bearded shrink"). He really wants reassurance that she loves him just as he is and isn't about to throw him over for some Jewish man who will meet all her needs. But the central paradox remains—if it all matters so much, why marry a non-Jew in the first place?

Even those Jews who did intermarry partly in reaction to negative associations around being Jewish, in order to get beyond this paradox, often have to come to terms with the fact that they themselves have a strong enough core of Jewish identity to "matter." For some Jews, once they are married it is as though they had made their statements of independence from the Jewish past and are then free to identify exactly as they choose. This identification almost uniformly includes some form of Jewishness. Conversion to Christianity is very rare, and attitudes toward Christian symbols remain more strongly negative than Jews' attitudes toward their own faith.

The religious differences that surface between spouses after the wedding may be a way of keeping some distance between them. It is a truism of late-twentieth-century psychology that many people have trouble with closeness and intimacy. An interfaith marriage contains the perfect rationale for separateness. If they need to, partners can maintain a certain distance by claiming that their differences are religious in origin. The religious issues are convenient ones around which to focus other conflicts, even if those may in actuality not be about religion at all. Ironically, this tendency to view all disagreements as an expression of interreligious conflict—even when religion is not really the issue—may exacerbate one or both partners' fears that religious differences pose a threat to their relationship. The fear that "our differences will split us apart," as one woman tearfully expressed it, causes some people to want to minimize those differences by eliminating the other faith's observances from the home. (This is compounded by the visceral discomfort many Jews feel about Christian symbols and liturgy in general.)

The loss that Christian partners feel when they are, essentially, forbidden to bring with them into the marriage elements of their own past is concrete: certain celebrations or past experiences are no longer available. For the Jewish partner, the parallel feeling is not so much loss as guilt. This guilt is highly abstract and may be more difficult to express than the distress about not having a Christmas tree. The fact that the Jewish partner may not even be able to articulate this feeling of being a betrayer may make the Christian partner feel rejected and angry. "Why should I give up something when my wife, who's Jewish but not religious at all, has given up nothing except the chance to marry a Jewish man?" argued one Catholic. A Catholic woman's comment on her Jewish husband's insistence that the tree itself was all he could tolerate of her religious observances in their family bespeaks both the rage and the confusion here: "Those Jews, they don't even know what they really want. They even took Jesus out of Christmas." There can be persistent underlying anger and resentment on the heels of feelings of loss or sadness.

These personal feelings of confusion, loss, and deprivation are mirrored in the partner of the other faith in feelings of guilt, uneasiness, and betrayal. The individual whose religion "wins" when one is chosen may still have to work through feelings of remorse at what the other partner has given up. Separately, Hannah said that she feels very threatened by her husband's Christian background, although she hadn't thought she would before they were married and shared a house. "I keep being afraid that he'll slip back, that his doing things Jewish is just giving in to me and that he'll soon want to have Christmas again. I hate hearing about his memories of Christmastime and other holidays with his sisters when he was a kid. I know I should probably be more sympathetic, but I just can't listen. I feel guilty because I'm the one who won't let him be Christian. I'm keeping him from his own past."

The characteristic image of the non-Jewish (especially Christian) wife of a Jewish man is that of the *shiksa*. The word actually derives from the term for something abominable, something to be avoided, but it has taken on the connotation of a woman who lures a Jewish man away from his origins.[3] For some couples the converse is true: the Jewish woman sees *herself* in the *shiksa* role, taking her Christian husband from his own people. For the intermarried Jew, even when the interfaith couple agrees to have a Jewish home, the issues of loss and deprivation, sadness, and fairness toward one's partner are all colored with feelings of guilt over betrayal—betrayal not of the partner but of the community. Actually marrying the taboo object is more powerful even than having one in the living room at Christmastime. The Christian partner is often cognizant of this as well. A New Jersey woman who converted from Episcopalianism to Judaism after her marriage to a Jew said that she had had her children converted at birth, when she was still uncertain as to whether or not she herself would convert, because "I felt I'd already taken one Jew away from his community, and I wasn't going to let these children be lost too." In reality, her husband was not "lost," she herself did convert, and they are now a religiously observant Jewish family; but in the beginning she had certainly picked up on her husband's feelings of guilt and discomfort and wanted very much to help heal them by making the children Jews from infancy and helping rear them as Jews, even in the years when she herself was still a practicing Protestant. When the non-Jewish partner tries to solve some basic uneasiness in the situation, at least one observer sees a pattern whereby the Jewish partner's own family conflicts are being dealt with via the spouse. "To a large extent, non-Jews change in order to solve the Jewish partner's problems with his or her family."[4]

In general, groups, like some extended families, have their "gatekeepers" and their "betrayers." The gatekeepers sit in judgment, and the "betrayers" find themselves looking over their shoulders to ascertain the extent to which they have violated the rules, to measure the damage they've done. The terms, of course, are self-explanatory, but in themselves fail to convey adequately the tone of disapproval and disappointment heard from synagogue pulpits, in the pages of Jewish newspapers, and around family dinner tables. The distress is real, and has its origin in part in very real fears about Jewish survival; but it also contains an element of control. The desire to control the choices of others is expressed so frequently and so forcefully that hardly anyone interdating or intermarrying is immune from its effect.

The personal tensions, felt largely in the immediate families of the individuals intermarrying, do seem to express themselves in terms of control. One commentator believes, in fact, that the intermarriage is just an excuse for the family to express its own powerful dynamic, and that religious traditionalism, which sometimes surfaces unexpectedly even in the most nonobservant families when a child's intermarriage looms on the horizon, is a smokescreen for other issues, including conflicts the parents have with one another.[5] Understanding this dynamic can be very helpful not only to the adult child facing a parent's disapprobation, but to the parents also, who may come to see that by staying cool they are able to keep the feelings warmer.

The feeling of betraying one's parents is not exclusive to the Jewish partner. Intermarried Christians reported having guilty feelings not about betraying a group but about going against the feelings of their own parents. A thirty-year-old woman whose parents had raised her in a small town in California's farm country said her fear "was not that my folks would see my engagement to a Jew as a threat to their religion or to the way they'd brought me up, but as a challenge to their own prejudices. They'd never liked Jews, and *that* was their problem." Of course, it was her problem too. Just as George, a Jewish man whose parents' florid protests over his impending wedding to a Methodist woman forced him to defend his choice vehemently and gave him no room in which to explore aspects of his own uncertainties, so this woman needs to see where her biases match those of her parents.[6] After all, we are all the children of our parents, and even if we spend our lives reacting against their views, we are shaped by them just as surely as if we mimicked them. The bias and the discomfort can be eased, but not until the partners can "own" some of the negative feelings themselves.

Commenting on the interfaith marriage of the late writer Shirley Jackson (best known for her exploration of prejudice in the short story "The Lottery") a psychiatrist who had known the couple when he was a premedical student commented that "an upstate kid taking up suddenly with a Jew . . . this is a big step. It's turning on your own heritage. She probably had not even known any Jews before. . . . When it's done against a prejudicial background, you know you're fighting against yourself as well, because kids incorporate the prejudices of their parents. After all these years, I find one thing—kids want to please their parents. This is what tears them apart."[7] Trying to separate out one's own views from those of one's parents, and trying to be frank about where those views converge, is a major task for the interfaith couple, both in the early years of the relationship and then, later, at the point when a parent dies and the issues surface again.

While parents are a major source of conflict for some couples, other feelings of having betrayed one's people or one's heritage derive from the mature individual, not necessarily from the community or the parents. The betrayal may be cast, for example, in political terms: "I have married a man who has to be convinced of Israel's right to exist," says a Jewish woman whose Christian husband, a journalist, has been an outspoken critic of Israeli policy for many years. There are moments, she confesses, "when I feel as if I have married the enemy." For Jews who intermarry, guilt over the betrayal of one's people often focuses on the Holocaust, or it may be more general. "I felt despair when I left the first session of this group," said a Jewish woman in her forties, planning her first marriage—to a Protestant. "How could I even consider marrying a non-Jew? Then I talked with my single Jewish women friends, and they're going through the same thing. I guess our attitudes change through time, as we age."

It appears not so much that people's opinions or values change, but that they are weighted differently. For a woman who has postponed marriage past her mid-thirties, as this woman has, the religious differences may be less of an impediment in the light of other compatibilities. She may now be surer of her own Jewish identity than she was twenty years earlier, and less sure of what her marriage prospects may be. Such feelings do not dissipate overnight but rather shift gradually as the Jewish partner accommodates to a new reality. This is a situation more common for Jewish women than men, since they are still more likely to be chosen than to choose, which means that some women may be faced with a choice between marrying out or not marrying at all. One response is to marry a Christian but to maintain strong feelings of group loyalty on many other levels: to the family, the known reference group, and the "biological" pool that makes up the long history of the Jews.

Jews feel a need to maintain their specificity for many reasons, two of which are especially pertinent in an intermarriage situation. One has to do with maintaining one's own psychic balance and not cutting off a past sense of self; the other has to do with group loyalty, which comes prepackaged with a component of guilt if one "passes" too easily as a non-Jew or marries one. And for Jews group loyalty is tied up with family loyalties (and conflicts, too). Family relations—including peaceful coexistence with one's own parents and marital happiness—are very important to the self-esteem of most Jews.[8] Understanding the importance the Jewish partner places on maintaining these ties may help non-Jewish partners see why, even in the face of parental opposition or unpleasantness, the Jewish partner persists in staying connected. Some people, of course, are more willing to cut themselves off from their families, especially if no hope of reconciliation appears likely. But from numerous interviews it became obvious that they are not the norm. The "integrators" are far more common than the "cut-offs." Because for Jews self-esteem is bound up with marital success and harmony, personal reasons parallel more abstract concerns over "Jewish survival." This may cause the Jewish partner to struggle over issues of loyalty and perceived betrayal—issues that the Christian partner can often just let pass.

In particular, Catholic-born partners of Jews express some variant of one man's proclamation:

> The Bible is all the same. I feel that the Old Testament is just the basis for the New, so I feel very comfortable with the idea that we'll raise our children Jewish; I'll be able to answer

their questions about Judaism because it's the first part of Christianity, and I have a good Catholic school background. I don't mind Jewish services. I just think Christ is "a step beyond." All I want is for any children I have to be good people, and I am satisfied that Judaism is an ethical religion and that they'll grow up good.

Few Jews said that "any religion" was fine with them, as this man did, and as two Christian women married to Jewish men articulated in almost identical language in two separate interviews, "Faith itself is very important to me. Whatever the specific manifestations are don't matter nearly so much. I want our children to be raised with some religion, that's all." The Catholic man continued: "The basic goal of religion is to give you direction in life, and an anchor. It doesn't matter to me as much which one. And the Jewish religion is very close to the Catholic religion." Commenting on this tendency of Christians to blend the two faiths, Presbyterian minister Richard Spalding admitted that "the stakes are always higher for the Jews. Among other reasons, Christianity can include Judaism; the converse is not true."

The Jewish partners married to Christians comment on the *differences* rather than the similarities between the two religious traditions. This may be because, unlike most Christians, who were taught in Sunday School that the so-called Old Testament is a precursor to the New, Jews are simply taught the Torah (the Old Testament) itself, and tend to view as alien that which came later, namely Christianity.

"Christ is the only difference between the two religions," one woman asserted, without mentioning how much flows from this essential difference. "Christians believe in the Old Testament, too." She feels a strong sense of her Jewish *identity* but no identification with Judaism as a religion. However, she did not say, nor did any of the other Jews interviewed, that Judaism and Christianity were alike. Even the Jews who are nonbelievers seemed to believe in the specificity and distinctiveness of each religious experience. The differences are real, and not just something the Jewish partners *feel*. "It is not an affective issue but a cognitive one," said a social worker who heads groups of intermarried and remarried couples. "Both Jew and Christian need to understand that the differences are real, and not just some neurotic prejudice on the part of the Jewish partner.''

New York writer Lee F. Gruzen, a Protestant married to a Jew, has helped create a mixed-faith religious-study group for the children of intermarriage at her children's private school.[9] Describing the program, she noted that the instructors, a minister and a rabbi, were very intent on delineating the *differences* among religious traditions and ideologies. According to Gruzen, however; ''The kids at this point want to know all the ways that the two traditions they're being raised in are the same, not different.''

This theme—that differences do not matter—was part of the exchange between partners in many interviews. With the comfortable air of a male member of the majority culture, a nonpracticing Lutheran journalist in his fifties, married to his second Jewish wife, told her that ''these things may have mattered to an older generation, to our parents maybe, but not to us. When I was growing up, my parents asked about the religion of the kids I played with, and it also mattered if you were Irish or German or Italian. These things just aren't a part of our lives at all.'' His wife, previously married to a Jewish man, her voice registering real shock, countered: ''Darling, I cannot *believe* you're saying that!''

Both partners have to recognize that their essential goals may be different. He is looking for a synthesis of their two traditions, so that they can be closer in their relationship. She is looking for separateness, so that as a Jew she doesn't feel swallowed up by the majority culture or—closer to the bone—does not feel that she has done something wrong by marrying out. For Jewish partners especially, creating that little bit of distance between the partners that allows them not to repudiate their Jewishness may be of crucial importance. Understanding this difference in operating style and in emotional needs can radically reduce the conflict between the partners.

The common term ''the Judeo-Christian tradition'' crystallizes this erroneous notion that the two faiths are contiguous, and that Jewishness does not need to be ''noticed'' as a separate and quite different religion and culture. Jews constantly struggle with the effort to maintain specificity in a world that is predominantly non-Jewish. Jews are always asking, one way or another, ''Please don't subsume me under Christianity!'' just as blacks may have to assert, especially to the allegedly ''color blind,'' that their skin color *is* important to them and has made a profound difference in their lives.

Not all people are sensitive to the fact that it may be no kindness to ignore or pass over characteristics different from their own. A Protestant woman whose husband is Jewish and whose children are being raised as Jews said that she wanted her children to respect all traditions. Thus she recounted proudly how her son, talking about a classmate for several months, "didn't even notice" that the other child was black. "He never separated him out as different," said the mother, unwittingly giving a perfect rendition of the "melting pot" theme—as opposed to the "mosaic" or multifaceted approach. Hearing this, a Jewish woman added, "The black child might have said, 'if you don't see my blackness you don't see an important part of who I am.' "

Christian partners appear far happier to have differences erased than highlighted ("Christmas is just a secular holiday, for heaven's sake.") There is nothing wrong with this desire to establish closeness and a similarity between two cultures, but often the Jewish partner doesn't know how to counter the assertion that Christmas is just a secular holiday, with a universal message. He or she may not feel this way and yet be embarrassed by having to burst the balloon and say, "It isn't *my* holiday, but I'll gladly share with you what I can, as a loving observer, just the way I hope you'll celebrate Passover or the High Holidays with me."

Christians who are religiously observant tend to feel reasonably comfortable in synagogue, or with such Jewish home observances as Sabbath prayers, a Passover seder, or Hanukkah candle lighting. (People who disdain any kind of religious rituals, of course, are the exception.) Christians tell of being quite comfortable attending ceremonies such as bar or bat mitzvah ceremonies or weddings in a synagogue, whereas many Jews say, as did Billy, a thirty-five-year-old whose wife is Episcopalian, "When I went with some college friends to Midnight Mass at Christmas I thought I'd really enjoy the music and the ritual. What took me completely by surprise was how uncomfortable I felt in the presence of that cross in the church. Liturgical music on my tape player is very different from hearing it while you're looking at that cross with Jesus on it, hanging there."

In every group, in every discussion about interfaith marriages—even those in which there has been a conversion—the discussion of church and synagogue and the respective religious symbols arises, partly at least because one must still deal with in-laws and extended family members who represent the nonparticipating religion of the new family grouping. That the issue comes up is no surprise. What is astonishing is that it is almost impossible for the Jewish partners to assert what the Christian symbols are about for Jews. Some Jewish partners have spoken about kneeling in church. A woman whose own mother is not Jewish, whose father is, and who identifies herself as a Jew in her marriage to a Christian man finally said that for her it must have to do with entering the world of those who have been seen historically as the main persecutors of Jews. Kneeling itself seems part of the act of "joining the Christians. It felt to me as if I'd be trying to pass as a Christian if I knelt, like a Marrano in Spain during the Inquisition" is how she characterized it.

"Get this stuff out in the open" counsel many of the authorities who consult with interfaith couples. "You have to talk about it if it's there—the Jewish person's negative reaction, the Christian's feeling that the Jew is distant or overreacting."

Marianne, a Presbyterian woman who is raising her children as Jews, asked Bill in a group of interfaith couples,[10] "Why is it when a Jewish person goes to Christian services they get so nervous? My husband said last time he thought the minister was giving him the evil eye. I think you're all being too sensitive about this."

BILL: You said you wanted to hear, so I'm telling you my thoughts.

LEADER: Do you often get told you're being too sensitive on this subject?

BILL: Only when I'm around Christians.

LEADER: Well, you're around one in *life*!

BILL: Look, Christian belief is so distant—the afterlife and all that. I just can't relate at all to what these people believe in. I cringe at it.

LEADER: One doesn't cringe for *ideas*, but for a visceral *feeling*.

The cloaking of strong feelings under an "intellectual" approach is a special pitfall for interfaith couples, since no one wants to deal with the central components of religion, which include belief and practice, prayer (to a Jew), or worship (to a Christian). Most interfaith couples are willing to talk about religious matters in the abstract but not to practice any religion.

Beyond theology, the religious differences include an uneasiness many Jews express about the political role of an absolutist church hierarchy, and the historical memory of persecutions waged against Jews by the Catholic church, from the Crusades and the Inquisition to the pogroms in Eastern Europe. From the other side, although official church policy has changed since Vatican II (1963–65), some Christians, especially Eastern Rite Catholics, may still, despite loving a Jew, erroneously hold Jews responsible for the death of Christ. The power of symbols to elicit strong feelings is most apparent in Catholic-Jewish couples. In fact, a higher percentage of interfaith couples interviewed had a Catholic partner than would have been predicted from random selection. (Those who work professionally with interfaith couples around the country also report this differential.) This may be because Protestants in interfaith relationships may be slightly less strongly attached to their own faith, more willing to blend into the Jewish partner's traditions, and therefore less likely to be facing observable "dilemmas" that would bring them into an intermarriage discussion group. It may be that on some level ethnic Catholics and Jews are more attracted to one another as marriage partners because of some cultural similarities unrelated to religious practice—for example, Italians and Jews have certain ethnic family characteristics that draw them together even as their religious differences are potential sources of conflict.

Scott, a young Jewish lawyer in New York, said that going to his fiancée's house for Christmas celebrations didn't bother him but that when Jeannie's mother gave her a crucifix to wear around her neck (with a representation of Jesus on the cross), he "freaked out." When Jeannie pointed out to him that he wears two Jewish stars on a chain around his neck his response was, "The star doesn't seem religious. The cross is. I don't have the same aversion to the Christmas tree, for instance, that I do to the cross."

An Irish Catholic man engaged to marry a Jewish woman responded: "The cross has always been the symbol of the religion that persecuted the Jews. Don't you think that's why you have such a strong reaction to it?" It took a non-Jew to focus on what a Jewish woman in the group then noted was "an anti-Semitic symbol" for her. "If I were marrying a Buddhist no one would object. There's no history of the persecution of Jews by Buddhists."

These strong reactions to religious symbols do not signal an unbreachable chasm between the partners. But recognizing them for what they are—namely, part of the cultural "baggage" one brings into the relationship—is the first step toward moving beyond them or living more honestly with them. Being able to say to a Christian spouse, "Seeing the cross scares me" or "I feel like I'm betraying my grandfather's memory if I go into a church on Easter because that was the time of the worst pogroms in the Ukraine, where he came from," is an important step in differentiating, in seeing one's partner as her- or himself and not part of the feared and persecuting enemy. If not out in the open, these responses of Jews to Christian symbols may seem instead like a rejection of the spouse on a personal level.

A Jewish man whose marriage to a Catholic woman fifteen years earlier had been postponed several times said that on a number of occasions when he and his fiancée were traveling—in Europe, in Mexico—they had decided to get married, and each time they walked into a church to do it, since she was somewhat religious and he describes himself as "a total atheist." But each time he took "one look at the cross with Jesus on it and decided I couldn't go through with it. It took me a long time to admit that was why." They finally returned to the United States and were married in a Unitarian church devoid of overt symbols, "thereby offending both her side of the family and mine at the same time." Nobody's religion was represented, and they liked it better that way. Religious celebration itself became taboo in their household. Symbols and images retain their power to come between the couple when they stay at the level of mystery, fraught with meaning and menace but without relation to any religious experiences the couple has in common.

The most potent representative image for the persecutions of Jews by Christians, and the metaphor for all others (though to call it a metaphor feels like sacrilege to many Jews), is the Holocaust—the murder of at least six million Jews by the Nazis during World War II. For the children of Holocaust survivors the Holocaust is no mere metaphor; this history has shaped them directly. Most children of survivors marry people of very similar backgrounds, often other children of survivors, but usually at least Jews with a strong and fixed sense of Jewish identification. The exceptions are fascinating: those who marry non-Jews, feeling at the same time the betrayal theme (and expressing it) and also the exhilaration of marrying a loving non-Jew and trying to heal the hatreds that allowed the Holocaust to happen.

The Holocaust can be a particular source of friction with a Christian mate, sometimes contributing to a fundamental sense of separateness. One woman, who came to a group for interfaith couples with her Protestant fiancé, said, "I feel as if I've lived the Holocaust, lived it myself. I think I am beginning to feel I can compromise without betraying everything. I always wanted to take my whole childhood with me, everything I got from my childhood, all the Jewishness. But I can't. . . . "

"The Holocaust just doesn't get to me viscerally," said a Presbyterian woman married to a Jew, "I don't see the Jews as weak. They have very good urban, verbal survival skills . . . the pushiness. My anti-Semitism isn't directed at a powerless people. When it comes out, it's a class thing, a sneer." This woman was at least able to get these feelings out into the open, so that they could be addressed. She was able to do so probably because she was in a small, supportive circle—she and her husband had become very friendly with another interfaith couple, and in the context of her friendship with the Christian man married to her Jewish friend, her remark came out sounding more confessional than condemning, as if she were telling tales on herself. But the remark itself certainly sent a chill through the Jews present, representing as it did some of her undiluted, unmediated anger at how she thought Jews "used" the Holocaust. At a subliminal level, the Holocaust may be, for some Christians, an emblem of Jewish suffering they would rather not deal with.

Other Jewish emblems have a negative effect on Christians— largely those that set Jewish *males* apart. Scott's fiancée said, "You react to the cross. But when you go to services you wear a *tallis* and a *yarmulke*. That's more religious than I get—I don't carry rosary beads or anything." A non-Jewish woman, a friend of theirs, also engaged to a Jewish man, added, "I have a problem with *yarmulkes* too." Jewish male ritual garb really does set Jews apart. The non-Jewish women who respond to it may be doing so partly out of uneasiness that their fiancées or husbands are different from the men of their own culture and partly because the *yarmulke,* especially, connotes to some an Old World Jew caricatured in anti-Semitic literature and cartoons.

As vivid as these anxieties seem for people marrying for the first time and making decisions about their shared home and life, all of these issues have a slightly different cast when they arise in a remarriage situation. So high a percentage of intermarriages are second marriages for one or both partners that one investigator claims "a previous divorce is the most powerful predictor of a future intermarriage."[11] People used to predict that intermarriage would lead to divorce; now it appears that the opposite is true: divorce leads to intermarriage. People widowed usually choose to marry someone of their own background in a subsequent marriage, but those divorced, Jews especially, perhaps in an attempt to start over in a different situation, tend to marry out of their own faith.

Every second marriage is in some ways burdened by the first. A special burden on the intermarriage—that of trying to be "better" than the first union—comes with its own set of complexities if there are children involved (see Chapter 8). The normal stepparent situation may be exacerbated by the religious differences or at least made more complicated. Not all situations are resolved as one might expect. One Jewish woman, raising her three children—from her first marriage—with a Christian man, told him she wanted no Christmas celebrations because of her children. Her children heard of this and told her: "We *want* to have Christmas for Jerry—he's so great about having our holidays with us."

Again, every situation has its own dynamic. Living with a non-Jewish man whose former wife was also Jewish, Marianne, in Kansas City, said she felt she always had to be the "good" Jew, because in subtle ways her boyfriend had linked everything that went wrong in his first marriage to the fact that his ex-wife was Jewish. How could Marianne express her Jewish identity without bringing forth his painful feelings of having been rejected by his ex-wife and her family for his reluctance to convert, among other conflicts? She simply asserted that she loved him the way he was and was not trying to change him, but that *she* had certain needs (to attend synagogue and light Sabbath candles, among them) that were totally independent of him. Perhaps her loyalty to her own traditions was one of the qualities he found attractive. She would be glad, she said, if he wanted to accompany her to services, but she didn't need him to come with her and she'd be back soon.

Marianne found that this kind of explicit verbal assurance worked very well in keeping their religious issues separate from the other adjustments in the relationship. Her approach might be a useful one for any couple to follow: First, she figured out what her own religious needs were at the moment; second, she stated how she personally was going to go about meeting them, without being angry or rejecting; third, she offered to have him come along or not, as he chose.

While all individuals have their own personal histories to weave into a marriage, histories of whole groups come into play in an intermarriage. Black-Jewish interfaith couples have to deal with cultural histories that often may appear incompatible. One Jewish woman married to a black Protestant reported being shocked that they were not accepted by either community. She said that although she had expected prejudice from whites, even within her own family, she was astonished that in the black neighborhood they lived in when they were first married, in the late 1960s, they were rejected or ignored by all their neighbors because her husband was viewed as an ''Uncle Tom'' who had sold out. The black women who might have been her friends and natural allies saw her as a usurper; she had become the *shiksa*, the one who had lured a man away from his own people.

Yet for many black-Jewish couples there is an acknowledgment of shared persecution that, if it does not translate into a competition of tears over which group has suffered more, can strengthen the bond between the partners immeasurably. This was true, at least initially, for many of the interracial marriages of the 1960s, in the wake of the civil rights movement that brought many American blacks and Jews together in a common struggle. In black Protestant–white Jewish marriages in the 1980s, the Jewish partner is almost always female, the black male. In one study of black-white marriages in New York City, half of the white partners were Jewish, most of them women.[12] The difference in the more recent marriages is that the black men are Caribbean rather than American.

Regardless of the background of the black in an interfaith marriage, one does not hear the calls for putting aside the culture of one partner that one hears from white Christian–white Jewish couples. The children's racial identification is almost uniformly black, even if the family's religious choice is Jewish. The issues for the couple are very much those of two people who want their children to grow up with two cultures. Because color is a visible fact of life, as well as a strong issue in America, it is likely that the children of such a union will identify as black. Ironically, this may explain why there is little resistance from the black Christian partner to raising the children Jewish or to having a Jewish home. For the children, Judaism can become the family's dominant religion, blackness their dominant racial-cultural identity.

For most interfaith couples, there is nothing static about their situations. There are times when one partner or the other wants to confront the differences head on, and times when circumstances force a reevaluation of past decisions. Couples may feel that things are "nailed down" when, early in the marriage, they decide how they want to handle Christmas and Hanukkah vis-à-vis the in-laws. But then a child is born, and the differences may surface in other ways or the questions may have to be answered a little differently to take new realities into account. Other events, in the family life cycle may trigger a reevaluation of these issues— the marriage of a sibling, the illness or death of a parent, the adolescent identity search of a child, even a job change or family move. "It's a bad plan which admits of no modification," said one man who had lived through with his wife several reevaluations of their mixed marriage. The process by which partners adapt to one another includes these sometimes critical life-cycle events, but is also affected by the development of the couple's personal history and of the trust between them.

The most important concern, of course, is not how each issue comes to a head and gets resolved but how the relationship fares in the process. Dilemmas like those presented by the couples in this chapter admit of no easy answers. But because the issues causing friction or concern often come out of differing traditions rather than individual personalities, a group discussion can provide the setting in which the search for compromise can begin.

"Having a sense of community will empower all the other moves you make," said Reverend Richard Spalding, although clearly the outcomes will at least in part be affected by the kind of community in which one chooses to work out the issues. A couple approaching Spalding in his church setting, for example, would probably "already have decided that the Jewish component of their lives together was going to be set aside." The same would probably be true of a couple approaching a rabbi, and many synagogue-based groups attract those already exploring the possibility of establishing a Jewish home, with the Christian partner considering Judaism. Those offered by nonreligious Jewish institutions, such as New York's 92nd Street Y or Jewish community centers nationwide, provide a setting open to all in which group participants usually do not feel they have to make any kind of Jewish commitment in order to participate—sometimes an advantage in helping both partners feel at ease.[13]

Discussion groups for Jewish-Christian couples are not group therapy, and they differ according to the setting, the skills of the leader, and the composition of each group. Groups organized by synagogues may have as part of their agenda keeping the mixed family within the Jewish fold or at least connected to a welcoming Jewish institution. Other groups stress study, or introductions to religious practices, or offer psychological support. One strength of meeting with other couples is that, in a safer context than the closed twosome, partners can hear and consider a range of solutions to every conflict discussed—simply because the participants themselves are usually a diverse lot (especially in non-synagogue-affiliated groups). In addition, the issues can be discussed with men and women together, moving some of the conflicts away from the gender battlefield and allowing couples to try to sort out what are the "interfaith" issues.

Since there are few historical role models for interfaith couples, they need to look around them to learn what their choices are. One pair, for example, deadlocked on how to proceed with wedding plans when each set of in-laws opposed the desires of the other, heard from a group of ten couples how each of them had handled similar crises, only to discover that they had several secular options for a wedding ceremony, and several religious ones also, which they had never even considered.

At the very least, talking with others can help a couple understand that situations they experience in their relationship are common to many interfaith couples. "In a discussion group I went to in my synagogue in Los Angeles," reported a Jewish woman whose Christian husband occasionally attends services with her there, "I met older couples who were also intermarried and—amazingly—Jewish couples whose children had married non-Jews. I could say things to them I hadn't said to my own parents, and I think that my husband and I helped them see some of the struggles *their* kids were having when they all got together."

Even in marriages where one partner has converted to the religion of the other, these "normal crises" can occur, because they arise not strictly from religious differences—differences in liturgy or ritual or theology—but from patterns of ethnicity, tradition, and values from one's birth family. The clearest popular representation of these perceived differences, mentioned frequently by interfaith couples, is the scene in Woody Allen's *Annie Hall* in which the Jewish hero appears at an exaggeratedly placid dinner scene with his WASP girlfriend and her family and flashes back to his own raucous Jewish family at mealtime. There really are differences in families of different ethnic and cultural backgrounds. Jews did describe more chaotic, emotionally expressive mealtimes than did WASPs or Catholics.

Without resorting to stereotype, which dictates that the characteristics of some are true for all members of the group, it helps to remember that Hispanic, Italian, and Jewish families, for example, express feelings more vociferously than do members of other groups, that WASP families place a higher value than most on self-sufficiency rather than interdependence, that family ties are pulled tighter in some groups than in others, that such powerful components of everyday life as food and money can have different meanings to a Scottish Presbyterian than to a New York Jew.[14] When differences surface in an interfaith marriage, couples find it helpful to remember not to take them personally, but to "check" the conflict against the norm for the partner's group. For example, a psychologist who has worked with interfaith couples suggests that "perhaps because many of the Protestants came from relatively disengaged families, holidays such as Christmas took on particular significance as symbols of family unity."[15]

The laughter of recognition that accompanies both the showing of *Annie Hall* and the recollection of this scene in the company of other interfaith couples demonstrates how much everyone involved recognizes that the differences (at least in *Annie Hall*) are not religious but stylistic and cultural. But whereas theology does not necessarily have to be lived with every day, cultural differences must be confronted more frequently. Because they are less specific, they are sometimes more difficult to see at first than strictly religious incompatibilities. Since partners compatible enough to consider marriage obviously see more similarities in each other than they do differences, and assume that the perceived similarities will carry them over the shoals of religious conflict, it surprises them to discover that even two people who on the surface appear to have much in common can find themselves at odds.

To find out exactly what their commonalities and differences are, some couples have gone through a whole series of self-administered "exercises" exploring how they respond to such questions as how or when to discipline a child, how to express disapproval, how much closeness each can tolerate. Most people learn these things about one another through living together, and no one has reported a couple who chose not to marry because of differences revealed in this way. Most useful is probably just the process of doing this together, one of the ancillary benefits of any formalized discussion in a relationship. Taking religious courses together also provides the benefits of a shared activity, as well as some understanding of the framework each partner is supported by (or trying to climb down from) when entering the marriage.

There is always some room for change and renegotiation. Couples *can* renegotiate the assumptions and contracts they began with, as did many of the people described here. The major task, of course, is to find the similarities, keep them in mind, and remind one another of them; and to feel comfortable expressing one's feelings and ideas even in the face of incompatibilities. "To do this requires," said a rabbi who sees many Christian-Jewish couples, "that you say it: 'I can enjoy Hanukkah and Passover even when I feel a little left out, but Yom Kippur services give me the creeps because they remind me of the intensity of the church services I hated as a child.'" Try to keep your analysis of the issues focused on your own feelings about them, not on the level of "All the Jews are . . . " or "All Christians think. . . . "

Recognizing that the issues lurking in the deep but narrow chasm between Christian and Jewish partners can be alarming, even risky, to inspect, the best advice in dealing with them is to avoid avoidance whenever possible. Shying away from examining the differences is a sure way of never being able to find deeper similarities, or true intimacy.

# 6

*Parents of Interfaith Couples*

It sounds like a joke, but it really happened: a Protestant minister ran into a Jewish woman he knew well on the street in their Midwestern town. "I just wanted to tell you that my son is engaged to marry a Jewish woman," he said. His friend smiled and asked polite questions about the wedding date, then went home and confessed to her husband that she hadn't been quite sure how to respond—perhaps the minister was upset about the engagement. "I'll tell you how to respond," offered her husband. "You tell him, 'It should only happen to me!'"

But to some parents it doesn't matter. The daughter of Episcopalians said: "My parents raised me to make mature decisions on my own. I'm sure they think who I marry and how I raise my kids is my own business. I'm surprised that other parents don't have the same attitude." Other people may use the children's choices to indict the parents: "It's no surprise that their son is marrying a Christian. What did they expect? They never participated in anything in the Jewish community, never insisted that their children go to Sunday school—so there you have it."

The Detroit woman who passed this judgment—in an offhand manner, no harm intended, she would assert—was not alone in her punitive response to hearing of an interfaith marriage. She suspected that the parents must be uncomfortable, and in an "I told you so" way, she was pleased. But what she didn't acknowledge was that even if the parents had done all she accused them of failing to do, their children still might not be marrying Jews.

What is revealing about this comment is not its content but its invective tone. Children's marital choices are taken as a measure of the parents' success or failure—as parents and, in some cases, as Jews or as Christians. Of the many parents he has counseled, theologian Richard L. Rubenstein says, with reassuring irony, "What they did not understand was that, though they had undoubtedly failed as parents at some level, their failures were seldom different from those of parents of young people who did not intermarry."[1] Almost all parents under these circumstances go through a whole range of emotions. A teacher who works closely with Jewish families points out that "only the rabbis whose children marry out have no guilt," suggesting that at least these parents cannot chide themselves for not having "religious enough" homes. But of course even in the families of clergy there can be— and is—guilt that perhaps the parents were too overbearing in their religious stance and for *that* reason the child married out.

For the Jews there is so much guilt because self-esteem is so bound up with family closeness. It is hard to imagine many Jewish families responding as did the parents of the Episcopalian woman: that their daughter would choose a spouse in a mature fashion and that was that. For Jews, a child's choice to marry someone of another faith is often felt to be a rent in the fabric of the family. How strongly a parent will react depends on his or her age and religious affiliation—the older and more religiously traditional, the more opposed they are likely to be to an interfaith marriage.[2]

Because Christians do not, as a rule, see interfaith marriage as a threat to group survival the way many Jews do, they usually do not feel the same kind or amount of personal anguish when their children marry out as do Jewish parents. Intermarriage in a Christian family is thus a less appropriate tool for children to use against parents or for parents to use for managing their children. Styles of parenthood come into play here as well. A man from a German Catholic family said that his father uttered not one word when he announced that he was going to marry a Jewish woman. "My father's way of showing dispproval was utter silence. Which meant that while I knew he wasn't happy with my marrying a Jew, at least I didn't have to get into any disputes with him over the plans." A woman described her Irish Catholic parents' attitude to her marrying a Jew as, "If you're adult enough to get married, you're adult enough to make your own decisions about religion and raising kids." (Not quite the same as the constant barrage of comment her fiancé was getting from his Jewish parents!) Christian parents express disapproval for personal, social, or theological reasons; Jewish parents feel pain, guilt, anger, and helplessness.

Christian reluctance to have children marry Jews seems to be based on three factors: a fear of the unknown (among parents who do not know Jews at all and see them as an alien culture); snobbery and even anti-Semitism; and a theology-based anxiety that their grandchildren will be damned forever if not baptized and raised as Christians or disappointment that they will not share a faith and heritage to which the parents are personally committed. The first objection is more easily dealt with—both by the couple and the Christian parents—than the latter two. Exposure to the family of the Jewish partner—or an introduction to a local rabbi or Jewish congregation if a visit with the Jewish parents is not feasible—can defuse some of the uneasiness that comes from ignorance or lack of exposure. One set of Christian parents responded so well to contact with things Jewish that they now go out of their way to find, in their small Arkansas town, Hanukkah and Passover cards to send to their Jewish son-in-law in New York. Not all stories conclude so happily and easily. The reaction of the non-Jewish parents will be determined in part by how "Jewish" their child becomes. Kerry McDevitt, now a cantor at a suburban New York synagogue, changed his surname to Ben David when he converted to Judaism after many years of marriage. His parents, he said, still write to his children as McDevitt; they've told him, "Your kids will live to resent it."

Sometimes a visceral distaste for Jews is so entrenched in the worldview of the Christian parents that it requires constant vigilance on the part of the Jewish son-in-law or daughter-in-law to lessen it. For example, one young man was frequently reassured by his in-laws that he was "not like" other Jews—to which he would reply, "I don't really take that as a compliment," and attempt, gently, to explain to them that what they thought of as "reality" was merely prejudice. A combination of his persistent unwillingness to be separated out as a "good" Jew and the fact that he and his parents introduced his in-laws over the years to a number of Jews whose company they enjoyed began to wear away at their preconceptions.

Anti-Gentile feelings on the part of Jewish parents expressed in hurtful comments and thoughtless prejudice also hinder smooth family relations. The difference is that anti-Semitism has a painful historical background and therefore often feels more threatening to Jews than anti-Gentile feelings do to Christians. (Unless, of course, these Christians impute to Jews a special power, which is the case with some forms of anti-Semitism; in this rather atypical situation, the Christian parents may actually be afraid of the Jew their child is marrying.[3])

Individuals deal with parental prejudice in different ways. One Jewish woman, married to a Methodist man whose mother had never known Jews before and was alarmed by Jewish traditions, lit her Sabbath candles in a corner of the living room rather than in the dining room when her mother-in-law was visiting for a few weeks rather than "offend this elderly woman." Another solution, worked out by a couple when the wife's Presbyterian parents came to dinner on occasional Friday nights, was simply to explain the traditions of their Sabbath observances so frequently that they lost their "toxic" quality. The Christian in-laws, who had known that "Jews do something with wine" and thought this mysteriously had to do with Christian blood and how the wine was made, learned from their Jewish son-in-law that "what you say over the wine isn't to make the wine itself holy, or to change it in any way. The blessing over the wine sanctifies the time, not the wine. It's a way of making the Sabbath day special. If you didn't have wine, you could even say the prayers over bread—it's not mysterious, it's just a way of saying that the day to come is holy time, not workaday time."

In addition to the pain of being the object of prejudice, the partner confronting his or her parents' prejudices struggles with the same issue that the spouse does: the possibility that these prejudices have been passed on to the children in some form. They are then bucking not only the biases of parents and in-laws but their own, often hidden, biases as well. Sometimes marrying a partner of a different race is a way of challenging parental prejudice directly. A powerful method of attaining—and proclaiming—distance from white parents' racial prejudices, for example, would be to marry a black.

Parents understand, sometimes intuitively, that a child's intermarriage can be a way of pulling away from the family of origin and that the harder they push for the child not to marry someone of a different faith, the more determined the couple may become. The very act of working together to fight the parents gives the couple that "dilemma" or problem to solve together which serves as a galvanizing task fusing them into a couple.

"Every time there was a problem with my parents," said Stanley, a Jewish man engaged to a Catholic, "Laura and I would talk it over; *we'd* be the ones to stay up all night discussing it. It *definitely* brought us closer together. We had just about decided that whatever happened we'd deal with it, just the two of us. Now that my family is being more accepting, like calling her up and asking her to come for the holidays, I feel that I have to include them again." This man had really been caught in the middle of a triangle between his mother and his fiancée, wanting to be the "good" son and the good lover. "I was always very, very close to my family. But that's changed. I see them less now—I guess to Laura it seems like a lot, but it's much less than it used to be, and I feel the difference." Becoming involved with a non-Jewish woman has given him some leverage as he tries to move away from his parents. The hard times they have experienced with his family have, Stan admitted, "glued" the couple together.

Some parents react so strongly against an impending intermarriage that they prevent the adult child from seeing any potential problems, blinded by the need to defend his or her choice against the parents' meddling. The couple is "protected" from "squarely identifying issues and conflicts in their own relationship."[4] From the parents' perspective, becoming embroiled intensely in the child's marriage choice—though it appears "natural" to some—may be a way of avoiding other problems or anxieties in the family while focusing on the couple. Parents are indeed entitled to express their opinions about a child's life choices, but observers of family systems point out that the style of the communication is enormously important. Concern should be conveyed in terms of the parents' own reactions: "I feel worried about your marrying someone who's Jewish because we've always felt especially close in this family over the holidays, and it will feel very odd to me, and in a way intrusive, to be sharing them with somebody who won't find any meaning in them," rather than "Your grandmother would roll over in her grave if she knew you were marrying a Jew."

Since Jews tend to stay in college and graduate school longer than most Americans,[5] and since number of years of education usually correlates with delayed marriage and childbearing, Jews in particular are likely to be older when they marry, and hence less susceptible to direct parental influences of any sort. If parental values and attitudes are not already incorporated into the adult child's psyche, any other influence is going to be perceived as coercive. Choices made to please the parents, in an overt way, are clearly not independent personal choices, and may be more damaging to the parent-child relationship than a disapproved-of intermarriage. A few cases came up in interviews of Jews who had married Jews who were not perfect mates for them at all—they were marrying within the fold in a mechanical way, as if to please their parents and to punish themselves as well.

When there are actual schisms between parents and children over an intermarriage, religion itself is often not the central issue. Loss of control and loss of a definable link to the future are the real concerns. When a son or daughter marries out, the parents are confronted with the reality that they can no longer determine their children's choices and actions. "I'm not sure at all how much religion itself even means to my mother," mused one man whose parents had been particularly vociferous in using religious constraints against intermarriage to buttress their objections. It is important for both parents and children to be able to separate the issues related to power and control in the family and the adult child's independence from explicit concerns over religious identity, practice, and transmission.

One clue in untangling the ties that bind is how the grandparents react. The older generation—grandparents or other respected elders in the extended family—are often able to be more accepting of the intermarriage than the parents, though the former are usually more religiously traditional. This may be a signal that the parents' reaction is not based on religion alone. Some distressed parents reacted to this observation by noting that the grandparents do not bear ultimate responsibility for how the adult child turns out. "It's fine for *them* to give their approval," the mother of an intermarried son responded.[6]

To help people sort out their religious feelings from family dynamics, participants in groups for Jewish parents of intermarried couples are sometimes asked: "How would you feel if your child married a person much more Orthodox than you are? A self-hating Jew who rejects all things Jewish? A Harvard law student who is Unitarian?"[7] From their answers, parents are usually able to learn a little about what their own biases are and where their feelings are strongest: class based? religious? fearful of how others will judge the situation?

In many cases one reason for parental opposition is a sense of loss. Parents experience loss in several ways of which loss of control within the nuclear family is only one example. In a more existential sense there is the experience of losing a definable future that comes when one is uncertain about what will be transmitted to the next generation. It is not just the daughter or son "lost" to a marriage that may feel alien but the feared loss of any prospective grandchildren. These feelings are exacerbated if the parents fear that they will be cut off from the couple, or feel guilty as a result of having expressed their feelings of disapproval insensitively. Interfaith couples have commented on how reassured their own parents have been to hear such statements as "We're not sure yet how we will raise any children we might have, but we want you to know that whatever happens we want you to be there as active grandparents, and we want you to tell them about your lives and your values and your traditions." The couple ought not to promise more than they feel they will want to deliver, but parents are clearly reassured to know that the plan calls for keeping the next generation linked to them in some way, however undefined at the moment.

Parents' objections to intermarriage may also reflect their own uncertainties about how a modern American Jew can express his or her Jewish identity. Even children of devoutly Orthodox Jews have been known to marry Christians, and two founders of modern Zionism—Theodore Herzl and Chaim Weizmann (who surely demonstrated enough "community involvement" to satisfy even the most punctilious keeper of records on these matters)—had children who married non-Jews. More recently, a study of leaders of the Reform movement in Judaism found that one-third of the married children of these leaders have married non-Jews.[8] This may be cold comfort to the individual family who had yearned for total continuity of the generations, but it may at least mitigate the feelings of isolation, inadequacy, and self-blame that some parents feel.

The pain and guilt and fury—and even the shame—of some Jewish parents is hard to overestimate. Responsibility for family outcome typically falls more heavily on mothers, but while the mother may be more expressive of the guilt or more obsessive about trying to figure out "where did we go wrong?" the sense of loss is there for fathers as well, of course. The loss felt when a child does not marry at all, or marries and decides not to have children, provokes similar feelings of the future being cut off that some parents (Jewish and Christian) feel when a child marries someone of another faith and presents the possibility of grandchildren who will be unlike the grandparents in some essential way. "It's the loss of the parents' spiritual immortality," said a counselor who works with the parents of intermarried couples.[9] Acknowledging the strengh of those feelings is necessary before moving on to a happier plane, but wallowing in them is obviously going to be counterproductive to any kind of reconciliation with the younger couple.

All responses emphasizing the parents' pain and loss are grounded in the illusion of parental control over children's choices. Whereas this might have been true in the popular imagination about some glorious past, literature and life abound with examples of children who have defied parental injunctions in order to marry nonsanctioned mates. Even the parents of the biblical Samson ask him plaintively, "Is there never a woman among the daughters of thy brethren, or among all my people, that thou goest to take a wife of the uncircumcised Philistines?" (Judges 14:3). The desperation of the parents' helplessness is highlighted by the classic threat of the Jewish mother: "I'll put my head in the oven," or the Jewish father: "I'll cut you off, I'll sit *shiva* [the traditional mourning period], it's as if you'll be dead to me." There are no reports of mothers really killing themselves after a child's intermarriage, although the feelings of loss may indeed be so severe for some families that it feels as if future hopes are dashed in the same way as when a loved one dies. A modern-day case of declaring an intermarried child dead actually did occur in 1984 in Winnipeg, Canada, when a father placed an obituary notice in a local Jewish paper stating that his daughter, mentioned by name, was dead, and that the family requested no condolence calls. "Would my father really prefer that I had died?" asked the daughter.

The imagery of loss and death comes up especially when the parents are survivors of the Holocaust. "If my sons intermarried, it would be like death for me," says one such woman. Yet almost all parents, unless the children want to keep them at bay for their own reasons, *are* reconciled after the marriage. In some cases, the same need for family closeness that caused the reaction against the impending marriage also draws the parents near after the fact. An Orthodox rabbi has said that more parents come to him for counseling when the child is engaged than after the marriage is a reality; most parents, of any faith, would rather accept the situation than lose the kids.

Even if some of the anguish abates after the marriage, parents do have to come to terms with residual disappointment. Traditionally, Jews expected the marriage of a child to link the extended families socially too. The Yiddish language even has special terms for the relationship: a *machuten* (literally, "binded") is the father of your child's spouse; a *machetayneste* is the mother. A binding relationship between the two extended families is not so likely to be established where there are religious differences, and the expectation may not even be there (there are no terms in English for this relationship that imply anything but a legal connection). When a child marries someone whose own family does not anticipate this additional set of ties, the Jewish parents may have another dimension of their expectations shifted, with some sadness as a result.

There may be disapproval from family and friends about the effect that the intermarriage could have on *their* children. One Jewish woman was angry with her sister-in-law for marrying a Methodist. "How on earth can I tell my sons and daughter not to marry a non-Jew when their adored aunt has already gone and done it!" Another woman, a Conservative Jew, refused to invite her best friend's children to her own son's wedding, although all the children, now in their twenties, had been close friends growing up. Her rationale? "I can't invite one of her children without inviting all four, and one of them is living with a non-Jewish woman, and I can't have him without her, so I don't want any of them at my son's wedding. It's a Jewish ceremony and I don't want to have it appear to anyone—my other children included— that I approve of the interfaith relationship."

Marriages that involve a clear-cut exchange of religious homogeneity for something of great perceived value—for example, social status—are less likely to generate powerful feelings of hurt and anger from the parents. When a Jewish man, Edwin Schlossberg, married Caroline Kennedy, the daughter of the late president, the groom's family made no statements objecting to the Catholic ceremony. Nor did the Jewish in-laws of Mario Cuomo's daughter when the office of the governor of New York announced the marriage plans of the interfaith couple. The status exchange works in both directions; the objections of non-Jewish parents to a child's marrying a Jew may be lessened if the prospective spouse offers advantages of education, social status, or money.[10]

Family dynamics being what they are, other children may indeed take their cues from a sibling's outmarriage, but in a paradoxical way. Several families interviewed mentioned that siblings went toward opposite ends of the religious spectrum. In one family, where a daughter became a religious traditionalist, in contrast to her parents' liberal brand of Judaism, and married a strictly Orthodox man, raising with him their religiously observant family, her brother married a non-Jewish woman and has consented to raise their children in the Presbyterian church. While such marriage choices could be explained as mere chance, they suggest that the adult children involved may be acting out the ambivalence that some claim is at work in every American Jewish family. In the other direction, younger children who see how displeased or wounded their parents were when an older sibling married out of the faith may try at some level to please the parents by selecting a mate of the same religious background as the family. This also happens in families in which a child has married someone who is of the same faith but much less observant than his or her own family; the next child to marry may choose a mate more in keeping with the parents' expectations—depending on who plays the role of ''good'' child.

Conflicts between parents and children over marriage choices are often the expression of conflicts that predated the child's choice of a mate. For one young man, who had been a pawn between his divorced parents, and was used frequently as his mother's confidant and ally, marrying a non-Jewish woman provided a route out of his triangular relationship with his warring parents. His mother's reaction of rudeness and outright hostility to a young woman who had behaved admirably toward her mother-in-law gives some indication of how much the mother needed her son to remain under her control. (Interestingly, this mother had not objected when another of her sons married a Christian some years before—that child had played a different role in her life.) Similarly, the woman whose Orthodox father ran the obituary notice marking her marriage to a non-Jew says that her relationship with her father had never been very good. ''I think if my father and I had had a better relationship for the last ten years, I might not have been able to go through with it."[11]

This woman's reaction supports the common notion that some children intermarry to rebel against or punish their parents, or the notion that if the child identified with the parents more the attraction to a partner of the same background would be greater. Intermarriage can be a distancing device for an adult child who is trying to break away from something in his or her past. A psychologist made the comparison succinctly: "More powerful circuits require more powerful circuit breakers,"[12]

In light of all the potential family dynamics, what can be useful to parents whose children have married people of another faith?

For all parents, the first task must be to recognize that the younger couple has feelings too. This is not as obvious as it may sound. "I'm in love, and my own parents aren't talking to me," one woman moaned. Many engaged or newly married couples have expressed the desire that their own parents could hear tapes of their conversations with others in similar situations, just to gain some understanding of the pain and rancor their actions are capable of creating. In one group of interfaith couples, someone described a strife-free interfaith couple who had no children. Skeptical of their alleged bliss, a young man countered, "Do they have *parents*?"

Children may be surprised, disturbed, or angry when parents who never expressed their identification with or commitment to Judaism suddenly react strongly against an intermarriage. A Jewish son said, after a puzzling encounter over his impending intermarriage, "I didn't really know how much religion meant to my father and mother." In one extraordinary example of faulty communication, Jewish parents who raised their son with no Jewish input, no bar mitzvah even, but as a committed liberal in an affluent New York City suburb, were horrified when he came home from college planning to marry a Greek Orthodox woman. His fiancée seemed to him in every way the very embodiment of his parents' own overtly expressed political and cultural values. How was he to know that their professed distance from their own Jewishness was merely lip service paid to what they perceived as the demands of modernity, and that beneath the surface lurked a profound loyalty to Judaism? They felt that his choice was a rejection of all that they were, while their son had assumed just the opposite.

For these parents, as for many Jews of their generation, inter-marriage presents ''a bitter series of dilemmas. . . . The American Jew has generally assumed a strong liberal stance toward social issues, particularly with respect to . . . the equality of all people regardless of race or religion.'' Parents do not want to be in the situation of affirming Jews as superior to other people, yet they do want their children to marry within the group. For people who are not religiously observant, basing this argument on a religious creed seems hypocritical or manipulative. It becomes very diffi-cult for a nonobservant liberal American Jew to deal with a child's intermarriage in any but irrational terms. Social scientist Marshall Sklare concluded that ''many of the value commitments of the Jew make it difficult for him to confront the issue of intermarriage head on.''[13]

If an interfaith relationship continues, or after an intermarriage takes place, the most useful tactic, as it is all along, is not to be punitive or threatening but to keep the door open at all times. Parents need to try to be clear about what it is that they object to. As the pop psychologists say, send ''I'' messages: ''I am really sad at the thought that you might not want to come to us for Christmas and Easter anymore.'' ''I am awfully nervous about having Christian in-laws, or about the possibility that you might not want to raise your children Jewish.''

As they were discussing wedding arrangements for her daugh-ter's marriage to a Catholic, one mother replied to the daughter's questions about Jewish wedding traditions with the oversimpli-fied observation and query, ''I don't understand. If all this mat-ters so much to you, why don't you just marry a Jewish fella?''[14] The mother's question brought to a head doubts the daughter herself had been expressing all along, and she broke the engage-ment. Far more engagements proceed to the finish line, but the mother's tone—a little tearful but genuinely puzzled—seemed to reflect back to the daughter some of her own doubts.

It is pointless, to say nothing of graceless, to talk about one's prejudices. It is far more useful to try, ''I respect your right to choose to marry anyone you want, and I'm sure that he [or she] must mean a great deal to you. Please tell me about him [or her].'' The answer to this could give some sense of the person the parent is going to be dealing with and some clues as to how best to pres-ent religious options to the couple. Whereas blanket disapproval is usually useless, presenting options or making offers is very important. Suggest and discuss conversion. Propose secular alternatives to having clergy perform the wedding ceremony, leaving the opportunity open for a religious ceremony later on, after the couple has had a chance to live through some of their religious issues.

Being available and supportive will usually prove the most useful approach in the long run, whatever the couple chooses. Useful for what? For maintaining family closeness, and in the end perhaps for providing the couple and their children with a conduit to religious traditions that could enrich their lives and that might otherwise be totally ignored. Mordecai Waxman, a Conservative rabbi who has counseled the parents of many interfaith couples in his large congregation for forty years, proposes two specific things parents can do. First, he says, a family does better with a single religion in the home. "Push for conversion. I cannot tell you how many non-Jewish spouses have said, long past the time of their marriages, that they would have converted except that nobody suggested it to them—neither the husband or wife nor the Jewish parents." This is borne out by recent data; conversion is most likely to happen in response to "the personal efforts" of Jewish parents or spouses.[15]

Rabbi Waxman's second injunction is *m'karev;* the Hebrew word means a bringing closer. "Bring them into a Jewish sphere of influence," suggests Waxman. Whether or not conversion is even being considered, Jewish parents should include the interfaith couple in holiday celebrations, Sabbath dinners, and synagogue attendance whenever feasible. The problem here is that for parents who did none of these things before their child married a non-Jew, their efforts after the wedding may smack of hypocrisy. One man said that the first Rosh Hashanah dinner his parents ever held was the year after he married a Catholic woman. "They were afraid of losing me to her side of the family, I think." Sometimes children surprise their parents in this regard. A Jewish man who had been unconcerned about having had a Christian wedding ceremony called his mother the first Hanukkah after the marriage to ask, "Why didn't you ever give me a menorah?"

Of course, no religious encouragement coming from the parents alone is likely to be effective without interest from their child. But since many families choose their religious orientation after the wedding—in fact, after the children are born—it behooves the parents to remain warm and resourceful models for the couple. It should not need to be said—but does—that bad be-havior on either side will come back to haunt the perpetrators, in addition to forcing the children to defend their choices more than necessary. One young Catholic woman had been treated very rudely by her fiancé's family when they were dating. They had refused to talk to her when she answered the telephone in his apartment, refused to allow her to accompany their son when they took him out to dinner, ignored her on the few occasions when they were face to face. After announcing their engagement, the young woman commented very frankly, "I admire his moth-er's strength, but I don't like her for what lengths she went to. . . . Now they've suddenly invited me for Passover. What am I going to do that's going to make them turn on me again? I don't trust them."

The only relationships that are really successfully broken up by this kind of protest are the relationships between parents and child. Obviously, once the marriage is a *fait accompli,* or on its way to being so, standing firm in opposition to the union is only counterproductive, though it is obviously so common that one advertisement for a parents' group sells its programs partly on the basis of providing suggestions for, "How can I rebuild a rela-tionship when I was so much against the wedding?"

Parental objections, carried to extremes, can have tragic conse-quences. A couple now in their forties met while in college in the early 1960s. Marty is Jewish, Marge is Protestant. They became lovers and Marge became pregnant. Though not yet legal in the United States, abortion was fairly accessible to college women. Marge decided, however, not to have an abortion. They planned to marry, but Marty's parents were horrified, as much because Marge was not Jewish as by the circumstances. They threatened to stop supporting him and paying his tuition if he married her. He acceded to his parents' wishes and the couple broke up. Marge had the baby and put it up for adoption. Some years later Marty and Marge met again, and this time decided to marry. They now have three children, and their marriage is a happy and lasting one, the children close to their parents and each other.

The story has variations. But the leitmotiv is always that the male—or his parents—fear that his life (read: *professional* life) would be ruined if he married the woman. In this scenario, the happiest of the outcomes is that the woman only thinks she is pregnant, or later miscarries. But the theme is the same—that

Jewish men ought not to let themselves be lured into marriage by non-Jewish women, although in real life these couples often, like Marge and Marty, find each other again after a separation—the unfinished business between them a powerful magnet. The inherent sexism in this scenario is obvious, and its victimization of women (who are the ones to ''take the consequences'' of an unplanned pregnancy) perfectly clear. There are no statistics to undergird the perception that these are not isolated incidents; nonetheless, this is a story familiar to many people in their forties and fifties now in mixed marriages. Though unplanned pregnancies might have spurred endogamous marriages, they did not elicit the same parental encouragement for intermarriage.

The examples of couples who eventually come back together, although they are initially persuaded to separate, should serve as a caution to parents that, even as they make their own feelings clear, they should not do so abusively or in a manner that either causes harm to one of the partners or will make cordial relations between parents and the couple impossible should they marry.

Parents need to be *menschen* (human beings), and probably want to be. Their own feelings of pain, foreboding, and, sometimes, embarrassment, are so strong that their good instincts may be overwhelmed by these negative feelings. The downside is that those who give free reign to their hostilities not only run the risk of losing a child and future grandchildren to another faith but may effectively preclude having any kind of relationship with them at all. Parents who, for example, continue to affirm actively their own commitment to Judaism, on the other hand, provide a role model for people who might want to convert later. (Sometimes it is the presence of a loving mother-in-law or grandfather that spurs this.)

While conversion may be the outcome parents have hoped for, it may bring unforeseen consequences. Although more children of interfaith marriages live closer to the Jewish than to the non-Jewish grandparents, some families, after the non-Jewish partner converts to Judaism, move farther away from the Jewish in-laws, leading one researcher to comment: ''Having satisfied their Jewish parents, conversionary couples may express a residual resentment by distancing themselves and their children from the parents.''[16]

In addition to these strains, intermarriage can also be damaging to the relationship between the parents of the intermarrying child themselves. One parent may object more than the other. One may talk about feelings of sadness and guilt while the other may want or need to deny the pain. The same way that good parent–bad parent dichotomies arise over other problems in raising children, here, too, one party may blame the other for what is imagined to be the failure of the parenting process revealed in the child's intermarriage.

It can be helpful for parents to remember their own histories as a source of perspective on this complex situation. They, like most Jews, probably express their own Jewishness in ways different from those of their own parents and grandparents. Each time their own family role changed, so did their views of Judaism and Jewish identification, and the role they played in the transmission of culture and religion.[17] Now they get a new chance—as grandparents. They can do it differently, and even better, than they did when they were parents. The need to determine what to do clearly does not end with the intermarriage itself. Parents (and actual or prospective grandparents) have an immensely useful role to play in providing their interfaith grandchildren with knowledge about their own traditions and about the family's history.

As grandparents, they no longer have to worry about their position on intermarriage. They only have to care about what of their tradition they want to transmit to the next generation. They also must find out what the parents will *allow* them to transmit. Even if the grandchildren are being raised in another religion, grandparents of the other faith can have a role. In such cases, as one grandmother put it, ''It's even more important for my Catholic grandchildren to have positive associations with things Jewish, and with Jewish people.'' This approach supports the view of some Jews that one of the positive aspects of intermarriage is the creation of many more homes in which at least one partner is Jewish, increasing the number of people who understand Judaism or have at least had some firsthand exposure to it. Following the same reasoning, Jewish grandparents should reach out to the non-Jewish grandparents on the other side to include them in Jewish holiday celebrations. In addition to furthering family harmony, such efforts can be viewed as creating non-Jewish ''allies'' for the Jewish community—people who have a chance to experience Judaism up close are less likely to have negative attitudes toward it.

The parents also have a role to play in supporting the children's marriage. More than one researcher has pointed out that inter-marriages are more likely to end in divorce than in-group marriages. While this correlation may have something to do with the religious differences between the partners, it also may partly reflect the tendency, in the face of less support from parents and others, to turn to divorce more readily than to less drastic forms of intervention such as counseling. Parents who are present and generally supportive, even when there are differences of opinion and judgment, can do their children a great service.

Parents should be careful of hidden negative attitudes. If there has been conversion, a convert should never be referred to as such—he or she is a complete Jew or a complete Christian. When grandchildren are being raised in one faith, it may be even more important to link the "other" grandparents to the family, to diminish the possibility that they will convey subtle negative messages to the grandchildren, out of ignorance. Jewish grandparents can create a double bind if, for example, they incite the feeling in the new family that no matter what happens in the family's religious practice the offspring of the intermarriage will "never" be Jewish.

Ideally, all this intelligence and goodwill should lead to harmony. But harmony is hard to come by. The three tasks for parents, the three phases they have to go through, are to make their own feelings clear in a courteous way; to be available to counsel the couple when asked for advice and to point out some of their own choices and the values they reflect; and, in the end, to accept the resolutions the couple reaches.

The parents' own value as human beings is not hanging in the balance when their children make marriage choices. Ultimately, the couple's choices are their own; parents need to try to wrest themselves free of any feelings of competitiveness over the couple or the grandchildren. If they find themselves really unable to "stay cool," they might benefit from refocusing some of their energy on other relationships within the family. Given some distance, the children, surprisingly, may move closer as they realize that they themselves have some control over the intergenerational dynamic. General advice on how to handle a triangular relationship—which the two parents and the intermarrying child surely create—pertains here. The essential ingredients are "staying calm, staying out, and hanging in."[18]

119

# 7

## The Wedding

DAVID (A JEW): I'd rather go civil and just not deal with these choices and problems.

JUDY (A CATHOLIC): A civil ceremony means we're just running away from the issue. And my family would really be hurt.

DAVID: We don't have to deal with all our potential conflicts at the wedding itself.

JUDY: Well, I'd rather have a rabbi than a judge.

DAVID: Okay. Let's just have a rabbi.

JUDY: No.

The interfaith wedding is a crucible in which are mixed an extraordinary array of ingredients, sometimes explosive when combined. Will the ceremony be civil or religious? If religious, whose religion? If secular, what traditional religious elements can be incorporated? Who will perform the ceremony? Where will the wedding be held? Who will the wedding attendants be? Who will say what at the wedding reception, and what food will they eat?

The negotiations of Judy and David exemplify the struggles involved when the partners retain their two separate faiths and have to structure the wedding ceremony to take this into account. Their story incorporates many of the elements common to others—the strong feelings of identification of each partner with his or her own tradition; the ambivalence of the Jewish partner ("I'd rather go civil") despite this identification; the familiar reactive dynamic in which the Jewish partner responds negatively to Christian ritual and symbol without being able to offer alternative

Jewish ones; the woman trying to remain true to what she wants spiritually while mollifying her husband-to-be. The Jewish partner wants to keep everyone happy—his family, his fiancée, the rabbi—and isn't even sure what he himself would like, except that it is not any of the possibilities they have so far come up with. "In the end," Judy groaned, "the only thing I'm going to get that I wanted is the band." (Judy is barely able to acknowledge that she is getting the man that she wants!)

DAVID: The dates are changing constantly. We can't figure out exactly how to do this. We were going to go ahead and have a Catholic ceremony because it mattered a lot to Judy, but my mother just got freaked out. It was too religious when we talked about having the priest there. And the priest freaked me out too when he met with us. [David is only touching on the fact that his mother was not the only one upset by having a Catholic ceremony.]

JUDY: I was wrong to take you to that priest. I thought all Jesuits would be liberal, like Daniel Berrigan. But no matter who the priest is, you have to realize that Christ is in the entire ceremony, like a baptism without a mass.

DAVID: How's a Jew supposed to know what that even means? My family is going to freak out if it's such a Christian wedding.

What is going on between Judy and David is not just the power struggle that one might think at first glance. Each really does want something different out of the marriage ceremony, just as the connection to a religious group means something different for each. Although they haven't articulated their search in these terms, they are looking for a solution that meets their individual psychological and spiritual needs. "In the ceremony, many individuals want to honor both traditions," according to Reverend Tracy Robinson Harris of New York's Community Church, who counsels and marries many interfaith couples.

In order to understand the wedding options—and the feelings of acceptance or of loneliness and alienation they may inspire in the couple—one must first understand how Christian and Jewish wedding ceremonies differ. A Christian ceremony, whether Catholic or Protestant, has at its core the sacrament of marriage, similar to other basic church sacramental rituals in that it is rooted in the Christian belief in Jesus as savior and in the salvation this belief will bring. This links the couple's relationship "to their commitment to Jesus Christ . . . their love for one another is a sign of the Lord's love for the Church," out of which they derive grace and strength for their life together.[1]

The Jewish ceremony is an elaboration of the marriage agreement itself. The *ketubah* (wedding contract) traditionally spells out the obligations incurred in, and the rights that flow from, this union. No particular faith in God is needed for two Jews to celebrate this marriage ceremony, traditionally held under a small canopy supposed to represent the groom's home. In fact, the idea of home is a theme permeating the rituals of the Jewish ceremony—evidence that the ceremony itself has more to do with the future of the bride and groom together as a new family unit than with their shared faith in God. Even the groom's breaking a glass under his foot, the traditional conclusion of the ceremony, is thought to signify that although the Temple was destroyed in the first century A.D., every couple has a chance to rebuild it in the form of their own Jewish household.[2]

The Jewish wedding focuses not on the religious beliefs of the couple but rather on their future as a political entity, so to speak, within the Jewish community. Because the ceremony signifies the creation of a new Jewish family unit, the wedding is seen strictly as a Jewish occasion; according to Jewish law (*halakhah*), it is the joining of two *Jews*. If one partner is not Jewish, the union is invalid; the religious laws joining the couple are binding only on Jews. This is why Orthodox and Conservative rabbis will not officiate at a mixed marriage. Reconstructionist rabbis may participate if it is not a Jewish ceremony but if they are there simply as a Jewish presence at a civil ceremony. While some Reform rabbis will perform a Jewish ceremony even when one partner is not Jewish, there are variations: Some rabbis will cofficiate with Christian clergy (as is clear from the wedding announcements on what one wit calls the intermarriage pages of the Sunday edition of the *New York Times*); others will not. Some require a period of study or counseling or a commitment to raise any future children Jewish or to maintain a Jewish home before they will participate in any way.

If one partner has converted to the religion of the other, and the religious content of the ceremony is pretty much determined in advance, many religious differences can be ironed out in advance of the wedding preparations. Since it is usually the Christian partner who converts to Judaism, a Jewish ceremony will be performed, although perhaps with variations to include the Christian parents and other relatives. The Conservative movement, for example, has guidelines that "permit" the non-Jewish parents to walk their child down the aisle to the ceremony. Non-Jewish friends or relatives can hold up the poles of the wedding canopy and act as attendants to the bride and groom; they cannot be witnesses signing the formal Jewish marriage contract. The role of Jews in a Christian ceremony will vary depending on the Christian denomination.

There are actually numerous religious and secular options for the Christian-Jewish couple wanting to achieve as painless and joyful a wedding ceremony as possible. Some of the choices have more religious validity or acceptability than others. Unitarian churches and the Ethical Culture Society have "nondenominational" marriage ceremonies that answer some couples' need for a traditional, yet neutral, wedding. Reverend Dick Leonard of The Unitarian Church of All Souls in New York has what he calls his basic service for the occasion, which includes readings from the Book of Ruth, Kahlil Gibran, and Shakespeare ("Let me not to the marriage of true minds/ Admit impediments"). The ceremony describes marriage as an institution "sanctioned by church and synagogue" and provides an opportunity, after the partners' brief pledges to one another, for a wine-sharing ceremony and the breaking of a glass. God is not mentioned in the ceremony, nor in many of the nonspecific ceremonies created by interfaith couples themselves. Not all couples choose religiously neutral ceremonies, however. Though at one time an intermarrying Catholic could not expect to be married within the church, now this is possible with a special dispensation. A Conservative or Orthodox rabbi will not perform a Jewish ceremony marrying an interfaith couple, but other rabbis sometimes permit variations. And couples have created scenarios that allow the presence of clergy from both sides—for example, where a minister performs the ceremony and a rabbi is present, perhaps in the role of family friend or witness. Arranging a ceremony where there is literally joint officiation is extremely difficult, and probably with good reason—because the blending or yoking of these two different theologies may be seen as canceling out the religious authenticity of each.

In addition to the theological problems, some interfaith partners have personal difficulties with joint officiation. Again, the objections here are not unlike those that relate to questions of worship or child rearing. For the Christian partner the marriage may feel invalid spiritually if it is not celebrated in a Christian ceremony. The Jewish partner may find the introduction of any Christian theology or mention of Christ repugnant but may still want the traditional features of a Jewish wedding to assert a link with the Jewish people for personal or spiritual reasons—to stand under the marriage canopy (*chuppah* in Hebrew), and to break the wine glass at the conclusion of the ceremony, signaling the couple's link to the historic destruction of the Temple in Jerusalem, connecting "the private moment under the chuppah with the public national event of the Temple."[3]

In the case of Judy and David, she wanted a spiritual dimension to her wedding for her own sense of the sanctity of the event. He wanted to feel connected as a Jew and not offend his parents. One solution, not the same as having joint officiation by a priest and a rabbi, would have been to have a small civil ceremony with a Jewish flavor, to satisfy the groom and his family, followed in another room by a small Catholic ceremony for the sake of the bride and her family. Since the civil ceremony has little meaning for Judy, she will not be disturbed by it if she knows she will be "really" married in a religious ceremony. And the Christian ceremony is unlikely to bother David at that point, because in his eyes he has already been married. Each ceremony might include just the couple and the appropriate family members, with the reception following the ceremony open to all the guests. Although this struck at least one observer as a "let's fool *both* partners" solution, it actually does manage to meet the immediate needs of both without creating friction over the wedding itself.

It may be (and has been) argued that a Jewish ceremony cannot legitimately be performed linking a Jew and a non-Jew, since the operative words of the Jewish marriage contract state that the pair is married "according to the laws of Moses and Israel," which are binding only on Jews. Yet experiencing such a ceremony, even in facsimile, or planning a wedding officiated at by a judge or other secular figure, which incorporates Jewish elements, may be very important not only to the Jewish partner—to give him or her the sense of still remaining connected to the Jewish community— but also to the Christian partner. Some rabbis suggest that the non-Jewish partner will have warm feelings about Judaism connected to the wedding ceremony and then may be more receptive to the idea of becoming Jewish through conversion. Rabbi Albert Axelrad, who has married many Jewish-Christian couples in his role as Jewish chaplain at Brandeis University, has written that if an interfaith couple committed to maintaining a Jewish household and raising Jewish children wants "a religious ceremony colored Jewish, I am prepared to participate, making it clear that I will not conduct the standard Jewish ceremony."[4] Axelrad makes a statement at the beginning of the wedding, as do several rabbis who officiate at mixed marriages, explaining that the ceremony that follows uses Jewish sources but is not "the normative Jewish ceremony."[5] Axelrad proposes a two-stage marriage, parallel in some ways to the tradition of Jews and some Christians of centuries ago, when the betrothal ceremony and the wedding itself were separate events. He performs the actual Jewish marriage ceremony—which includes a *ketubah*, or wedding contract—only after the Christian spouse has converted to Judaism, should this take place. In any case, the "ceremony colored Jewish" is a legally binding secular marriage.

For David and Judy, however, a ceremony that omitted any reference to her strongly held Christian beliefs and Catholic practice would not have been satisfactory. She wanted her tradition represented explicitly in the marriage ceremony, and in some ways—commented a social worker who had led a group in which the couple had participated—"this is a very authentic position. The two religions are different and can't be blended into one, and they had to figure out a way of celebrating with that doubleness."

Why the Jewish content mattered so much to David and his family—though he himself said "I'd have much more trouble marrying a Hasidic Jew than marrying a Catholic," was that a ceremony with explicitly Christian content would have signaled to his parents and even to himself that he had lost something of his Jewish identity. For the Christian partner, the loss experienced if the Christian rituals (different from denomination to denomination) are not followed in the ceremony is an individual, spiritual forfeiture. This was why Judy had said that to have some religious input in the ceremony she would even have settled for a rabbi and a Jewish ceremony rather than a strictly secular one. A Christian college chaplain who counsels interfaith student couples distinguished the Jewish partner's concerns this way: "A Christian family does not give up the Christian identity of one of its members even when that member marries outside the faith.

Christian identity can only be surrendered by an intentional act of apostasy. Christians cannot understand why Jews do not see things the same way."[6] Since to most Jews, Judaism signifies more than faith alone, even a Jew who has relinquished formal religious ties often feels bound to Jewishness.

This strong desire to have the marriage ceremony stand as a link to what one Jewish intermarrying man referred to as "the long march of Jewish history" is what makes it so important for some prospective brides and grooms to have a Jewish presence at the ceremony, however symbolic or unofficial. Responding to this need (and to the Jewish community's desire to maintain some connection with interfaith couples), it has been suggested that, if the Christian partner evinces a desire to live a Jewish life and "become an associate member of the Jewish people" even without converting to Judaism, the rabbi should serve as a witness in a civil marriage.[7]

Some rabbis assist the couple in creating a "facsimile" service. Rabbi Leslie Gutterman of Providence helps interfaith couples "write their own service to be officiated at by a judge. These couples usually come away feeling that . . . what we have done is honest and written with an integrity that the couple can convey to family and friends."[8]

One Reform Rabbi conducts a "Jewish-style" wedding in which there is a wedding canopy and Hebrew blessings are pronounced over the couple by the rabbi, yet the marriage contract is a civil one, not the *ketubah*. Such a wedding has no standing in Jewish legal terms, but it does provide a way for the couple to mark their link to Judaism.

In this vein, Rabbis Rebecca Alpert and Linda Holtzman and rabbinic instructor Arthur Waskow have created an example of a secular ceremony with a Jewish flavor and New Age overtones. The wedding instructions begin with the suggestion that "if at all possible, the setting and symbols of the ceremony should reflect the motif of the Rainbow Covenant, that not only the whole human race but all forms of life are in the covenant with God."[9]

Many interfaith couples arranging civil ceremonies, interfaith services, or even Christian weddings try to incorporate something of the Jewish tradition, especially the breaking of the glass, which is uniquely associated with the wedding celebration, since it is not used anywhere else in Jewish ritual or custom. A Jewish woman married for fifteen years to a practicing Episcopalian described their wedding: "We had a leader of the nonreligious Ethical Culture Society preside. My husband read from the New Testament. I read from the Song of Songs. He broke the glass and that was that." Although it has virtually no formal religious significance, the act of breaking the glass has become the characteristic Jewish wedding symbol, concluding the solemnities and indicating that the festivities and rejoicing are about to begin.

The glass that is broken is not the glass used for the *kiddush*, or blessing over the wine sipped by groom and bride, which takes place earlier in a Jewish ceremony. But perhaps linked to the idea of the glass at the conclusion, some Jews who are intermarrying in a ceremony that is either secular or Christian attempt to incorporate some blessing over wine in a kiddush cup. The very presence of this familiar ritual object, linked to weekly Sabbath celebrations, may make the Jewish partner feel more comfortable in the face of alien Christian symbols or, in a setting that has carefully been stripped of any religious symbolism, provide a link with the past.

Before 1970, when intermarriage rates rose steeply, rabbis were more uniformly opposed to performing intermarriages. One of the most common forms of rejection a Jew felt came from his or her own rabbi and synagogue. A rabbi who initially refused to marry the couple was sometimes pressured to do so by congregants; a willingness to perform intermarriages was reportedly a factor in whether or not a rabbi was hired. One Conservative rabbi claims that he is never asked anymore to officiate at interfaith marriages—not that they aren't taking place among members or children of members of his congregation, but that his congregants "know enough not to ask." Sometimes congregants erroneously assume that rabbis who seem less traditional will be more amenable to such requests. A Reform woman rabbi who does not perform intermarriages says that she is always approached by interfaith couples: "People think that because I'm in an untraditional role I'll be liberal in all areas of Jewish practice." Even if they do endorse traditional thinking on interfaith marriages, however, women rabbis are still frequently sought out by intermarrying couples—either for counsel or to help plan the wedding. A rabbi often in this situation says, "Because people don't know many women rabbis, they can't dump all their prejudices and anti-rabbi feelings onto [them]."

The arguments made by Reform rabbis on both sides of the issue offer some insights into the reasoning behind the decision to officiate or not to officiate. Reviewing these rationales might be helpful to interfaith couples struggling to find a comfortable wedding procedure. Basically, those who officiate at mixed marriages do so out of a desire to keep the couple close to the Jewish community; they do not want to alienate the Jewish partner from the synagogue and may even suggest a synagogue wedding without the traditional Jewish ceremony. Many Reform and other rabbis who do not themselves officiate at intermarriages regularly recommend colleagues who do, so a couple looking for a rabbi should not hesitate to approach even one who is known not to officiate him- or herself.

The risk involved in approaching a member of the clergy "cold" —what one woman called the "telephone-book method"—is that one may indeed find someone on the other end of the line who is very much opposed to interfaith marriages and who will take the opportunity to announce this fact to the couple. A common complaint is that "rabbis are so hypocritical. I want to draw near, I want to be married by a rabbi, after all, and they're saying 'go away.'" The rabbis are likely not being hypocritical. The situation is complex for many of them, who want to keep the couple close but feel that they cannot perform the ceremony itself. Rabbi Alexander M. Schindler, president of the Union of American Hebrew Congregations (the central body of Reform Judaism), has said: "The Rabbi who chooses not to officiate should spend extra energy striving to convince the couple that there is no rejection involved. I invariably spend more time counseling the couple to whom I have to say no than with the couple whom I will marry. If possible, I will attend their wedding to demonstrate symbolically my embracing them even though I could not myself officiate."[10]

One Reform rabbi makes his case very poignantly: "It is impossible to stress too strongly how bitter the Jew feels when the rabbi refuses to marry him. He feels he is being rejected by the Jewish people, leaving a scar from which he rarely recovers. If a religious marriage is refused, it does not stop the couple from getting married—it only turns them away from the synagogue."[11] Yet this probably reveals more about the conflicts rabbis themselves feel about turning people away than any accurate assessment of the aftereffects of such a refusal. The latest figures indicate that being married by a rabbi has no effect on the partners' rate of conversion to Judaism or disaffection with Judaism after the ceremony.[12]

Conservative rabbis are specifically enjoined from officiating at a wedding in which the non-Jewish partner has not converted, "or to be present in any way in which the rabbinic role might be noted," according to the Rabbinical Assembly Committee on Jewish Law and Standards. In most states cantors are legally able to perform a marriage, but Conservative cantors are under the same strictures as Conservative rabbis.

Although the Reconstructionist movement (a twentieth-century offshoot of Conservative Judaism) has set forth its position that the Jewish wedding ceremony be reserved for the marriage of one Jew to another, it adds two interesting elements to this. First, that a Reconstructionist rabbi, after determining that the couple intends to establish a Jewish home and educate their children as Jews, may attend a civil ceremony and after its conclusion make a statement "welcoming the couple's intention to create a Jewish home."[13] Second, that the synagogue arm of the Reconstructionist movement will actively try to develop a marriage ceremony for interfaith couples that differs from the traditional Jewish ceremony.

As the Reform guidelines for rabbis note, the promises couples make—to each other and to clergy—before the wedding are not always kept. Even in the best-intentioned individuals, feelings and motives change, especially on issues as sensitive as how the children will be raised. Several interfaith couples noted in interviews that when a child was born they were astonished by the strength of their desire to raise that child in their own faith. In an attempt to reinforce the couple's early pledge to raise their children Jewish, Reconstructionist rabbi Susan Schnur, who does officiate at some mixed marriages, but only if there is no coofficiation with clergy of the other religion, said: "I begin by making it all overt—that they'll raise their kids Jewish and have a Jewish home. I make a statement at the beginning of the ceremony telling the guests about this; the couple contracts with me from the beginning of our discussions that this will happen, that their decision will be overt and public."

In Christianity, too, there is an obvious concern with what will happen in the next generation, a concern made manifest in the traditional Catholic priest's insistence that a Catholic marrying out of the faith actually pledge—and have the partner pledge—to raise any children in the Catholic faith. Recognizing the difficulty of enforcing such pledges, and the hypocrisy they sometimes encouraged, many Catholic clergy today do not require any binding commitment from the partners, though their wishes are made quite clear in premarital counseling, often required if a couple are to marry in the Catholic church.[14] If this counseling will be difficult for the Jewish partner to accept, the Catholic should perhaps review the material to be taught in advance and prepare his or her partner for what is to come, thus averting an encounter in the priest's study—like the one that made David (and Judy) so uneasy—in which the priest disparaged David's discomfort about having a strictly Catholic ceremony. Many Catholic priests and laypeople are more sensitive now than ever before to issues of concern to Jewish partners in interfaith marriages because of the concerted effort made to educate Catholics about Jews and Jewish history in the wake of the conciliatory efforts of Vatican II in 1963.[15]

The struggle to find an appropriate clergyperson or venue for their interfaith wedding is one of the first major tasks the mixed-faith couple faces together. It provides a laboratory for problem solving, and some couples decide that the experiment is not worth the effort. One couple, discussing their relationship in a group setting, decided after the Jewish woman could not overcome real feelings of sadness and loss at not having a Jewish ceremony that they would break their engagement. (Her Christian fiancé was equally strongly attached to his own Polish Catholic roots.) Premarital rabbinical counseling is not necessarily geared to this goal, but often does propose that the non-Jewish partner consider converting to Judaism before the wedding.

To avoid confronting their differences head on before marriage, intermarrying couples are frequently drawn to secular solutions— for example, a secular ceremony presided over by a Jewish judge—infused with custom-made details, such as personally selected readings or comments by each partner and pledges about their future together. Given the tremendous tensions that may emerge in trying to accommodate two different religious systems in one already highly charged occasion, a secular solution "seemed much cleaner, more honest" to one Protestant woman characterizing the decision she and her Jewish husband arrived at.

Even a secular ceremony contains potential pitfalls. A Congregationalist woman described how, at the dress rehearsal for her nondenominational wedding, the cleric who was organizing the service greeted the wedding party in the chapel by saying, "Welcome to the church center for the United Nations." Her Jewish father-in-law said, "Wait!" And the cleric changed his greeting to "Welcome to the religious center for the United Nations." Language is tremendously important in a service designed to offend no one; people who have experienced such ceremonies advise others to "go over every word."

There are several advantages to a secular ceremony, incorporating whatever aspects of each tradition the other partner won't feel uncomfortable with. First, some priests and rabbis will not perform a religious ceremony at a later date if the partners have previously been married to each other in a religious ceremony of another faith (should one convert or should circumstances change and the couple opt for a unidimensional religious ceremony). Second, a secular service should offend the least number of relatives on both sides. Third, a secular wedding allows the two partners to reach compromise together without having the decision linked to parents' wishes and pressures from either side.

Numerous conventional and unusual locations have been the settings for the secular ceremonies uniting Jewish-Christian couples, aside from synagogues or churches: college chapels (nondenominational), museums, clubs of various sorts (including country clubs), academic facilities, catering halls, parks, boathouses, and private homes. In some ways, the more unusual the setting the less likely the guests are to expect a conventional wedding in the first place, so out-of-the-ordinary locations may be appropriate for these weddings. The music and even the food convey a message—to the partners, their families, and the guests. Serving obviously nonkosher food (shellfish or pork products) at a wedding between a Jew and a Christian, even if the Jewish participants may not themselves be strictly kosher, sends a message that Jewish traditions are being blatantly flouted. And if the ethnic background of either partner calls for special music, particularly for group dancing that can make everybody feel part of the festivities, the couple would be wise to include this in their planning. The guests at one Jamaican Christian–New York Jewish wedding still talk about the great reggae music and the great Israeli dance tunes that the band played.

Whatever the modality of the ceremony, the parents and close relatives on both sides should be included if they feel comfortable participating. This is, after all, supposed to be a happy event, and one of the goals in creating it is to provide happy associations in years to come. Excluding significant family members (or not encouraging them to get over their uneasiness and attend the wedding) may burder the partners' memories with some sadness later. One couple said that they were forever having to explain the missing characters in their wedding photos, telling their children that "Grandma and Grandpa just couldn't make it."

The issues that arise around the wedding are not so different from other choices and negotiations the couple will experience, but they are more complex, intensified, and involve the clearest act of differentiation from the two families of origin. In contrast, by the time childbearing and child-rearing decisions are being made, the couple has had a little more distance from the older generation.

It is no surprise that the families on both sides are involved, and that the partners are striving to accommodate their needs as well as their own (if they are lucky enough to be able to see what their own needs are). It is to be expected that parents will care who their children marry and how the wedding goes, but also—and maybe more importantly—because this is often the rite of passage that defines for the older generation their success as parents and their ability to launch their children as independent adults. ("My parents played 'good cop–bad cop' for three months when we were planning our wedding. One week my father would be upset that I was marrying a Jew and the next week it would be my mother," said a Methodist woman whose mother had been trying to orchestrate her wedding from a distance of two thousand miles.) A transition like marriage creates a degree of shifting—or even havoc—in the family system involved, even when the partners are of the same faith.

Parents who go crazy (*freak out* is the term the engaged couple frequently uses) over the wedding arrangements may well have other issues of conflict with their children—or with this child in particular—that make reasoned discussion of the wedding itself extraordinarily difficult. A rabbi-cum-family therapist, who has for decades dealt with interfaith couples in both roles, states "categorically" that "the cause of almost all severe parental reactions to marital choice is the failure of the reacting parent to have worked out something important in other relationships."[16]

Even when both families have been reconciled to a secular wedding, the interfaith couple may encounter problems because of religious laws on other occasions. A Catholic who is married without the church sacrament of marriage may be forbidden to receive Communion. A Jew who is married to someone who has not converted to Judaism, regardless of the kind of wedding they had, may be kept from holding office in a synagogue. The non-Jewish spouse will usually be denied complete membership privileges in the synagogue (though welcome at services and synagogue events). And under traditional interpretations of Jewish law, a non-Jew may not be buried in a Jewish cemetery, which means that a married couple might have to anticipate being separated after they are both dead.

Just as there are choices beyond confrontation in working out the other details of their shared lives, so there are options in planning the wedding ceremony, which can serve as the emblem of how well the couple are able to deal with their disparate religious traditions. The easiest option to carry out may be, in cases where there has been no religious conversion, to find a secular solution that incorporates enough of each tradition to help the partners feel connected to their own past associations. Respecting the double (and essentially unblendable) nature of their backgrounds even in the ceremony that marks their union is a way of encouraging that same kind of authenticity as they move on to other occasions together.

134

# 8

♦

# *Raising Children*

How to raise children in an interfaith marriage has been *the* conundrum for intermarried couples. It is an issue debated between partners even when they are still at the dating stage, not yet seriously considering marriage. Discussions about how they will raise any future children are used by some women and men as a litmus test, in fact, of whether or not a relationship ought to continue. The children represent all the compromises and choices and forfeitures the partners anticipate having to make.

Preparing for parenthood, Jewish-Christian couples confront several general anxieties. Jewish partners might have been warned since childhood's religious school classes "not to break a 5,000-year-old chain"; they may have a special concern about what raising an "interfaith" or "neutral" or Christian child might mean in the continuum of Jewish history. A Christian parent may have deep uneasiness and unexplored feelings about introducing "Jewish blood" into the family line, or fears—overt or buried—that a child raised as a Jew will not go to heaven.[1]

The children of earlier intermarriages faced different situations than do such children today. In the early 1960s, for example, only about 3 percent of Jews married non-Jews; for children of these uncommon unions, a few scenarios were possible. In the first, the Christian parent converted (in those days almost always the mother, since the Jews who married out of the faith were then almost exclusively men) and with the collusion of her husband and children may have kept her Christian heritage somewhat under wraps, usually not making reference to it. In earlier, noncon-

versionary marriages the identity of the Jewish partner was sometimes kept secret—giving the children the shock of recognizing
the Jewish component in their own identities only in adulthood.[2]
In less dramatic cases, the Jewish parent in a mixed marriage
might simply "forget about" any expressions of Jewish identity.
In fact, a 1954 study of Harvard and Radcliffe students who had
one Jewish and one Christian parent found that not a single *mischling* recalled a Jewish parent expressing a desire that they receive any education in Judaism or attend Jewish services.[3]

In another scenario for interfaith families of the past, the Christian parent maintained his or her (usually her) own identity, and
the children were raised "neither." Their mothers—certainly in
the 1940s and 1950s and early 1960s the chief establishers of the
household's "culture"—were not Jewish, and in many cases
were overtly something else, either Protestant or Catholic. With
Christmas trees in the house and little public celebration of Jewish
rituals, the children themselves were usually not entirely welcomed into the Jewish community, neither by their peers nor by
adults. These children would obviously tend, for example, to
have much less affiliation with Jewish organizations—even secular ones—than their fully Jewish cohorts. However, since most of
them were likely to have Jewish surnames, they didn't quite pass
in either world.

Today, with intermarriage rates much higher, the children of
marriages like these face quite different issues. For one thing, a
parent who has converted to Judaism is likely to have done so
while keeping his or her ties to a birth family intact, and the
religion-of-origin is no secret. And most children of mixed marriages feel some connection to the religion of *both* parents.[4]

Because the issues are now more overtly expressed, the prospective children who are so common a source of anxiety absorb
couples in discussion groups around the country for session after
session. Some even talk about the possibility of including in a
prenuptial agreement provisions for the religious upbringing of
a child in the event that the parents divorce, although in most
jurisdictions such an agreement wouldn't stand up under the
law. It might be argued that individuals often project onto these
hypothetical children many of their own fears about a partner's
religious expression. "How would the child feel walking into a
fancy suburban synagogue not knowing the language of the prayers?" could just as easily be the anxiety of the Presbyterian

woman who voices these concerns in the name of her as-yet-unconceived child.

What goes into the parents' choice to have children in the first place? Interfaith couples typically have fewer children than partners whose religious backgrounds match. This may be because these couples also tend to be older, and to be in a second marriage, possibly with children from other unions, but it may also be an expression of how challenging they perceive raising such children to be. Hostilities do seem to surface with children, but this finding should come as no surprise to *anyone* who has had children—regardless of the parents' religious backgrounds.

Children precipitate decision-making statements about religious identity, however. Couples could probably avert confrontation on many of the issues that potentially divide them if they put off having children indefinitely. A household can avoid "choosing" a faith if there is no third party around to be affected. The Hanukkah menorah can give way to the Christmas tree, or the partners can just, as one man put it, "do their religious thing" outside the home, each attending services and celebrations elsewhere. Couples who have reached some sense of equilibrium, at least for a while, may not want to recalibrate their religious decisions. So it is no surprise that interfaith couples are less fertile.[5]

Parents become so uncomfortable about their children's religious identity—even when they thought they didn't care—because religion is indeed different from other parameters against which one measures one's identity and places oneself in the world. The nearest analogy would be professional identity: I am a doctor, I am a teacher. In another generation (and perhaps in some circles even now) a political identity would have come close: "I am a Republican," "I am a Socialist," "I am a Southerner." But religious identity is not defined as something one *does*. The answer to "What religion is your child?" is not "He belongs to the First Methodist Church" or "She goes to High Holiday services at the Reform temple."

The power of the conflicts stirred up by the prospect of children was conveyed by a thirty-eight-year-old Jewish woman who has had a hard time talking to her Italian Catholic husband about having a child: "It's getting later and later for me, but I'd rather have no child at all than have a Catholic child," she said and started to cry. At the other end of the continuum from this woman are those who feel stimulated and challenged by the possibility of creating a family unit that tries to integrate two traditions under one roof. In between are those who simply, like one Jewish man married to a Christian, father of two teenage sons, "would never have been able to think about having children if we'd had to worry about all this stuff beforehand."

Some people prefer to clarify their positions in advance, even knowing that the ground might shift over time. Clarification—out loud—is very useful, if only because it allows the partners to take the critical step of thinking about who *they* are before trying to figure out what their unborn child will be. Once the couple marries and children are on the scene, they make manifest the parents' struggle to blend two identities. One Jewish woman reported in outrage a playground incident in which a Jewish neighbor casually mentioned that "your four-year-old doesn't look Jewish," knowing that the child's father was, indeed, not a Jew. Her fury over this intrusive remark was fueled in part by her own unexamined ambivalence and uncertainty about having a daughter who *does* have a dual identity even though she was being raised a Jew.

Larry, a Jewish man in his twenties, wrestling with what his own Jewish identity is and means, was trying to figure out how he and Beth, his Catholic fiancée would raise the children they planned for: "I *am* observant, but I'm not religious. What am I observing? I'm observing being Jewish." This tautology gave him a lot of trouble as he tried to imagine what he would communicate to a child—that is, what mattered most to him about his Jewishness. Larry wanted his hypothetical child to be a Jew because he wanted the child to be part of the universe he himself was familiar with. He felt—viscerally—that he didn't want the child "swallowed up by the majority culture" and somehow swept away from him, beyond his control. Beth wanted the child to have a Christian sense of faith in a higher power, and not to be adrift in existential *angst* at every moment, which was how she perceived Larry.

Ritual and belief had very different meanings for the partners in this couple. To the Catholic, Beth, the rites of prayer and church attendance and receiving Communion had to do with her personal and private relationship with God. For the Jew, Larry, religious ritual had little of what he might define as spiritual meaning but was entirely bound up with reinforcing his identity as part of a group; in his case, ritual observance became almost a political act. These differences in how one views religious activity have a great effect on the way one selects from among the options available in raising children. The issue is not only competing (or overlapping) theologies, but also complexities of meaning that are not precisely theological.

One possible resolution of their dilemma that Beth and Larry considered was raising the child as part of the Jewish people, but with an understanding of, and attachment to, Christian holidays and rituals as well. It is understandable that this interplay of both traditions may, for all its paradoxes and difficulties, be in the end appealing to couples—not only because it obviates the need for the partners to make painful choices but also because it seems to eliminate the problem of having a parent raising a child in an unfamiliar religion.

Each partner may be concerned about raising a child in an alien religion. But it is also quite possible for each to feel ambivalent about his or her own religious tradition and to be equally anxious about having to be the expert or transmitter of that tradition. Parents who are uncertain about or afraid of their own connection to a religious tradition may expect their children, magically, to provide some resolution. Steve, from a Mormon family in Utah, wanted his child to have a Christmas tree—*that* he knew—but when he and his Jewish wife Elaine discussed what religious principles they would honor in their home it became clear that Steve hated the idea of church attendance and everything else to do with organized religion. He just wanted his children to have "a connection with nature when they're older." Debbie, a Jew, made no stand on introducing any Jewish observances into the home she created with her Christian husband, but she wistfully suggested that maybe their young son "will inspire me to go back to Judaism."

Indeed, this does often happen, though sometimes not until the children themselves are preteens and request or demand more religious input. A Protestant minister described how a family became involved in her church simply because the teenage son of Protestant-Jewish parents joined the church youth group, wanting to participate along with his close friends from school. In this case, the child made the choice and the mother followed his lead back into her own religious tradition. The father, reported the minister, "was holding on to his Jewishness very strongly.'' The concern that their children receive dual religious instruction has, ironically, led some parents back into their own churches or synagogues—they have started to study not only their partner's faith but their own as well. Others may focus their Jewishness completely on their children—''I'm just holding on to a bit of religious tradition in my life because I don't want my kids to be deprived of part of their heritage.'' A Christian would be less likely to focus all the family's religious activity around the child, since Christianity is based on individual salvation (even the adults count here) whereas Judaism is strongly linked to ''peoplehood'' and generational continuity. Usually Jews are the ones who express greater concern over the children's religious participation than over their own, partly because Judaism does not require individual faith for salvation. However, this ''being Jewish for the sake of the children'' places a great burden on the child, and masks parental ambivalence as well. Parents leave to the child the responsibility of enunciating and living out the family's religious identity, because they are unwilling or afraid to say that their own heritage means something to *them*.

Pained by the historical oppression of Jews, and perhaps knowing little else about Judaism, many Jews are afraid of identifying too closely with a suffering people.[6] Some many even have married a non-Jew as a way of escaping from a collective Jewish past that they think has consisted only of pogroms, enforced exiles, and death camps. Yet the Jewish parent him- or herself may be able to relate to nothing but Jewish suffering—not a very positive message to transmit to a child. The history of Jewish oppression is better known than the tenets of religious Judaism. A large proportion of American Jews consider themselves secular, yet Jewish, with few ties to religious practice per se.[7]

For some Christians, especially those who were raised in homes where religious activity was chronic and mandatory, and closely associated with overcontrolling parents and a claustrophobic home atmosphere, all religious activity may be suspect. One man, from a pious Southern Baptist family, had rejected organized religion altogether in his late teens, and was incredulous when his Jewish wife, not an overtly observant woman, began attending synagogue services every week after their marriage— evidently something she felt she had to do to reinforce her own sense of not having sacrificed her Jewish identity in their marriage. She wanted to raise their child Jewish, and felt very strongly about it; to him all religious expression was poison, and he preferred to raise their two-year-old as ''a secular humanist with good ethics.'' For both Christian and Jew, ambivalent and even strongly negative feelings about their *own* backgrounds are more common impediments to happy compromise in an inter-faith family than is conflict with the religion of the spouse.

On the other hand, where religious feelings are strong and are respected by each partner, the child can be exposed to a richness of understanding about both traditions. Although their situation may be uncommon because of his wide-ranging understanding of different religious traditions, Baptist theologian Harvey Cox and his Jewish wife, Nina Tumarkin—raising their young son as a Jew—light *Shabbat* candles together each Friday evening. Cox said, ''I hold him while she lights the candles. He feels something in it, perhaps because I do. I've never had, until now, the weekly familial reminders of the tradition. And we pray every day at supper, thanking God for food. We mention special things—a friend who is sick, a special visitor. Our son sees that we can pray *together* and that prayer is part of our lives.''

The most difficult child-rearing situations occur when one partner is strongly religious and the other is not.[8] Some nonreligious partners treat a spouse's religious observances or personal struggles over faith with scorn or teasing, undercutting the child's sense of what is important. Not only are there two competing traditions the child must try to integrate, but in addition, the child will feel disloyal to the nonreligious parent or inauthentic, an object of a parent's derision, whenever he or she attends to any religious material.

This conflict is resolved much as it is in same-faith marriages, assuming that there is some degree of goodwill and open communication between the partners. ''There should be no silent communications,'' said one teacher who worked with several inter-faith children. The parent who wants the child to learn about religion needs to make this clear: ''This is important to me. I can understand if you don't want to provide our child any religious or spiritual experiences yourself, but please don't sabotage what I'm doing by calling it irrational or superstitious; when you do it really hurts me, and it damages my credibility as a parent. Anyway, we can't presume that the whole world is known to us, so it seems to me a mistake for us to imagine that religious feelings have no place in it.''

One Protestant man quoted to his Jewish wife a justification for faith in some divine power that he had heard novelist I. B. Singer give in a lecture to scientists. It worked to convince her that there might be some rational underpinnings to his faith. His version of the Singer metaphor for why he himself believes:

A man is washed up on a deserted island, on which no human habitation has ever existed, nor has any ship ever stopped there or plane flown over. He crawls onto the dry land and finds—for example—a wristwatch! How can he explain this? By the Big Bang theory? How did a watch come to be in that place? Accidentally some sand melted to form the watch face? An animal died and became a leather watch strap? He might have tried to justify the fact of the watch by saying that it was all accidental, but no bang created that watch!

For this couple this story helped to resolve some of the uneasiness the nonreligious partner felt about religious faith generally. But such unease or ambivalence is rarely eliminated by an anecdote alone. There are other denials or, more likely, silences. Many interfaith partners have been afraid to address clearly the issues around raising their children, both in order to keep the marriage and the family on a stable course by avoiding a schism between the partners *and* in order to avoid peeling back the layers of negative feelings they harbor about their own religion. A woman who since her teens had been in rebellion against what she saw as the constrictions of her Catholic upbringing, and who counted among her siblings a nun and two priests, found herself yelling at her nine- year-old son, "I am *not* Catholic! I am not any religion at all. You can tell your friends that Daddy is Jewish and Mommy is *nothing*, and that'll be the truth!"

This woman and her Jewish counterparts hate a part of what they come from, and these feelings get expressed to their children one way or another. Often religion gets mixed up with general feelings about one's family of origin, and it becomes hard to sort out where the hostility to parents leaves off and hostility to religion itself begins. For example, one Jewish man was so angry with his own parents about his upbringing that when his son said he wanted to go to Hebrew school with his friends the father screamed, "I am putting my foot down. Absolutely not!" Not all cases display the conflict so clearly. But especially for people who

142

are trying hard not to be exactly like their own parents (and this may be part of the universal human condition), the distancing can include not wanting to pass along the previous generation's religion to the children. The children then get several messages: that religion is a dirty little secret in the family, that it makes Mom or Dad angry, that their own family does not respond on this issue the way the child imagines other families do.[9]

Kids pick up on the "fear and loathing" theme in some parents' lives, their terror of being, as one father put it, "sucked back into it." Afraid of not being able to assert one's individuality vis-à-vis one's own parents may still be an issue for some interfaith partners. What happens when these people have children of their own and those children want to connect with something of their parents' dual spiritual heritage? It may spark a search for positive aspects of the past. Children often reach back to the people for whom the questions will cause less pain—grandparents or other relatives or a clergyperson. Thus, what happens at first—especially if religion is an overheated issue for either parent—is that the children get caught in the crossfire, as pawns; the second stage is that the child's reaching out can heal rifts with the grandparents' generation in the process.

Children of any age respond as much to the unspoken as they do to the explicit. A child in an interfaith marriage early on figures out what issues must never be talked about at home. For example, a son may be terribly uncomfortable about telling his parents that he wants to go to after-school Hebrew classes like the Jewish kids in his regular school class. On some level a child may sense that the parent—in this case the Jewish parent—actually desires a reconciliation with his or her own tradition but may be fearful of acknowledging this.

A daughter in her midteens had a real spiritual awakening when she went to church services with her grandmother, yet was afraid to tell either parent, understanding how concerned each was that her religious decisions might suggest a preference for one of them over the other. She might have wanted to explore one of the two household religions but was afraid that the parent of the other faith would feel rejected. One man, raised by a Jewish father and an Episcopalian mother, rejected both, studying yoga instead. "The struggle for me was that if I pursued my spiritual life as a Christian, I would be unfaithful to my Jewish background, and if I pursued my spiritual life as a Jew, I would be unfaithful to my Christian background.''[10] The task of the child in these situations is apparently to foster family unity by keeping the lid on areas of potential conflict. Hence the children of interfaith marriages often find themselves mediating between the two parents and their two cultures, even in cases where the parents have consciously chosen to make one religion the official family tradition, or at least the official religion for the offspring.

For some children of interfaith marriages, a symbol of this mediation is their need to ''explain away'' their names. The children of Jewish fathers and Christian mothers who are reared as Christians face a special dilemma if they have recognizably Jewish surnames. For example, a sister and brother who were raised in the Dutch Reformed church but whose last name was Cohen found themselves explaining to their teachers throughout their school careers why they were not staying out of class to attend synagogue on the Jewish holy days and, more significantly, explaining to their friends, ''why we're not Jewish.'' All children, but particularly children like these, should have an opportunity at home to discuss religious differences and religious prejudice. Even grade-schoolers need to stockpile enough verbal ammunition to be able to say, ''I don't like that joke. That hurts my feelings. I am a Christian and my father is Jewish, and I don't like to hear you say bad things about anybody's religion.''

A majority of children in mixed marriages where the mother is Jewish are raised as Jews, and in families where the father is the Jewish partner there is often significant Jewish involvement for the children and the parents.[11] When an interfaith couple chooses consciously to raise their children as Christians, this is usually because the Christian partner feels strongly religious and the Jewish partner feels little or no allegiance to religious Judaism, and in addition wants to move away somewhat from his or her own Jewish identity. In families where the Jewish partner does care, there is usually an attempt to raise the children as Jews or to incorporate some Jewish content into their lives.[12]

For a child to be or become a Christian, faith or belief is involved. There is no universal prescription for how this is to come about, although most mainstream Christian denominations consider a belief in Jesus as Messiah and savior or in the historical life and teachings of Jesus as necessary conditions for identifying as a faithful Christian. Christianity is a community of belief and adherence to that belief, and does not have anything to do with biological descent. A child born of non-Christian parents, adopted by Christians, and raised as a Christian is considered to be one by most churches. Formally, the birth family is not a necessary or sufficient determinant of the child's religious identity.

In one sense, raising children Christian is relatively easy for the Jewish partner. When the outside culture matches that of the home—for example when it is Christmas outside, in every shop window, it is also Christmas inside the home—no special care need be taken by the non-Christian partner to reinforce Christianity. So much about Christianity is part of daily life in the Western world, from the texts studied in high school and college to the art in museums to the near-universal celebration of holidays connected to Christian observances, that the Jewish parent at least has some basis for relating to or participating in Christian celebrations. The hard part is finding a way to explain where the Jewish parent's own allegiances reside.

On a personal level, it may be very difficult for the Jewish parent to rear a Christian child because much of Jewish history in the past two millennia has involved the struggle with Christianity and with individual Christians. Residual guilt about defaulting on—or betraying—this struggle, plus a sense of uneasiness about losing one's identity and that of the children to the popular culture, feeds the uneasiness many Jews report. And yet, many Jewish men married to Christian women make very little direct argument in favor of raising the children exclusively Jewish. The passivity of men in this regard is quite remarkable, especially in light of the fact that most major decisions in a household are weighted in favor of male wishes. Men's reluctance to make a case for Judaism may have to do with not wanting to rock the marital boat or not feeling comfortable with Judaism themselves, but it may be even more influenced by the understanding that if the mother is going to do the majority of care giving she herself has to be familiar with and comfortable with the religion—usually her own.

Jewish parents in interfaith marriages have to be aware of what their visceral responses convey to their children. If a Jew who has decided to raise children Christian has a reaction like one woman who said, ''I cringe every time that tree goes up in our living room,'' the kids will get a message of disapproval that may be far more confusing than if the parental feelings were made more explicit, allowing for questions and explanations all around. How the family celebrates may remain the same, and one partner's discomfort may never be resolved, but when conflicts are acknowledged at least the children will know what that discomfort is about and not imagine that they themselves are its source. Whatever the parents' choices, making the reasons for them clear—if possible—and even articulating any uneasiness they feel is more useful to the children than denial or concealment. Harvey Cox pointed out, "It is important for kids to know that people disagree on these questions. As in the Jewish rabbinic tradition, through the disputes you're invited into the conversation."

The problem is, of course, that people are not always aware of their feelings about religious identity in advance, and even carefully wrought decisions made before a child is born don't always hold in the face of the reality of parenthood. "When I became pregnant in 1962 with my firstborn child," said one woman discussing the first of her two intermarriages, "I was astounded to find that I was not pregnant with a citizen of the world, but with a Jew."

Since the dominant culture exerting its strong pull is Christian, it is surprising how many intermarried couples choose to raise their children Jewish. While this "tenacity of Jewishness" in the lives of intermarried families has been termed a major trend,[13] it is not always easy for a Jewish woman to assert her desire to have Jewish children. Women's assertiveness is beginning to emerge, however, and Jewish women are able to say that it matters to them very much how religion will be expressed in the family. A Catholic man admitted, somewhat wistfully, "If I'd said I wanted the child raised Christian, she never would have married me. I *know* that."

It may be that the demographics make even nonreligious Jews feel so strongly about Jewish survival that they can "win out" even over Christian spouses more religious than they are.[14] This marks an important change from the child-rearing practices of most Jewish-Christian couples two generations ago, a healthier attitude toward their own identities on the part of intermarried Jews, and an important step also in keeping some of the offspring of these interfaith marriages affiliated with the Jewish people.

More than two-thirds of Jews who are now intermarried say that they feel positively about their own religious background, while less than half of the Christian partners feel that way. And because you don't have to convert formally to experience Jewishness, the majority of interfaith families do have some degree of Jewish identification—even if they also celebrate Christmas and Easter. In a family in which the non-Jewish partner converts to Judaism, there may be pulls toward aspects of Christian ritual that seem as much a link with the family of the converted partner as with faith itself. In one case, the Jewish-born partner encouraged her husband, who converted to Judaism before their marriage, *not* to drop all his Christian observances, and then changed her mind. "When Richard first said he didn't want the kids to have Christmas, I disagreed with him. Now I think he's right. Especially because he's a convert, I think it's important not to have a Christmas tree or anything like that. Instead, we go to his parents' house at Thanksgiving and for other strictly family times with no religious content; this keeps it clean for the kids." This family lives in a small Midwestern academic town, one of only a few Jewish households, and raising Jewish children in this milieu, they say, means that they have to be "pretty authoritarian. Otherwise, it's hard for people like us who've come out of the sixties"—that is, whose own ideology would lean toward religious and cultural relativism—to maintain a clear position on Jewish identification.

For the intermarried couple who choose to raise their children exclusively Jewish, and where the Christian partner has not converted to Judaism, raising Jewish children may mean entering an alien culture. It's not quite the same exchange as a Jew raising a Christian child for the simple reason that much of Judaism is unfamiliar to Christians, despite the fact that some Christians believe Judaism is the sacred precursor to Christian scriptures.

Jewish identity is linked to descent rather than to affiliation or belief in a specific dogma. Conservative and Orthodox Judaism consider a child to be Jewish if he or she has a Jewish mother; Reform and Reconstructionist denominations recognize that a child born of a Jewish father and a non-Jewish mother is a Jew if that person expresses an intention to live as a Jew. A child not born of a Jewish parent but who is adopted into a Jewish home must undergo conversion in order to be considered Jewish, even if both adoptive parents are Jews. Similarly, if the Christian-born mother of children who are being raised Jewish decides to convert to Judaism *after* the children are born, her conversion in no way affects them. They must also convert if they want to be considered Jews by Orthodox and Conservative standards.

But while it is obviously simpler if conversion and the creation of a unified family identity take place before parenthood, couples should not feel that they've missed the boat if they decide to consider this alternative later on. Similarly, a Jewish parent who becomes heartsick when a son is five years old and didn't have the ceremony accompanying a ritual circumcision in infancy can always arrange for a ceremony at a later date. Doors are never closed on any of these matters. Naturally, it can be terribly confusing for a child who already understands about his or her religious identity to have that changed suddenly. But parents can sometimes alleviate their own anxiety by understanding that they can become more involved in their children's religious upbringing along the way even if they did not start out thinking they wanted to be.

Those who wish to raise a child Jewish in a family where the father is a Jew and the mother is not may consider converting the child at birth. Conversion at birth is simple—prayers, a brief immersion in a *mikvah* (ritual bath), and, for a boy, circumcision. Since most parents who intend to raise the boy Jewish would have him circumcised anyway, the actual conversion ceremony is little more than that. The advantages of conversion here are twofold. First, it eliminates any possible confusion or trauma for the child who later discovers that he or she is not considered a Jew by some authorities; second, it solidifies and makes concrete the parents' decision. The child *is* a Jew, and is not merely being raised *as* a Jew.

Whereas it is uniformly agreed that there is no question about the presumption of Jewishness if the mother is a Jew, there are now disputes in the Jewish community over whether having a Jewish father makes a child a Jew. The Christian woman in a Jewish-Christian marriage is blamed, as it were, for the fact that her children are not considered Jews by the majority of Jews at the same time that she may be trying her hardest to help the children experience Judaism. She may resent the apparent lack of appreciation for her efforts and the additional burden of responsibility for her children's non-Jewish status.

Not unexpectedly, women who are going to raise children in a faith not their own express far more concern than men do over whether or not this is humanly possible. First of all, women still, traditionally, are responsible for most of child care. This means that they are responsible for instilling religious values, arranging for the child's religious education, and so forth. Even where both parents work outside the home all the evidence shows that a mother will still spend more time with the child than a father. Second, if the mother of the child is Jewish, she will be raising the family in her own religion if she raises that child Jewish. The Christian wife of a Jew may be expected to raise Jewish children although she herself may be actively practicing another religion. When a child asks about belief, is this mother to say, "Well, dear, I believe in one set of values and history, but you are supposed to believe in another"?

A Catholic woman in her twenties, personally very devout, wondered:

> How is it possible to raise a Jewish child—and this is very important to my fiancé—while I practice another religion? Not just that it's confusing to the child, but just how does he expect me to do this? Somebody in his family suggested that if the child ever asked me about my own religion I should try to answer without making reference to Christ. Now how on earth am I supposed to pull that one off if the holiday the kid asks about is Easter? But it's not just the information. It's that I'd be one thing and my very own child is supposed to be something else. I'm not sure I'd even feel like the child's own mother.

One woman interviewed noted that she felt "like a dictator" when she told her Jewish child "what he ought to believe," since she herself believed differently. "Sometimes I feel as if I'm telling the kid the world is flat when in my heart and mind I know that it's round." People have children for a whole constellation of reasons, but usually because, at some level, they want to pass along something of themselves. Raising a child in a tradition other than one's own, that child, one's very own offspring, can feel "other." A Catholic woman raising her child as a Jew told of how her son casually asked her one day, "Mommy, what's a crucifix?" She said she had been "shocked that my child didn't know something which had been so essential to me," then realized that—for her own sake—she needed to explain to her son the symbols and meaning of *her* faith, so her child would not seem so distant from her because of his lack of knowledge.

In most cases the confusion is greater when the mother is the one raising a child in a faith not her own, which is one reason why many prospective fathers who feel strongly that their children be raised in their faith make every effort to encourage their wives to convert to their faith before they have children. This minimizes some of the confusion and pain. Another Catholic woman wept and said, "It's hard to raise a child who's not like you." To resolve some of these feelings she took a course in basic Judaism along with her husband and reported that she "really felt a new respect for the Jewish tradition. It's still not my tradition, but I have a much better understanding now of what I'm supposed to be transmitting to my son. Some of what we've learned—for instance about the Sabbath and making the time into something special—I like having in my own life, not just as something for my kid."

Mothers usually have to engage themselves one way or another in the lives—including the religious lives—of their children. Men, especially if they do not want to share their wives' religious observances, sometimes respond by distancing themselves from all religious activity. Thus, the father whose religion is not chosen is most likely to feel like the "odd man out." He may then choose to cut himself off from family celebrations altogether, reinforcing his isolation. This is usually the man's way of handling the situation, since family dynamics, in the past at least, have usually favored the mother's religion as the faith of the children. But the cutting off raises more problems than it solves. Is our religion not good enough for Daddy? Is Daddy not good enough for our religion? A parent who chooses this method may have difficulty communicating any feelings about being left out, and sometimes the other partner, or the children, end up reaching out to him or her.

The spouse whose religion has been chosen usually feels some guilt, and some anger, too, in response to passive-aggressive behavior from the left-out parent. Especially in a situation where the spouse with the stronger religious feelings is given carte blanche in raising the child religiously, it can be irritating when this authority is then undercut in an indirect way by the partner. Often people who think that they do not have strong religious feelings of their own, but who in fact may feel very ambivalent, have the most difficulty saying both what they would like to include in their family's life and what they do not feel comfortable with. Since they can't express it, nobody can do anything to improve matters; their withdrawal may seem quite incomprehensible to their children.

The challenge is to find some way for people in this situation to be integrated into the family's rituals or learning. In the case of the family in which children are being raised as Jews the logical way to get the "excluded" parent to draw near would be to involve him or her in study of some sort, or to provide some ritual participation, for example, at the weekly Sabbath table. In one family the wife and the children approached the father, a scholarly man, to ask him to prepare some comments on the part of the Bible being read by his children at school. In another, the father said his own grace before the Friday evening Sabbath dinner they all had together; everyone understood that it was not a Jewish prayer but was the father's way of sharing *Shabbat* with them in a way that felt authentic to him.

There are many variations on this "inclusive" solution to the parents' feelings if one religion is chosen for the family to practice. There are categories of "fellow travelers" in many faiths, and it has been proposed that in Judaism the use of the term *gertoshav* (literally, "the stranger who lives among you"), an ancient word for a "potential" Jew, be recast for modern use.[15] For complex emotional or familial reasons, a spouse in an interfaith marriage often does not feel comfortable converting or even assuming directly the practices of another faith. But he or she also feels no hostility to the rituals or celebrations that the other family members observe, and participates as much as he or she wants to, with enjoyment and sincerity.

Obviously this is a choice that will create minimal friction in the marriage and on the family as a whole. Sometimes it can be achieved as simply as one Jewish woman managed it when she asked her Episcopalian husband to accompany her and the children to a Friday night service at the synagogue. It was "low key," meaning largely in English, and with very pleasant music and a sermon relating the biblical portion for the week to current political events. She simply said to him, after several weeks of going herself and ascertaining that the atmosphere would be comfortable for all of them, "I'd really be so happy if you would come with us for an hour or so." She was so pleased that he came just because she and the children had wanted him to that their home was sunny for days afterwards, and the family participation at Friday night services was repeated frequently.

Not all attempts at inclusion work as smoothly. For some interfaith families any kind of formal religious experience in an institutional setting disrupts their harmony. "I hate going because they always have a vested interest in getting us all over to their side— whether it's a temple or a church," said one woman who claimed that the only happy celebrations she and her husband could find were those experienced with other interfaith families. Even though they had decided originally to send their child to a Presbyterian school, where despite his obviously Jewish surname nobody took him for a Jew, the Jewish husband and father could not bear to attend even the watered-down chapel services that preceded various school functions. He was so clearly miserable on these occasions that his wife rarely pressed him to attend. When they held or attended Christmas parties or Easter dinners even within their group of intermarried friends, he made a point of talking only to other Jews on these occasions. Ultimately, the couple decided to send their child to public school and to try to neutralize the husband's very negative feelings by introducing some Jewish observances at home.

The most successful and rational responses from men and women raising children in a faith not their own seem to come from Christians who understand and respect religion generally. It appears that those individuals who know the most about their own faith are the ones who can tolerate with greatest equanimity the situation where their children are being raised in another religion. This emerged in numerous interviews, typified by one in which a Catholic man in his late twenties told of being quite comfortable with his wife's desire to raise their daughter exclusively as a Jew. He himself continued to attend Mass regularly, but he altered his own schedule so that his church attendance didn't interfere in any way with his young daughter's schedule. Theologian Harvey Cox said that when he and his Jewish wife went for counseling on how to raise their young son, he told the rabbi, "I know that Jewish law says the child of a Jewish woman is Jewish and should be raised Jewish, and I think it is right. The only thing I insist on is I want to help raise him Jewish."[16]

A statistical analysis of how intact interfaith families handle child rearing suggests that most couples are able to agree on child-rearing practices. The only significant exceptions occur in families in which Jewish women are married to Christian men. Non-Jewish men are more likely to report being in disagreement with their wives.[17] Given the power imbalance in most marriages, with the husband as dominant figure, when a Jewish man inter-marries, his wife may assume at some level that her husband will play a dominant role in most decision making—no surprise (and hence no real disagreement) when the husband wants some Jew-ish input into the children's lives. When a Jewish woman marries a non-Jew and insists that Jewishness be a factor in the home in some way, her husband may be uncomfortable with her assertive-ness on this issue not because he is anti-Jewish but because he is taken aback by a woman's assumption of a decision-making role in such an important aspect of family life. Jewish women who intermarry, then, have to be prepared for more conflict over child rearing than their male Jewish peers.

When children are raised as Jews in an interfaith family, whether by Jewish or Christian mothers, there are special compli-cations if the parents divorce. Children raised Jewish who stay with a Christian mother after divorce are especially likely to be-come pawns in the divorce process. There is an emerging body of rabbinic and legal scholarship on this issue, since rates of di-vorce *and* intermarriage have been rising so steeply.[18] One of the arguments mustered in favor of recognizing patrilineal descent suggested that courts might be more receptive to awarding cus-tody to a Jewish father after divorce from a Christian woman if it could be proved that the children were also Jewish.

Remarriage after divorce brings with it an entire subset of issues and choices for all the parents involved. Religion may become the focus of family conflict in a stepfamily situation, in which, for example, the Jewish mother and father, divorced from one another, see their child as a prize to be won. The child, born and raised a Jew, may find his or her religious experiences affected by a parent's remarriage to a Christian. "Dad and his new wife want to take me skiing on the weekends; my mother is making me stay home to go to Hebrew school," complained one ten-year-old. All the happy activities appear to be centered around the nonreli-gious activity. Unless the new parental dyad is strongly commit-ted to making as little change as possible in the child's life, the possibility for confusion may be even greater than for a child raised with birth parents of different religions.

## Can You Opt for Both? Or Neither?

Given the complexities of negotiation involved between Christian and Jew, husband and wife, if children are going to be raised exclusively in one tradition or the other, it is not surprising that so many families choose not to choose. Two-thirds of interfaith parents do not make a choice of religion for their children.[19]

Some parents believe that bringing up a child with access to both religious traditions enriches the child's life considerably and spares the parents from having to make painful choices to give up something very special from their own lives. But Christians are more likely to be the ones embracing this all-inclusive attitude of ''the more celebrations, the better'' and Jews are likelier to see the blending as a dilution of the family's Jewish component. ''You just have to learn to make choices when you're deliberately creating an interfaith family,'' said a Jewish woman married to an Episcopalian who, like her, feels very strongly bound to his own religious tradition. With their interfaith seders and multiple-faith holiday celebrations, they are ''making something that's trying to work for everybody.''

If issues of personal belief are not salient for the Jewish parent, it's more likely that he or she could tolerate certain Christian rituals both in the home and for the child, and still consider the child to be living in a partly Jewish environment. This is not an either-or situation, as would be likely between Protestants and Catholics, for example. In fact Christian-Jewish households in which there has been no conversion are likely to have aspects of both practices—for example, celebrating Christmas *and* Hanukka, Easter *and* Passover.[20]

Parents who *consciously* choose to raise their children with aspects of both faiths, not as an avoidance technique but because they each feel they have something of importance to pass on to the child, have to give holiday celebrations and religious education much more thought than those parents who more or less drift into the ''both'' option. If from the beginning both partners feel equally strongly about their religious identity—even it their desire to practice their own religion has been spurred on by the very fact of being in an intermarriage—the ''both'' option is possible. One advantage of this approach, done with commitment, is that the whole family becomes involved in religious study and exploration, and this in itself may, paradoxically, bring the family members closer. However, raising a Christian-Jewish child requires twice as much work, if the parents are committed to doing it rigorously. If both parents are involved with explaining their own or each other's religious traditions, the child gets the idea that religion itself is a serious matter, and does learn to take religion seriously. Otherwise, "both" becomes "neither."

Many families give the children a *de facto* taste of each parent's religious heritage without making the choice to do so explicit. Parents who end up with this kind of covert compact may do so because they fear that if they discussed a program of duality the other partner might insist that his or her religion reign supreme. If the parents "do both" just because they are anxious lest the child violate the family's unspoken laws of religious neutrality, the child soon gets the idea that religion is a subject that makes Mom and Dad nervous. For both parents there is the fear voiced by the as-yet-unmarried man who pleaded, "What are the statistics? What does the research say? Are these children raised as both going to grow up normal?" The parents of the more than 750,000 offspring of mixed marriages in the United States often do express what one rabbi described as "tremendous guilt" over what they have "done" to or with their children.

The common wisdom holds that children raised in a blend of two traditions will grow up confused in important ways. The same wisdom says that "letting the child choose" won't work either. The newly popular image of the child of an interfaith marriage is of someone who, even if confused and "uncentered," is accustomed to moving back and forth between two cultures, growing up to be an excellent negotiator and communicator.[21] Indeed, since two-thirds of the children of mixed marriages have no specific religious tradition chosen for them by their parents, the origins of these feelings of mobility are quite clear. One woman, raised as a Protestant by a Christian mother and a Jewish father, and herself the mother of Jewish children, converted first to Catholicism and then to Judaism. She said, "As far as my own identity is concerned, it is going to be a lifelong process to figure it out. I'll never feel that I belong one hundred percent in either place."[22]

Sometimes the choice to raise a child in both traditions and the choice to adopt neither, cutting loose from religious ritual and identification altogether, are just two sides of the same issue— how parents can deal with their desires to avoid conflict. Some interfaith couples have proposed (before there were any children on the scene) that they would raise their daughters in the faith of their mother, their sons in the faith of the father. On the eve of her wedding one Christian woman told her friends that she and her Jewish husband had agreed to raise the children in alternating religions—that is, the first child would be Catholic, the second Jewish, a third—if they got that far—would be Catholic again. A friend queried, "What will you do when you're pushing both of them in a supermarket cart and they start to ask you about the Christmas decorations? Are you going to give two different answers?" The fear of confrontation, or the fear that compromise of any sort could be personally inauthentic and crippling, led this couple to a decision that, on the surface, can only seem absurd. "It'll be like teams," suggests her husband, as if there were no problems inherent in raising two siblings with two different worldviews in the same family. "One child for the soul, one child for the people; baptism and *brith*" quipped Esther Perel.

But *how* to do the right thing when raising children whose ancestry "dates back to the *Mayflower* on one side and Moses on the other," as one Jewish woman put it about the three children of her intermarriage? The modus operandi can include many variables, but the need to find a group with which to identify emerges as the most important. Some families join a synagogue that is particularly receptive to interfaith couples—and there are reports of more and more of these from coast to coast. Others choose to belong to a traditional synagogue *and* a church; this is not a particularly common choice, since most traditional synagogues do not count non-Jews as members, though all are welcome at services.

Now that their numbers are growing, people strongly committed to raising their children in both traditions are finding that their "reference group" is neither the synagogue nor the church but rather a group of other likeminded families. Parents are creating their own support communities. One synagogue in New York City has spun off a small group that consists exclusively of families in which one parent is not Jewish and one is. The group itself has become the locus for holiday celebrations (such as an annual interfaith seder) and life-cycle ceremonies, a place where the couples and their children feel increasing comfortable. A similarly supportive situation evolved out of a discussion session for inter-married parents at a private school—becoming a form of *cha-*

*vurah*—the informal friendship-group format for prayer and study that has become increasingly popular for Jewish worshipers since the late 1960s.

Jewish community centers—in reaching out to interfaith families through discussion groups, retreats, and holiday celebrations—have provided another conduit through which these families can find one another and also find a connection, however tenuous, to the larger Jewish community. Families without these options find themselves on their own, inventing and selecting from a range of religious and spiritual possibilities at home and in public, ad lib, depending on which traditions are important to each parent.

Some parents feel that they would rather ban religion from the home altogether than tolerate the imperfect "both" system, but others are clearly challenged by the opportunity to try integrating aspects of both. "This year I have to figure out what to do," said a Jewish woman living in Brooklyn. "Our synagogue *chavurah* group is coming over for *latkes*, and our Christmas tree is up in the living room." Integration requires a lot of explanation—not just in a social context, but especially to the children, at every stage. Well done, the advantage may be a respect for diversity, although a cogent argument could be made that a child pays a price in identity confusion in order to learn this lesson. In terms of human ecology there may be more efficient ways of teaching tolerance.

Some families have an inside-outside rule for how they celebrate two traditions, usually observing Jewish traditions at home and Christian ones outside—because, as one partner in such a marriage put it, "Judaism is a home-based religion," and Christianity is all around on the outside anyway. This man observes the Sabbath laws and keeps a kosher home, in which he lives with his Roman Catholic wife and their three teenage children. His wife is a practicing Catholic outside their home. One of their three children, a daughter, decided to convert to Judaism, but their sons are still searching for one faith; their father calls this "religious roulette." The parents' desire to blend two backgrounds is understandable, but to raise a child simultaneously Christian and Jewish is something of an oxymoron—to be a Christian, you must believe that Jesus Christ, as the son of God, came to earth to die for the sins of humanity. Jews do not believe in the divinity of Jesus, or in many other central tenets of Christianity.

In a lively dialogue over the Christmas story with fourth- and fifth-graders in a special program for the children of interfaith families at Trinity School in New York City, one child asked who was the real father of Jesus. A minister answered, "Christians believe that God was his father. Jews believe that Joseph was his father." The student persisted. "But since we're both Jewish and Christian, are we supposed to believe that God *and* Joseph were his father?" Rabbi Lavey Derby of the 92nd Street YM-YWHA in New York City, who has also taught children of interfaith families, says that the test he proposes to his young students has to do with Easter and the story of the resurrection of Jesus: "When you go to the cave on the third day, that's your identity. If the body is there and dead, you're a Jew. If the body is missing, you're a Christian, and you have experienced a miracle. . . ."

A fifteen-year-old says, "I'm a religious orphan. I was told I was both. Then I was told that I couldn't believe in Jesus and still be Jewish. My parents really messed up." There are certainly ways in which ritual and celebrations from each tradition can be incorporated into one household. It would be intellectually dishonest—"mental contortions"—to imagine that these divergent theologies, religious philosophies, and beliefs can be incorporated seamlessly into one person, though Lavey Derby remarked that "these children *are* both, and their issues are different from the issues of the two parents of different traditions who decided to intermarry and have a child."

Out of concern that this dualism may be too hard for a child to sustain, many interfaith parents say that they expect their children to choose one religion at some point. To "expose the child to both" and let him or her choose can lead to an irresolute state, as described by a Baltimore woman from such a background. Now in her twenties, she grew up in a Jewish-Protestant home in which she and her brother were raised "so that we were supposed to choose when we grew up." She recalled an incident from when she was five or six: In December the teacher passed out a "generic" holiday crafts project; the Jewish children were to make Hanukkah decorations and the Christian children, Christmas decorations. The little girl froze. She simply could not decide what to do. She probably imagined, as so many kids her age report, that to choose one holiday over the other would mean favoring one parent, too—a very scary choice at any age. In the end, she talked her way out of doing the project altogether.

An audience who listened to this woman tell of her own confusion as a child had two disparate responses. The interfaith couples who did not yet have children claimed that her "problem" was a "communications problem"—that is, her parents failed to explain things correctly to her. Those with children responded by saying, "Yes. That confusion and panic could happen." The problem is that each tradition usually demands exclusive loyalty (no such thing here as maintaining dual nationality) and says things that contradict the dicta of the other. There really are cognitive differences between the two faiths. Before interfaith partners have children of their own they may believe that these differences can be stifled, ignored, or denied; in fact, one woman in this situation said, "These are not issues that a child would be grappling with." But they *are* significant differences that affect how a child perceives the world. For example, Judaism believes that guilt arises from doing something wrong and that it acts as a behavioral corrective so that one can move on. Christians believe that sin is part of every person's makeup and can be corrected by faith or, in the case of Catholics, by confession.

The extensions of these differences get expressed in areas that may be important to the child—for example, ideas about the divinity of Jesus or about what happens to us after we die, or about abortion (even the most traditional Jews believe that abortion is justified to save the life of the mother; Catholics believe it is a sin under any circumstances), or even about the importance of believing in a divine being altogether (many Jews would claim that belief is less urgent than living one's daily life righteously and according to their views of the political and social extrapolations of Jewish law; Catholics and mainstream Protestants would be likely to say that *faith* is of the utmost importance.)[23]

Children of intermarriage will probably always carry something of both religious traditions as part of their family associations. But all children, especially while they are young, probably need a unified religious identity, not, "My mother is this, my father is that and I'm half and half." In a perfect world, it might be possible for children to sort out that certain observances and holidays come from one parent or the other, but one of the ways children—especially in the years before adolescence—sort out their reality is by naming it and by cross-examining others. To the question: "What religion are you?" it is certainly convenient and reassuring—if not strictly necessary—to have a simple answer rather than having to "explain" one's family's bifurcation, however rich in options this might seem to one's parents.

Raised with both religions, understanding that the parents' lives are a blend of sometimes disparate religions, most children in this situation will, however, ultimately choose one religion or the other as the primary one with which to identify. (And not all siblings will necessarily make the same choice, as interviews with adult children of interfaith marriages demonstrate.) One choice can be to "split"—to feel a little of each; another choice may be made by history, as was the case for mixed-marriage offspring in Germany in the 1930s and 1940s when the Nazis made the choice for them. (The Nuremberg Laws passed in Nazi Germany in 1935 began the legally sanctioned cruelties against Jews and other "non-Aryans"; a consequence of these laws was the development of strict definitions of who was to be considered Jewish, including those with one Jewish grandparent.) Psychotherapist Esther Perel asks the interfaith parents of young children, "Do *you* want to make the choice or do you want to leave it to the kids or to history?"

And yet the choice to choose is obviously not an easy one, since in choosing one faith, the partner whose faith is not chosen gives up a great deal; and in choosing to live out both religions, each partner gives up something. Wrestling with her Jewish husband's feelings, a Catholic woman trying to choose a faith for their future children, asked: "Religion is a part of culture; to give up one's religion, for whatever reason, means relinquishing a part of oneself. Don't the children get a mixed message from *that* that's more confusing than being raised in a home with both traditions?"

The conscious decision to raise a child systematically in two religions may be justified on the grounds that it is better for the child, but in many cases the choice seems to be motivated at least as much by a desire to avoid confrontation between the parents. Parents want very much to be able to have it all. Perel challenges those who would consider this option: "Do you want to expose your children to both so they know what you have lost, what you are missing and mourning for, or do you want *them* to have an identity?"

There is a sense of loss, certainly, if one parent does not transmit specifically what feels important about his or her religious tradition. "Religion was very central to me growing up," says a

Baptist man from Missouri. "Christmas was a wonderful family feeling, which it's hard for me not to have with my son." The pain experienced by the individual parent whose child will not share his or her faith depends in part on what it is he or she would ideally want to pass on of his or her specific religious identity. For this man it was the family closeness of Christmas, which perhaps could be replicated in other ways. For a Jewish woman raising her two children in a carefully planned dual-faith household, the sadness was expressed as, "I would have loved to have seen my daughters be bat mitzvah, as I was."

Because every parent whose children are being raised in an alien religious tradition experiences some degree of loss, it's important—for the child and the parent—that there not be an artificial, clean-slate approach to the religious background of the parent who is "odd one out." Raising Christian or even religiously "neutral" children in an intermarriage may mean that the Jewish parent, for example, provides access for the children to aspects of the Jewish component of their makeup, though perhaps via cultural or ethnic connections rather than through ritual or belief.

For a Jewish man in the Pacific Southwest, bedtime chats and stories provide the vehicle for him to transmit something of his own heritage to his Presbyterian daughter. He sings her Yiddish lullabies, tells the stories of Jewish communities in Eastern Europe that his father had told him (what it was like to have goats sleeping in the house at night, among other things). Like the Christian father who doesn't talk specifically about Communion with his Jewish son, this man doesn't tell his daugther many of the Bible stories he himself remembers, feeling that they are almost always specifically linked to Jewish history—Jews who were forbidden to study Torah and defied the ban, holidays celebrating Jews who vanquished more powerful oppressors, and so on. Rather, he gives his daughter a kind of cultural anthropologist's approach to Jewishness—a bit removed, but very much in details of daily life. "As she get older, and starts school and understands more," he says, "I can probably tell her more."

One could clearly speculate endlessly on what might be a more nearly perfect solution, but in practical terms, different solutions work best for different families. A basic ground rule that emerges from discussion with interfaith couples of various ages and backgrounds is that intensity of religious feeling is the most sensible determinant of which religion is chosen for the home. The special pitfall here, however, is that sometimes religious feelings are dormant, especially in a secularized, intellectual society, so that decisions based on the level of religious feeling present before marriage, or before children are born, or even before a parent dies, may feel invalidated by the powerful emotions engendered by these major events. It is wise, therefore, for partners to consider the possibility that their own level of attachment to a religious tradition may increase as they age, and with this in mind, to reach an understanding that religious decisions about children made early in a relationship may be subject to alteration later on—when children are born or are in the early preschool years. Obviously, once a child has reached the age when he or she can make statements about religious identity—age three or four—the decision to alter that identity cannot be taken lightly. Accommodation is one thing; religious conversion of the child is something else. If the decision about child rearing cannot be changed, perhaps the whole family can accommodate itself somewhat to the religious needs of the partner whose religion is not chosen.

Even with a commitment to expose the child to both religions, there can easily be residual feelings of discomfort on the part of the husband or wife. The Jew may feel that the Christian has the support of the entire Western world. For the Christian partner, the Jewish part may be particularly hard because "Jewishness" may seem so overwhelming and all-encompassing. And if, as sometimes happens, the Jewish partner becomes culturally *more* Jewish after the children arrive—using ever more Yiddish phrases in everyday speech, making more frequent remarks, as one man did, about how much smarter Jews are than other people—this can be viewed as hostility or insult or at least as an irritant and an impediment to cheerful interfaith child rearing. The Christian parent may feel anger at a pervasiveness of Jewishness—in terms of language, foods, even politics—without there necessarily being for the children the specific advantages of Judaism itself, as a faith.

Because of the potential confusion and pain inherent in choosing one faith or both, some interfaith partners try to find other unifying principles for a family that has deliberately chosen to raise their children without an explicit commitment to either parent's religion. One choice is to find a "compromise" religion. For some, this is Unitarianism or Ethical Culture, both humanistic, intellectualized offshoots of Christianity and Judaism in which neither liturgy nor ritual is so overtly religious that a born Jew or a lapsed Christian might be offended. Some parents prefer entirely nonreligious choices. Although it lacks a spiritual or transcendent dimension, one such "neutral" choice is political ideology, a "secular religion" such as socialism, or even generalized political activism. What does it mean, as so many atheistic parents phrase it, "to be a Jew without God"? A secular Christian may have a residue that relates to personal behavior salvation, and responsibility; a secular Jew has often absorbed some aspect of the Jewish mission of *tikkun olam*—improving or repairing the world, and whatever "Jewishness" is passed along to his or her children comes in on this frequency. This was a choice that worked better thirty years ago than it does today; then, a mixed-marriage family could have rituals of a sort with compatible others, and the children could feel part of a warm and caring community just as church or synagogue members do today.[24] The community came together for union activities or political concerts and rallies around various causes and ideologies. The title of Arthur Koestler's book on communism in America, *The God That Failed*, suggest the religious passion that informed political ideologues of a previous generation. The same sense of unifying purpose appeared in the lives of interfaith couples raising children in urban or rural communes in the sixties and early seventies; here, again, a unifying ethical and political sensibility provided a structure for what was to replace the "neither" choice regarding religion in the lives of interfaith family.

In the less-ideological present, where there are few strong communal holds on people, and in fact an increasing interest in spirituality and the place of nonrational matters in our lives, the "neither" or totally nonreligous choice can have negative fallout for children. (This is true even in a family where both parents share the same religious background but are committed to having no vestiges of religious ritual or expression in their home.) The fallout has to do with the fact that most children growing up, even in progressive or academic communities where religious expression has been thought to have a bad name, identify with one religion or another. In fact most receive some kind of religious instruction, celebrate bar or bat mitzvah, Communion, Confirmation, or other religious marker events. An advice columnist put it this way to parents who want to leave their children free of all religious affiliation: "The child who gets no instruction at all . . .

can develop notions of personal unworthiness and the general inferiority of non-affiliated families.''[25] Or they may be vulnerable to incorrect or distorted views of Jewish (and Christian) history, beliefs, and practices. Grandparents can play a crucial role in providing ''unaffiliated'' interfaith children with a sense of their heritage and history, if not of a faith itself.

When one partner has converted to the religion of the other, the extended family provides an exercise in integrating emotional and cultural and ethnic differences rather than theological ones. Grandma's Swedish meatballs that she makes when she comes to visit from Minnesota may have to be adapted to the newly koshered kitchen of a family in which the born-Lutheran husband has converted to Judaism, and she may feel that there is no rational need for her to eliminate dairy products from meat dishes as she cooks for her grandchildren, but presumably the children know that Grandma is just accustomed to doing things a little differently.

Children may hear questions about their holiday observances even from their own relatives who identify with another faith. A wise move for parents would be to avoid having contact with grandparents of another faith during a holiday time that might be particularly trying for all concerned. For example, parents raising their child as a Christian, who know that the Jewish grandparents will have a difficult time with Christmas carols or holiday decorations, will make life easier for the child if they keep the grandparents at bay at this season. The grandparents may truly be unable to control their negative responses to seeing a Christmas tree in their child's home, and the grandchildren will certainly pick up on this; if they are young they will only understand that their grandparents have negative feelings about them, without being able to comprehend that the religious symbols themselves, not the children, are the objects of disapproval.

In some families there is a struggle if grandchildren will not visit over a holiday time that might put them into conflict with the religious observances in their own home. But most families report an easing of these tensions over time, with grandchildren very much part of the process of healing any rifts that the interfaith marriage might have caused. One woman who coverted to Judaism recounted how her own mother—originally pained by the fact that her grandchildren were being raised as Jews and therefore would not be coming to decorate the tree each year—

came to help her Jewish son-in-law make the house kosher for Passover when her daughter was recovering from an illness and could not do it herself. Even this Protestant grandmother, married to a minister, became engaged in Jewish celebrations as a way of drawing near to her grandchildren.

Nothing, however, is carved in stone. Even a person who has converted to another religion still carries his or her cultural "baggage." This baggage may at times feel lighter, at times heavier, depending on circumstances. For example, upon the death of one's own parent one questions one's choices and behaviors *as* a parent. For a convert, or someone who has agreed to raise children in a faith not his or her own, the death of a parent can precipitate a crisis of identity as well as a crisis of faith.

Regardless of which religious choices are made, grandparents and other members of the extended family play an important role. For grandparents and others of the faith the couple has chosen for the family, the role is to reinforce the choice by being a supportive presence through holiday celebrations and other marker events, while at the same time being respectful of the backgrounds of both spouses. For grandparents whose religion is not now represented in the couple's life, there is an opportunity to provide not only support for their child (whose new family is now of a different faith) but also important resources for the grandchildren, who will probably want a safe way to find out what Mommy or Daddy's past was like and what the "other" religion is about without being so threatening to family stability as might be the case if they found out through the parent. At a remove of one generation, the children can question and observe the other religion safely. Where one spouse has converted, so that the children at least perceive that at present their parents share the same faith, child rearing is considerably simplified. While it is likely that the parents will still differ on at least some aspects of theology, practice, or worldview, these differences can be discussed in a more academic way, rather than as fundamental identity issues.

Aside from the formal issues of belief and more important to most children, is how the parents *feel* about these differences. Even if the household is effectively living one tradition, the differences should neither be exaggerated nor glossed over. The children should be told about the religious and cultural background of both sides of the family—for the sake of their own identity. For young children this can be done in the most natural way simply by anecdote. For older children, genealogical tracking, such as making a family tree or producing "oral history" tapes with the older relative on both sides, may be effective.

No matter how clear the parents are in discussing their own traditions or how good the religious school, there are certain built-in conflicts for the child who has ties to both Christianity and Judaism, particularly when learning about religious persecution, a subject that arises in conjunction with many holidays which celebrate historical events. For example, a seven-year-old boy who had just learned the Purim story of political oppression of the Jews in ancient Persia came home and asked, "Will Haman come after me too, or just Daddy and Grandma and Grandpa?" Children of intermarriages are often amazed and troubled to learn that the organized church, and people identifying themselves as Christians, were responsible for so much persecution of the Jews during the Holocaust and the Inquisition. It is important for all children, but especially these, to learn that there *were* "Righteous Gentiles"—Christians who took risks to save Jews.[26]

Tolerance might arise as a theme in a household where Advent, the season of four weeks before Christmas, is celebrated, with candles, wreaths and songs each Sunday before the major holiday. Part of the preparation for the Christmas holiday can include a discussion of how people then and now respond to those whose beliefs are different. How the parents themselves respond will be a model for the children, as always.

Even when a parent has converted, his or her life presents two distinct strands for the children to weave together. If Dad converted to Judaism in his thirties, the stories he tells of his own childhood may resonate with memories and descriptions of Christmases spent around the hearth at a vacation house, or Easter breakfasts with an extended family. And the Dad telling the stories may not be able to help sentimentalizing or even longing for the experiences of a boyhood that are no longer accessible to him, and that he has decided, with his conversion, not to pass along to his own children. The Christian-born parent may be theologically comfortable with Judaism after his or her conversion, but not everything changes utterly with the assumption of a Jewish religious identity. One man, sensitive to this, says that when he talks to his kids about his own childhood he tries to make parallels to their Jewish experiences, like, "I used to really enjoy seeing all my cousins when they'd come over at Christmas, just the way you do when the family comes over for *Shabbat* dinner or for the holidays," focusing more on the good family times and not so much on the rituals themselves.

Children in nonconversionary families find so many of their peers in the same situation that, at least in urban areas, there is no dearth of companionship around this issue. Reflecting the new reality that interfaith couples want to address the issue of their children's religious faith somewhat more openly now, some Christian institutions have developed special classes in religion for the offspring of Jewish-Christian marriages. The Jewish community, too, has reached out to this population, understanding that it represents a significant pool of potential and actual Jews. The Reform movement, in particular, following its decision in the early 1980s that a child with one Jewish parent (of either sex) is considered Jewish, has tried to sensitize religious-school teachers and others who deal with young children to the fact that a child in class may come in one day describing his or her Christmas tree or a church service attended with the Christian parent or stepparent. "Don't just ignore what the child is saying; address it, and try to make some time for a discussion of the double heritage of some of the children in the class," is the advice one Reform rabbi gives his teachers. Jews in other branches of Judaism have always felt much uneasiness about showing even this much acceptance of the interfaith child's situation; the fear here is that discussion might imply sanction or approval.

## Cultural and Ethnic Differences

Some issues in raising children in an interfaith family are cultural and not strictly speaking religious, although they often get subsumed under the category of religious differences for reasons of convenience or prejudice (or both). First of all, in addition to a religious identity, we all carry an ethnic affiliation. One may be a Catholic who is Irish, Polish, Italian, Australian, Chinese, and so on. One may be a Jew whose ancestors came from Germany but who is Sephardic, or descended from fifteenth-century Spanish Jews. Race and nationality, to say nothing of individual character, all play a part in defining both "who" we are and what are our expectations about family life. "Even if you reject your religion," comments a Jewish man about his decision to marry a Catholic and their attempt to raise their children in neither tradition, "you can't reject your own background."

For Christians, who encompass many diverse forms of "peoplehood"—that is, cultural and ethnic and racial identities—religion and these other identity cues can be separated, making it possible to identify the different component parts. This is not so simple for Jews; with religious faith often apparently unimportant, religious identity is nonetheless tightly bound to culture and ethnicity in ways that make it hard to sort out what (never mind how) various factors will be passed along to the next generation.

Different religious traditions (as cultural entities, rather than the belief systems themselves) have given rise to different ethnic attitudes toward child rearing. Understanding that cultural "styles" differ takes some of the potential parental conflicts out of the personal realm. The family that believes that children have opinions worth listening to may be a family in which, a generation or two ago, the children were the immigrant parents' conduit to information about the strange new world they were living in. In other families, sometimes those with a firm belief in divine authority and its replication in the family structure with father at the head, parents expect strict obedience from their children, not opinions expressed at the dinner table. And apropos of a dinner table, food—the quantities, who gets served first and last, what constitutes proper mealtime behavior—is an excellent metaphor for calibrating the different expectations a couple has about child rearing. Families of Swedish stock who grew up in Minnesota during the twenties and thirties report that children were served at the "second table," eating what the grownups had left over. In Jewish families in the United States at that time, the mother typically pretended to adore the bony neck of the chicken so that the children might have the choicer parts. These differences extend beyond the dinner table to color many aspects of child rearing. For couples of different backgrounds today their differences are expressed around such comments as "You're babying this kid" or "You're so distant—you aren't tuned in enough to anticipate your son's needs" or "my Protestant in-laws are very low-affect people," in the words of a Jewish woman in Oklahoma.

The jokes about Jewish mothers' intrusive behavior toward their children (sons in particular) are matched in quantity only by those jokes that have to do with coddling and overprotectiveness, as in "Yes, he can walk. But thank God he doesn't have to." Just as different cultures inculcate different attitudes about food, they also place different values and interpretations on this issue of helplessness versus autonomy. A Jewish partner might interpret a spouse's behavior toward a child as cold or uncaring if the non-Jewish partner, for example, expected a child to work during the summers rather than to go to camp, even if there was money for camp:

> I felt our son should have fun now because later life will always bring work and more work. On the other hand, my husband really feels strongly that work builds character and that if his character isn't built when he's thirteen he'll never adapt to the world of work later on. I see this attitude in other members of his family. His own father and mother wouldn't give him one cent once he was out of high school, although they had the money. They expected him to work his way through college, and he did.

What the Jew in this example considers standard parental generosity, the WASP disapproves of as immoderate, excessive, or damaging. Studies show that Jews are more liberal parents, allowing more verbal exchanges and a broader range of acceptable behavior in their children than other parents do.[27] Members of different ethnic groups also have different ideas about what constitutes pain, how one should express distress (if at all), and where one should go for help.[28] Sometimes these issues prove thornier than the strictly theological ones, because formal religious observance in most families can always be postponed from week to week or holiday to holiday, but these other complexities of child rearing demand to be dealt with on a daily basis. Every day parents in an intermarriage must decide, for example, what will be the family's standards for restaurant deportment or the expression of opinions different from those of a parent.

Two sets of examples will bring home how some of these differences are expressed in the raising of children. Italian Americans have a fairly high correlation between the occupations of fathers and sons. Italian children are expected to replicate their parents' lives. An Italian Catholic man in his twenties who wanted to become a history professor described his own father telling him, "Plumbing has been good to me; it'll be good to you too." Jews, on the other hand, have been called, in America, a one-generation proletariat, encouraging their children to move on and up; this meant that the children of the working class had some geographic mobility and portable skills or professions, even though parents recognized that the acquisition of such skills might mean separations from home. Jews, more than Protestants or Catholics, value self-direction and intellectual autonomy over conformity to any external authority.[29] These cultural differences can be highlighted in families where overtly expressing the religious differences would be too threatening. One Jewish man, disappointed because his son didn't have a bar mitzvah ("My Catholic wife wouldn't have felt comfortable in synagogue," he said) displaced his hurt feelings onto their son's school choices, and took an active role in convincing his wife that the boy should attend a very competitive prep school; at least in this arena the father felt he had passed on to his son something important to him, and even, the father confessed, something "Jewish" in that the value was placed on academic excellence.

While the so-called enmeshed Jewish family, both in the Old Country and in the New World, permitted and even encouraged its young to leave the nest in pursuit of educational or professional goals, children were expected to maintain family closeness by frequent communication. Therefore, imagine the reaction of a Jewish woman married to a Canadian "lapsed WASP" when, early in their courtship, they were strolling through a department store and her husband stopped for a moment of idle chatter with a man who passed them in an aisle. No introductions were made, and when she questioned her partner he said, yes, that had been his father, and he'd been inquiring about the health of his mother, with whom he'd not been in touch for several months, though they all lived in the same city. Clearly, different expectations about closeness affect the intermarried couple's child rearing. Sometimes negotiations bring the couple to a middle ground, but more often the parent who desires greater closeness wins out—even if he or she has to defend to the other the long-distance phone bills.

"Our cultural differences are greater than our religious differences," said Janet, a Jew in a New York suburb, married to a Baptist from a small town in Virginia. "But despite it all, I'm happier with him than I was with my first husband, who was a very suitable Jewish lawyer." The issues that divided this couple, regarding how to raise their eleven-year-old son, were articulated by her husband, Bob, "It's usually around the question of what is an appropriate amount of risk to allow a child. I said, 'He's eleven and he's going to visit my dad. It's time—it's way past time—for him to learn to shoot. Dad can teach him.''' As he spoke, Janet grimaced fiercely, but they had obviously worked out a comfortable distance between her anxieties and his derring-do.

Inherited family styles can be very different indeed. This becomes clear in a setting where cross-cultural comparisons are possible. For example, two families were observed when they were seeing off family members at an airport. In one family group, Irish Catholics, the young mother and two-year-old son were going on a vacation to visit Grandma. The father's final exhortation to the little boy as they boarded the plane was, "Be good, now." A Jewish family was similarly sending off a mother and young child for a visit to Grandma. The father's last words before they boarded the plane were, "Have a great time." Each loving papa emphasized a different goal for his child. In an interfaith marriage, similar differences in expectation surface around the children.

Although these differences in outlook and behavior may ultimately derive from some religously linked worldview or from a history of religious persecution or expression, they are not actually religious differences. And ironically, the parents' cultural differences over how to raise the child need to be discussed, yet the very differences that are at issue prevent them from debating fair and square. Conflict expression and resolution differ among different ethnic groups. While a Protestant may use silent withdrawal as a way of expressing disapproval, his Jewish wife, who may be used to disapproval being accompanied by raised voices, doesn't realize that he is angry. She thinks he is being cold; he thinks she is being hysterical. Often, once the partners can tune into the way each one reacts to anger or stress, they are able to reach some compromises over what they expect and desire from their children.[30]

There are no uniform nor easy answers. But it is helpful to remember that the child is an independent being whose unique perspective, personality, and experience, along with parental influence, significantly affect the child's ultimate decisions regarding religious identification and practice. His or her interest in religion—pro or con, Christian or Jewish—is not necessarily a personal response toward the parent of either faith. The very best to hope for is that whatever choices the child ultimately makes will not be in reaction against an uncomfortable atmosphere created by the interfaith couple, but will instead reflect an informed understanding of him- or herself and both strands of his or her religious and ethnic heritage.

Perhaps the most important guideline for the parent in Christian-Jewish marriage is not to be fearful of the child's expressions of interest in either faith. One Protestant mother raising her child with both faiths said, "I know I might lose him to Judaism when he grows up, but it's not going to help matters any if I try to squelch his interest." Parents need to guard against adding secrecy and toxicity to the situation of "doubleness" the child may already experience.

# Cycles, Ceremonies, Celebrations

From the struggles that individuals have in reconciling diverse religious backgrounds, it might appear that religion itself is merely a burden. But the purpose of religion for most people is to enhance life, not to encumber it. Judaism and Christianity have developed rituals and liturgy for many occasions—life-cycle transitions, calendar celebrations, and individual spiritual growth—which may be able to provide pleasure, inspiration, and some comfort for interfaith families.

For the couple trying to meld two traditions in one household, or trying to help the grandparents whose traditions may not be represented in the younger family feel part of family celebrations, there are options, creative solutions, and much information that leads towards greater understanding of the religious issues that can arise in marking familiar life-cycle events. Even if the interfaith family chooses not to celebrate any religious holidays or to mark any stages of life with religious ceremony, still knowing what one's own and one's partner's religious faith provides in the way of spiritual and communal "enhancement" gives one a sense of continuity.

## Birth

Faced with the prospect of impending parenthood, many people who felt earlier that their own religious traditions had no hold on them find themselves wanting to mark the arrival of the new family member in a traditional way. A Jewish parent may suddenly feel that a *brith* is important; a Christian may have unexpectedly strong feelings that the child must be baptized. Or each may have been firmly commited to his or her own faith all along and must make the earlier negotiated settlement concrete now that a child is expected.

Ritual circumcision, a ceremony that usually takes place when a Jewish male is eight days old, is a stumbling block for some couples. This is a ceremony that marks the child as a Jew—not simply a physical act (there is no parallel physical marker for female children, and they are equally Jews), but a public affirmation of his Jewishness.

For a Methodist man who had made a prenuptial promise to his wife that they would raise their children as Jews, the prospect of having a son who would be circumcised, and hence different from himself, made him very uneasy. The idea of the circumcision itself, not the religious ceremony, repelled him and made him feel, he said, as if he'd be an outsider in the life of his own son because he himself was not circumcised. "It's so basic and it sounds so crude, but I don't want us to be different in that way. It might even scare him later on, to think he lost part of his penis." A sympathetic rabbi who spoke with the new father in the hospital shortly after his son was born explained, first, that the foreskin is not part of the penis; second, that the child would be different anyway because they had agreed to raise him Jewish; and three, that the objections to the *brith* might be a way of rethinking his original pledge to his wife about their children. The man accepted the rabbi's explanations and advice and agreed to the *brith*.

In other families, especially where the non-Jewish father has himself been circumcised, it is the religious nature of the occasion that can be a problem. (Circumcision was a fairly common practice in North America from about the 1940s to the 1960s for non-Jews, usually because it was considered hygienic. Since the 1960s this practice has become less popular with non-Jews, and it is now the source of much debate among pediatricians.) One woman resolved it this way: "My husband is not Jewish, and while he thought the circumcision was okay, he hated the idea of having a big fuss made because of this 'operation' on our baby. I didn't mind having the doctor perform the circumcision in the hospital—with no fuss and no witnesses—and then we had a celebration at home later, on the traditional eighth day, with a *kiddush* and an acknowledgment that this child was a Jew.''

The idea of a secret or covert circumcision is a little ironic in light of the fact that circumcision is supposed to represent a convenantal joining of this new person to the Jewish people. The implications of the ceremony are communal and public; having it done in private is something of a contradiction in terms, though it worked for this couple; they got what each needed from the occasion. Although much is made about the physical aspect of the circumcision, its point is not merely to mark Jewish males physically. *Briss (brith milah* in Hebrew) is a covenantal ceremony, marking the covenant *(brith)* binding Jews to God; it is a way of saying ''I am one with the Jewish people.'' It is this overt statement of identification that makes a traditional *brith* an especially important event for the interfaith family if Judaism is their religion of choice and identification.

Circumcision was less an issue of contention in the past, when most intermarrying Jews were male, and therefore were likely themselves to have been circumcised. Now that Jewish women are marrying out in equal numbers, they are forced to consider very carefully the powerful psychological associations their husbands make with this physical marker on a boy's genitalia. This potential physical difference between father and son need not be a barrier to circumcision, but the parents need to feel comfortable discussing this both with each other and, later, with the child himself.

(Circumcision, for so many centuries the distinguishing physical mark of a Jewish male—although occurring also in some non-Western cultures—was sometimes deliberately not performed on the sons of Jews who had escaped the Nazi Holocaust. These traumatized parents felt that by not circumcising their sons they were somehow giving them an added shield of protection should Jews ever again be persecuted as they had been under the Nazis. Some of this feeling of vulnerability to attack may come into play when a Christian father does not want his Jewish son to undergo circumcision.)

From the mid-1970s on, families have become more conscious both of the sexism involved in celebrating only the birth of a boy with a major ceremony, and of ways this can be mitigated. Today most Jewish-identified families have some kind of birth ceremony for welcoming a newborn Jewish daughter. The ceremony itself usually consists of blessings, songs, and a festive meal. Because it is not yet fixed in its rituals, and because it involves no physical marking of the child, some interfaith couples feel more comfortable with this baby-naming ceremony than with a *brith*; one woman commented, "If you're intermarried it's so much easier if you have a girl."

As the *brith* and, less definitively, a girl's naming ceremony signify that the parents intend this child to be a Jew, so baptism marks the dedication of a child to Christianity. The ritual of infant baptism consists of immersing the child in water or touching the child's forehead with holy water. The ceremony usually takes place in a church. Unlike circumcision, which is a rite of identifying a (male) child with a *people*, baptism is the ritual in which a person is identified with a *faith*, connected to a divine being. As such, it is essentially a private covenant. One young mother, a Catholic, said that she was surprised at how strong her feelings were about baptism. She and her Jewish husband had decided to raise their child Jewish, but when the child was born, she said, "I suddenly got scared. What if by not having my baby baptized I was condemning him to eternal damnation? On the one hand, I thought this was superstitious, and on the other hand, what if it were true?"

While Catholics do believe that a child who dies without being baptized will go to purgatory, there is, according to Presbyterian minister Richard Spalding, "no room for this fear in Protestant doctrine. Baptism is a sign of a relationship that already exists [between the child and Christian faith]; it's a badge, the way marriage is a badge of a relationship that already exists." Most Protestants believe that an unbaptized child is still "spiritually secure." In addition to these theological definitions, the eagerness of some parents to consider infant baptism may also reflect a desire to compensate for having transgressed a taboo by marrying a Jew—just as we have seen examples of intermarried Jews becoming more religiously observant after their marriage. Jewish partners reported no such feelings that a child might be jeopardized by not having a *brith*. Not performing a ritual circumcision means only that the child will not be identified physically as a Jew; it is a ceremony that can be performed later in life, as it is for converts. The uncircumcised child is not considered to be spiritually at risk in any way.

Because of baptism's potent associations with damnation and salvation in the minds of Christians, many Jewish partners in interfaith marriages have permitted their children who were being raised as Jews to be baptized in order to lessen their spouse's anxiety. Whether this is possible or not depends on the clergyperson involved. Under these circumstances, some will offer a form of Christian blessing instead of actual baptism, believing that the baptism itself represents a commitment to being Christian. Many Jewish grandparents have the same visceral response to the idea of a Jewish child's baptism that some Christian men have to the rituals marking circumcision. If the baptismal ceremony (or christening, as the naming that may accompany the baptism is sometimes called) doesn't matter very much to the Jewish partner, even though its underlying rationale is completely dissociated from Jewish theology, a simple baptism may be an accommodation acceptable in some families in order to satisfy the Christian parent and the grandparents. One Jewish woman said that she decided to permit baptism for her Jewish daughter (who would be raised as a Jew, she and her husband agreed) because, *"that is something that's over in a few minutes; my child will be Jewish the rest of her life."*

## What to Name the Baby?

Naming the newborn can be more divisive than the ceremonies surrounding birth rituals. The ceremonies may be forgotten after a while, but the child's name stands forever—sometimes as a reproach to the grandparents on either side, sometimes as a neutral factor, sometimes as a way of noting the blending of two ethnic or religious identities. One Jewish man contemplating having children said, "My mother might be upset before the child is born, but as soon as she sees that baby she's going to be thrilled. Unless we call her Mary. My mother-in-law would feel the same way; 'Here's your new grandson, Mrs. McLoughlin; his name is Hymie.' "

The naming itself is a matter for negotiation. In Jewish tradition, a child is named after a dear relative; for most Jews the tradition is to name after a *dead* relative or friend, and the name is considered a way of keeping that person's memory alive. Sephardic Jews with customs that came originally from Spain and other parts of the Mediterranean, name children after grandparents, even if the grandparents are still living. The custom among some Christians to name a child after the father or mother may feel very alien or even frightening to Jews of European descent because of their taboo against naming a child after someone alive. The Catholic and Eastern Orthodox practice of giving a child a saint's name may also make the Jewish partner feel uncomfortable. Recognizing the power of names, and handling the sensitivities around them, goes a long way. Since there are no real religious "rules" about this, it is wise to keep the names as neutral as possible, for the sake of the child's relationship to grandparents, as well as to minimize conflicts for the parents. The Jewish father of a grown son remembers telling his own father the boy's name at birth. The new grandfather's incredulous response: *"Christopher?* As in *Christ?"* Knowing that the boy's mother was Catholic, the name Christopher had such powerful Christian associations for him that the grandfather did not even realize the child had been given a name his father thought was an apt memorial to the deceased Jewish grandmother, Charlotte.

## Religious Education

As the child grows, the parents face choices about how to teach the religious tradition chosen for the family, and what to teach of the other tradition. Regardless of what is taught in religious school, the child will still contend with a dual religious heritage, which should be respected by whatever educational setting the parents select. The primary goal for formal (or informal) religious education for these children should be, like the physician's dictum, *primum non nocere*—"First, do no harm."

It is imperative that whatever religious instruction a child receive helps him or her feel worthwhile, and that, even if the child is the product of a conversionary marriage where the home is all of a piece practicing the same religion, there is no scorn for the religious traditions of the other parent's background. Christian teachings should never suggest to the child that Judaism is a less developed faith or that Jews are ripe for conversion to Christianity; Jewish instruction should not make the child feel disloyal to a beleaguered people because his or her parents intermarried or because he or she feels close to non-Jewish grandparents or other relatives. A woman raised as a Catholic described in the third person her experience of this scorn during her Catholic school exprience: "She was a model student despite the fact that the nuns told her that her mother would not be joining her in heaven because she's, well, you know, Jewish."[2]

Parents would be unlikely to send their children to Catholic school if they were not already committed to raising the child Catholic. The ambiguity is therefore less than for children of mixed marriages who might attend Hebrew school to get what one Jewish father termed "a taste of Judaism." Perhaps out of fear that the educational options available would not provide a welcoming environment for their children, only a minority of mixed-marriage families have in the past offered their children Jewish education; only 20 percent of the children of non-conversionary marriages have had any formal Jewish education, compared to 85 percent of the children from conversionary famil-ies.[3] Some programs under Jewish auspices are trying to improve this through curricula that respect the interfaith child's circum-stances (see Resources).

Motivated by concern for the comfort of children and their fam-ilies and also by their concern with numbers, some educators want to go out of their way to make the offspring of intermarriage feel at home in a Jewish setting. Today the issue is chronically under discussion in Reform and Reconstructionist Judaism, with video guides and teachers' manuals stressing the needs of these children. Demographers predict that by the year 2000 more than 50 percent of the students in Jewish schools will be the offspring of intermarriages. The process of drawing these children of mixed marriage closer to the Jewish community has been dubbed "in-reach." Now that there are more sensitive curricula—and more sensitized teachers—one might hope that interfaith couples would want to seek them out. Especially if they are trying to raise their children in both religions, a good Hebrew school curriculum with sensitive teachers may be more effective in imparting Jewish knowledge than a Jewish parent who may be underinformed, ambivalent, or both.

To be sure that the school environment is sensitive to the needs of intermarried families, parents may ask directly, in a face-to-face interview with the principal or teachers, for example, "How would you handle a situation in which a child in your Hebrew school comes in and says, 'You asked for a family tree. My mother's side is really interesting; her grandfather was a Lutheran minister who fled to the United States because of religious persecution'?'' What parents should be looking for is a response similar to one set forth in a manual for sensitizing teachers to this issue: ''That is a very interesting story. Since we're focusing here on Jewish ancestors, would you please tell us also about your father's side?''[4]

Sensitivity around this issue is especially important in blended families. With an increasing number of intermarriages being remarriages, households may be trying to raise children in different traditions—for example, his children are being raised as Jews, hers as Christians, because that's how each set of children started out in the parents' first marriages. Religious school educators now find themselves examining their own responses so that there will be no sharp intake of breath when a child speaks, in Christian Sunday school, about having gone to his stepbrother's bar mitzvah training class with him or to services with Jewish relatives. Similar tact is, of course, required from Jewish educators who, when dealing with such Jewish concepts as ''all Jews are responsible for one another,'' point out that this by no means suggests that they are not also responsible for others too, and that such Jewish organizations as Mazon (meaning ''Food'' in Hebrew) ask Jews to contribute 3 percent of the cost of all celebratory meals (at bar and bat mitzvahs, for example) to help feed the hungry and homeless around the world.

The hidden agenda in a religous school is much more important than the actual course material. Concerning public school, parents can tell their children: ''Never mind if the teacher is a rat; you have to learn the material; doing well is the best revenge.'' Not true here. What goes on in religious training is the establishment of an identity, and if the child of an intermarriage is made to feel like ''a half Jew'' in a Jewish context or like a ''pagan'' in a Christian setting, all that will happen is that the child will feel inferior or unworthy, with neither religious tradition well served.

There are a few places parents can begin their search. Most are under Jewish auspices—again, because many Jewish educators see the children of intermarriage, now estimated at between 400,000 and 600,000 in the United States, as an important pool of potential Jews. Parents looking especially for a Jewish educational experience for their children that will respect their bireligious background can seek out *chavurah* (fellowship)-type schools, usually informal and relatively small, as well as religious congregations that specialize, either deliberately or de facto, in interfaith families.[5]

When parents choose a religious learning situation for a child, some of their own uneasiness may come through. (This is true, among Jews especially, even in some families where both parents were born Jewish.) Some parents want the formal curriculum to give the children what the parents themselves have had to give up in order to maintain stable marriages. Others may want the children to learn about the very aspects of their own tradition that they themselves have quite consciously rejected—and for this reason, the children's religious education often engages the parents emotionally and intellectually, sometimes in unexpected ways.

## Bar and Bat Mitzvah

After birth, there are a few other ceremonial occasions that provide opportunities for the interfaith couple to express how they're raising their children and what their goals are for them. Bar mitzvah, the ceremony marking the entry of a male Jew into adulthood, and bat mitzvah, its equivalent (but far more recent) ceremony for females, provide such an occasion. By the time the child is thirteen (the usual age for this ceremony, though Orthodox girls often celebrate it at twelve), the religious aspects of the ritual obviously have an intellectual impact on him or her that the birth ceremonies did not. The parents have had thirteen more years to experience the joys and conflicts of their marriage and to influence the child's religious identity. Complexities of feeling arise at this time even in endogamous Jewish families, partly because of the age of the children—thinking beings, but still not fully formed, with all the ambivalence and vulnerability that adolescence brings. Even caterers comment that feelings run much higher in planning bar or bat mitzvahs than weddings, because, one of them said, "The parents feel so responsible for what happens to the kid; they feel that if anything goes wrong there will be negative feelings about Jewish stuff forever." Bar and bat mitzvahs are the only life-cycle events that do not change the family structure in any way; they "do not mark the leaving or entry of a family member.''[6] and provide a very clear occasion for the whole nuclear family to make a statement about its own unity or religious identity.

For couples who have not settled on one household religion, or who have chosen to minimize the presence of religion in their lives, it is less likely that their children will celebrate this marker event. Only 15 percent of the children born to mixed couples (where the non-Jewish partner has not converted to to Judaism) celebrate bar or bat mitzvah, whereas nearly 75 percent of children go through the ritual in families where the non-Jewish partner has converted to Judaism.[7]

The ceremony usually consists of having the youngster participate in the regular Sabbath services, say blessings over the Torah, and read from it. As a public occasion, it needs to be held with a *minyan* (a quorum of at least ten Jews), and is usually done in synagogue, although there are innovative ceremonies held at home, out of doors, at campsites, and so on. Because study and the preparation of prayer material are involved, the Jewish parent in an interfaith marriage ''may not want to push it,'' says one rabbi. Because bat mitzvah has been popular in North America only since the late 1950s and is not yet a universal Jewish ceremony, some women in interfaith marriages may not have had the ceremony themselves and so do not feel its loss for their daughters. Bar mitzvah is an almost universal experience for Jewish males.[8] Religious significance aside, bar and bat mitzvah provide an opportunity to go public and to display the family's religious convictions. Sociologist Egon Mayer notes that ''bar mitzvah has emerged as the signal Jewish ceremony by which an intermarried family publicly proclaims that their child is being raised as a Jew.''[9]

A child born of a Jewish mother is automatically considered Jewish and therefore entitled to celebrate bar or bat mitzvah in any denomination of Judaism; so is a child of any parentage who has converted to Judaism. In the Reform and Reconstructionist movements, a child of a Jewish father who indicates his or her Jewishness by expressing a desire for the ceremony is considered to be Jewish and can celebrate with full honors. In Conservative and Orthodox Judaism, the unconverted child of a Jewish father and a non-Jewish mother (one who did not convert to Judaism before the birth of the child) is not a Jew, and therefore would not mark this Jewish life-cycle event.

The ceremony itself has been under discussion by religious groups to determine what should be the role of a paarent who is not Jewish, since the ceremony focuses on assuming the obligations of a Jewish adult. In Orthodox Judaism, the tradition lets the mother off the hook in some ways, since in any case in Orthodoxy women do not participate with men in most synagogue-based religious ceremonies; in a Conservative synagogue, assuming that the child had converted, the mother's role could be a symbolic one—she might say a blessing in English, or present some special object to the child, perhaps even a family Bible from her side of the family, noting in her remarks the child's dual heritage. Her presence, either in the synagogue proper or on the *bimah* (platform from which prayers are read), is usually not a problem for religious authorities.

For the non-Jewish father, adaptations have been made in the service, with appropriate blessings said over the boy or girl, but with the Jewish component of the blessings taken care of by a rabbi or Jewish relative of the celebrant. In a Conservative or Orthodox ceremony, a non-Jew would not be called up to the platform to say the blessings over the Torah, the argument being that to do so would "secularize" the Torah reading. A non-Jewish father could come to the *bimah* to recite English blessings giving thanks that the child has reached this milestone. To avoid diluting the religious aspects of the ceremony, regardless of the policy of the individual synagogues, it is probably wise to restrict the participation of the non-Jewish relatives to areas not strictly associated with Jewish ritual or prayers not especially associated with the assertion of Jewish identity.

Dealing with the children's and the adults' emotions around this issue is hard for all families, but especially so for "nonnormative" families, where divorce or intermarriage make the negotiations around the event more complex. In a blended family where the birth parent(s) and the stepparent(s) may be of different religions, there are a variety of solutions if the celebrant wants a role for all these significant adults. The Jewish father or mother, for example, might drape the *tallis* over the shoulders of the celebrant (since the attainment of religious adulthood marks the first occasion on which one is obligated to wear the prayer shawl). The non-Jewish stepfather or stepmother might say prayers in English or make a speech at the festive meal that is supposed to follow the religious ceremony.

Until the early 1980s, when the Reform movement in Judaism declared that any child with one Jewish parent who decides to identify as a Jew is considered Jewish, a painful situation arose for some children of interfaith marriages.[10] The situation still comes up now in Conservative synagogues; less so in Orthodox ones because there are far fewer mixed-marriage families in Orthodox synagogues. The problem is this: A couple raises their child Jewish, but the mother does not convert to Judaism before the child is born, nor is the child converted to Judaism. As the age of bar or bat mitzvah approaches, the child prepares for the ceremony just as all his or her Jewish contemporaries are doing. Then the family is made aware of the fact that unless the child undergoes formal conversion to Judaism (despite having been raised a Jew, gone to Hebrew school classes, and so on) he or she cannot become bar or bat mitzvah, as this is a ceremony marking a child's acceptance of adult *Jewish* responsibilities.

The religious authorities, the "gatekeepers," are within their rights in wanting to maintain boundaries between Jew and Christian, and in their desire to uphold the meaning of a religious ceremony. But the pain inflicted on the child and his or her family is great, and the child's sense of unworthiness may be devastating, and—a not insignificant issue—the child and family may become totally alienated from the Jewish community as a result. For interfaith couples affiliating with Conservative or Orthodox synagogues it is crucial to discuss the situation when the children are still young, so that adequate preparation can be made either for their formal conversion or to find some alternative marker ceremony for entering young adulthood, ensuring that the encounter with Jewish law doesn't come as a shock a few months before the child reaches thirteen. "The agony surprises me sometimes," said a rabbi well known in the Conservative movement, "since there is a simple solution to the problem—convert the child formally at birth or as soon as there is a manifest desire for the child to be a Jew, and the problem disappears."

The situation is especially upsetting for families where the mother has herself converted to Judaism, but after the birth of the children. The offspring are then left in a kind of limbo—raised as Jews by two Jewish parents, but not born of a Jewish mother, so their own religious status is in doubt in two major branches of Judaism. To avoid this and other similar conflicts (including potential conflicts over the raised-Jewish child's eligibility as a marriage partner for an Orthodox mate), if a couple chooses to raise their children as Jews it makes a great deal of sense to have each child formally converted at birth if the mother is not Jewish. Conversion in infancy obviates the need to deal with problems such as the bar or bat mitzvah dilemma later on.

An interesting aside to the issue of bar and bat mitzvah ceremonies for children is the rise in the number of women who, never having had the opportunity to celebrate when they were younger, choose to have a bat mitzvah as adults. Rabbi Avis Miller reported that in her congregation in Washington, D.C., adult bat mitzvah is especially popular among Jewish women married to non-Jewish men, since the preparatory study and the event itself are done alone, not with a spouse. Adult bat mitzvah thus provides what is in some ways an ideal ritual experience for such women: both authentic and independent of other family members.

## Confirmation

Typically, the confirmation ceremony in both Jewish and Christian institutions marks the point when the child has become a young adult and puts the seal on his or her commitment to live as a Jew or as a Christian. (Although the term used is the same in both traditions, the ceremonies are not; they reflect the goals and norms of each faith group.) The ceremony has many variations but is usually performed in a group, almost as a parallel to a secular graduation ceremony, which in a way it is, marking the completing of the "childhood" phase of religious education. Confirmation usually takes place between twelve and fourteen for Christians, and around fifteen or sixteen for Reform Jews (the only group to celebrate confirmation on a large scale; originally it replaced bar and bat mitzvah among American Reform Jews; during the last two decades, both bar or bat mitzvah and confirmation have been marked in Reform congregations). Because there is no specific age at which confirmation would be celebrated, and because it is considered optional by many denominations of Christians, it can present less difficulty for the interfaith family than, say, bar or bat mitzvah. Although for a family grappling with integrating the traditions of each spouse, confirmation for the children is a ceremony often dismissed precisely because it is not usually considered mandatory in any tradition.

## Holidays

More complex are the issues that arise over holiday celebrations, which come around each year. Families can and do develop their own ways to deal with conflicts that arise, but a general rule of thumb, endorsed by both Christian and Jewish clergy, is that blending the holidays and the symbols is both a devaluation of each tradition and confusing to the individuals involved. Paradoxically, the more involved one becomes in authentic religious expression—distinct from intellectual study of the two religions—the more conflict both children and adults may experience. Making the spiritual dimension concrete through worship, prayer, and ritual celebrations mandates for most people that they choose one tradition over the other—another factor for the intermarried couple to consider in weighing whether or not to maintain a single religious tradition in their home.

The festivals that commemorate events in Jewish history—Purim, Passover, and Hanukkah most obviously—are easiest for the intermarried couple. In part this is because Christians recognize some of the precursors of their own faith in Passover, and because the themes of liberation and religious choice that are so strong in the other two holidays resonate with meaning for Protestants and Catholics also. Festivals rooted in celebrating nature, such as Succoth, the "Festival of Booths" that marks the autumn harvest, or Tu B'Shevat, a planting festival usually celebrated in February, have themes that are accesible to all faiths, though of course the prayers and rites that mark them are specifically Jewish.

Certain festivals allow themselves to be shared more than others. Easter is expecially hard for some Jews, with the intensity of historical memory it may bring as the classic time for anti-Semitic pogroms and blood libels against Jews, particularly in Eastern Europe where most North American Jews' ancestors came from. In addition, Easter encapsulates theologically exactly what Jews do not accept in Christianity—the resurrection of Jesus as the Messiah.

Similarly, the High Holidays—Rosh Hashanah, Yom Kippur—may be trying times for non-Jewish partners in interfaith marriages because they are marked in synagogue rather than at home and they are, literally, Days of Awe, of self-examination and moral seriousness. As an accounting of the soul, so to speak, they are highly individualistic, although they are experienced in a collective setting as part of a community. They are focused on prayer, not on ritual (as the Sabbath is) or on history. These are "inward" occasions, and even partners in an endogamous marriage, or parents and children, or siblings, may not feel particularly close to one another at these times, even as they are in synagogue together. While introspection knows no religious boundaries, here the personal accounting is expected to take place within a community, in the context of Jewish tradition and ritual.

Yom Kippur, which is a day of fasting and synagogue prayers asking forgiveness for sins committed wittingly or unwittingly, individually or collectively, is reportedly very difficult for Christians to witness or experience. The Christian husband of a Jewish woman said that he has no difficulty attending services on Rosh Hashanah, the Jewish New Year, which falls ten days before Yom Kippur, but is loath to accompany his wife to services on Yom Kippur, the Day of Atonement. "It reminds me too much of the talk of sin I had to listen to in the Baptist church my folks took me to every Sunday. I know the liturgy and the purpose here are different, but I just have such a painful feeling of revulsion when I hear all that talk about what we've all done wrong. . . . " His wife, glad to have him in synagogue with her on the New Year, made no plea for his presence on Yom Kippur.

Reinforcing the social bonding and boundaries of the Jewish community, the High Holidays are the paramount public annual occasion when all members of the community are expected to appear. The other major holidays are celebrated by the most American Jews in their own homes, but coming together in synagogue on these holidays is an important way of being counted as a Jew, and of seeing and being seen by other Jews—marking changes in people's lives over the intervening year, seeing others' children and grandchildren perhaps for the first time. For interfaith couples and for the Jewish parents of someone who has married out there may be an additional level of self-consciousness in presenting oneself before the community, which can precipitate hard feelings if the discomfort is not addressed.

Less dramatic than the big holiday celebrations is the weekly rhythm of life: for Christians, attendance at Sunday services, for Jews the setting aside of the twenty-five or so hours from sundown Friday to sunset Saturday as a day of rest. Sunday worship services in every denomination of Christianity are a means of affirming one's faith in religious tenets. Sabbath for the Jews is related not to a statement of faith but to a sanctification of time—"making the Sabbath day holy" is how one of the blessings says it. Because *Shabbat* does not conflict with the day of Christian worship, intermarried couples find that if each wants to maintain the weekly rites of his or her tradition it is possible to do so with little temporal conlict. A Jewish woman whose husband is a non-practicing Lutheran began to light Sabbath candles every week after her marriage—she had never done so when she was single, although Jewish law and tradition make no distinctions between single and married persons in this obligation. Her husband, far from objecting, very much liked the fact that after the candle-lighting his wife would say a blessing over wine and *challah* and they spent the rest of the evening quietly at home together. Their own ritual included a commitment to stay at home on Friday evenings, alone or with friends, having *Shabbat* as an island of repose they both appreciated.

This couple's accommodation to one partner's need for ritual did not take place overnight. Initially, although he made no objections, the Christian partner was taken aback by his Jewish wife's need to have some element of Jewish ritual in their home. For some couples the ritual distinctions are expressed through foods. One Jewish man in an interfaith marriage told his wife that he was repelled that she should want to cook ham or pork in their house—although he would occasionally eat both in restaurants. Pork products, like shellfish, are forbidden foods, and a religiously observant Jew will not eat them. But some Jews who do not characterize themselves as observant also avoid pork. "Shrimp, that's different," this man said. "No Jew was ever told that he could save his life if he ate shrimp or lobster," referring to the practice, during the Spanish Inquisition and at other times, of giving Jews a choice between violating Jewish law (by eating pork) to stay alive or refusing and being killed. Thus, there are vestiges of these Jewish religious observances even in the lives of Jews who do not celebrate the full cycle of Jewish holidays or who routinely work on the Sabbath. Understanding the blurring of boundaries between culture and religion when it comes to the religious observances of some Jews is often a challenge for the Christian partner in an interfaith marriage—and sometimes also for the Jew who has never clearly articulated even to him- or herself what observances feel important, and why.

The parent whose holiday is not the one being celebrated may be able to view the preparations and the event itself comfortably from a distance, as an observer. If there are strong negative feelings—as some Jews have about Christmas and Easter, or some Christians have over the emphasis on individual responsibility for sins at Yom Kippur, it is best that these be overtly expressed as the reason why that partner is not going to participate in the event.

## The December Dilemma

The issue that most often drives intermarried couples into the arms of a discussion group or support group is the question of how to integrate two religious traditions in one time frame. A calendar coincidence has created an artificial juxtaposition of Christmas and Hanukkah, and the differential responses to these events are not just a measure of how religiously identified the household is. How the holidays are celebrated also has to do with family, with tradition, and with how the parents feel about both.

One child of an intermarriage told his Hebrew-school class: "Yes, we celebrate Hanukkah by lighting candles every night for eight nights, but we save our presents and put them under the tree and we open them on Christmas morning." The sensitive response from the Hebrew school teacher might be a model for intermarried couples trying to teach their children that maintaining a religious tradition doesn't mean choosing one parent over the other. This teacher replied: "Honor your father and your mother' is a Jewish value. If both holidays are observed in your home, that is your parents' decision. Here, we focus on Hanukkah, because this is a Jewish school.''[11]

Every family works out its own method for dealing with the sharing of time and space for the parents' differing religious traditions. (In a conversionary marriage the questions have to do with how to relate to the in-laws and grandparents of the tradition not being celebrated.) Parents go to discussion groups partly because they cannot figure out for themselves exactly what to do about the holidays, but also because these choices are fraught with emotion and overlaid with feelings of anxiety about how their choices will affect the children. A community of people who have shared this struggle can provide crucial support for parents who, especially at holiday times that test everyone's emotional stability, may feel especially vulnerable. Just being able to light Hanukkah candles with another family where there is also a Christian partner unfamiliar with the Jewish traditions can help both the Jewish and the Christian partners feel less isolated.

One family has decided simply to go away from their "problem." Each year as the December holidays approach, they plan a family vacation, pack the children off to some neutral resort setting and exchange presents as generic "holiday gifts" during their vacation. Putting aside for a moment that this "solution" may not be available to most parents for financial or scheduling reasons, this entirely begs the question of how to pass along to the children something meaningful from each parent's religious and cultural heritage. The goal should *not* be avoidance. Pretending that the two holidays really aren't there (which never actually works anyway, because even at resorts people wish one another Merry Christmas, even on Tahiti where there are no pine trees) is conveying a message of the hidden, the secret, the avoided— which makes the children think both that traditions are unimportant and also that they must be very important and powerful indeed if Mom and Dad are so nervous that they have to leave home to escape them.

Secularizing these holidays "is a cop-out," said an East Coast rabbi who numbers interfaith couples among his congregants. "Painting Easter eggs or hanging a Jewish star on a Christmas tree and saying 'this is a time of giving' isn't what any of the holidays is about, and if you just do presents you're telling the children that there is no other dimension in life than the here and now; you're depriving them not just of the specifics of one religion or the other, but of a whole long-range view of human existence which they're likelier to get if you can infuse some sense of a religious tradition into their lives." It is confusing as well as diminishing: If the holidays have only secular meaning, why the pain? Mom and Dad are both human, so if these are just "human" holidays, why the conflict?

If the parents have made a decision that one religion will be celebrated in the home, part of the negotiation preceding this decision may have been that the other parent will be "entitled" to celebrate his or her holidays, with the clear message articulated to the children that this is a holiday that they can help Mom or Dad enjoy but that it is not *their* holiday. Depending how successful the parents themselves have been in adjusting to their differences (and this is the big "depending" for everything that relates to children), the children may be able to accept this with perfect calm. The family is Jewish, Dad is Jewish, they all belong to temple, but Mom has a Christmas tree. One woman in this situation says, after fifteen years of marriage, "I was the one who insisted that the children be raised in one tradition, and that was Judaism. But I wasn't at all ready to give up the things that were really important to me. My kids know when they have a tree it's for Mommy. When I don't have the need anymore, the tree will go."

The tensions around the "December dilemma" are most severe when the holiday season highlights or crystallizes the parents' still unresolved conflicts over whose religious tradition will be observed. Under these circumstances, the children have little chance to be comfortable with either (or any) holiday celebration. Imagine how a child feels if at every holiday occasion one or the other parent feels uncomfortable and makes this discomfort known, however subtly. Armed with empathy for their child, intermarried adults have an obligation to modify their own expectations somewhat until a balance is struck that both can live wth. Obviously, if one parent is positively allergic (metaphorically) to living in a home with a Christmas tree, it might not be a bad idea—if the family has not declared itself Jewish—for everybody to go off to Grandma's house for Christmas day to enjoy an undiluted holiday celebration.

A Jew may legitimately be uneasy about Christmas, especially because it is a holiday from which he or she may routinely have felt excluded, and may experience what Rabbi Harold Schulweis calls "Santa Klaustrophobia."[12] Not everyone considers "Merry Christmas" a routine salutation. Hanukkah has taken on much more importance as a Jewish historical-religious holiday than it deserves because of its proximity to Christmas on the calendar—Hanukkah gives Jews a chance to have a "big" occasion that, for the children, is coming to rival Christmas in gift-giving. A Christian partner is unlikely to feel uncomfortable on theological grounds, but may feel uncomfortable about having a unfamiliar holiday celebrated in his or her home. The holidays provide the ideal occasion on which the spouses can do battle, if they are so inclined, which is why the December dilemma season should be subtitled "power playoffs." To avert confrontation, there should be ways the non-practicing partner can become part of the celebration; with Hanukkah, for example, a Christian father can learn to play *dreidel* (spinning top) games with the children, a traditional holiday pastime that will keep him part of the action yet not force him into religious participation. The children should be helped to understand that the two holidays are not competitors but celebrations of two different views of reality and spirituality. Hanukkah commemorates a military victory and has come to represent the struggle for religious freedom, culminating in the reconsecration of the Temple. Christmas celebrates the birth of a man thought to be God incarnate. Jews do not believe that there is any other God, or manifestation of God, than the One, so for a Jew to celebrate Christmas would be a contradiction. But a Jew can certainly help or observe someone else celebrating Christmas—including his or her own parent.

It is helpful for parents to keep in mind that the children stand to gain a great deal by witnessing how their parents resolve a difference such as this one. If decisions and compromises are made with mutual respect, with neither parent undercutting the other with snide remarks or attempts to manipulate the children to one side or the other, the children will have learned an important lesson in religious tolerance and marital compatibility. They'll also be strengthened when they come to explain to their friends what they celebrate and how and why.

## Death

With holiday celebrations one has the feeling that if change is needed, or if things don't work out satisfactorily this year, there is always next year's calendar to be observed. Even with the wedding ceremony, if a couple has a secular ceremony they can, if they choose, have a religious one later on, or a reaffirmation of their marriage vows to mark an anniversary. Not so with death, an especially painful time for intermarried families, who often have conflicting loyalties—to the tradition of a deceased parent or spouse, and to their own needs for comfort in a time of grieving.

For everyone, the death of a parent raises questions about one's own choices and behaviors, both as a child and perhaps as a parent also. For a convert, or someone who has agreed to raise children in a faith not his or her own, the death of a parent can precipitate a crisis of identity as well as a crisis of faith. For someone who has converted out of the religion in which he or she was raised, the death of a parent can be expecially traumatic, since the sources of present comfort are likely to be at variance with what the deceased parent would have chosen. One woman, a convert to Judaism, was told by her own rabbi after her father's death not to say *kaddish,* the traditional mourners' prayer recited daily for the first year after the death of a loved one and on specific occasions each year thereafter. As a Jew, she very much wanted the balm of regular prayer in a community; as her father's daughter, she felt guilty that she would be doing something her father might not have appreciated or understood. Her rabbi's feeling was that it would not honor her father's memory to do so; other rabbis would disagree, since the *kaddish* is really an affirmation of spiritual transcendence and is intended as a comfort to the living.

Lydia Kukoff, herself a Jew by choice, tells of her own experiences in mourning her Christian father. "I have no easy answers. I can only tell you what I have done. I say the *yizkor* prayer [a prayer of remembrance recited at the anniversary of the death and at selected commemorative occasions each year] for my father but do not light a *yahrzeit* candle [lit on the anniversary of the death, at home, and burning for approximately twenty-four hours]. On the anniversary of his death I make a contribution to his church in his name and I recite a psalm in his memory."[13]

Because the Jewish rites surrounding death and mourning are intended to be psychologically supportive of the living rather than to ease the transition of the dead into the next world, they are particularly appealing to many non-Jews. One Christian woman claimed that her desire to convert to Judaism was spurred by her experiences with Jewish mourning rituals. In an odd twist, a lapsed Protestant man married to a Jewish woman was able to mourn his own father only with Jewish rituals. He had felt estranged for thirty years from his father's brand of fundamentalist Protestantism, and could not bear to return to express his grief in the church in which he had been raised. Instead, he went with his wife to the local Conservative synagogue on the Sabbath morning after his father's death and stood with the other mourners when the *kaddish* was said. He did the same thing at the *yizkor* (general memorial) services held the next month at the synagogue. He said, "I don't feel swallowed up by the Jews the way

I do with my father's Christianity." He was able to connect with his own father respectfully without going back into a situation in the church that for him would have offered no succor. As a nominal Christian in a Jewish situation, he was safe in another way also—no one could have accused him of doing too little to honor the memory of his father. He was guaranteed that his grief would be respected and that he would be left alone to express it.

More painful may be the death of a spouse whose faith was different from that of the survivor. Laura, an Episcopalian who was married to a Jew reported that after her husband Mitchell died of cancer in his mid-forties the family sat *shiva* (observing the traditional seven days of mourning) at his parents' house. Her two teenage sons, converted to Judaism at birth, said the appropriate Jewish prayers with their grandparents. While Laura was not in any way excluded from the family closeness at the house of mourning, she had no family members with whom to do any formal grieving. The minister of the church she attended recognized this after visiting Laura at her in-laws' home, and thereafter made a point of spending time there with her each day during the week of mourning.

For Larry, a Jewish man whose Greek Orthodox wife Becky died suddenly in her late fifties, the rituals of her church did not feel particularly comforting at all. Her funeral was conducted in the church, and even the graveside rites, which included having flowers on the grave, were alien to what Larry recalled from Jewish funerals, which usually are quite simple, with mourners placing stones on the grave rather than floral offerings. They had no children, and while Becky had remained a fairly regular churchgoer throughout her married life, Larry had no affiliation with any synagogue or rabbi. One of his Jewish colleagues at the magazine where he worked asked him, shortly after Becky's death, if he wanted to attend a Saturday morning synagogue service with him to say the *kaddish* prayer; Larry went, and reported that he found himself tearful but "surprisingly comforted" just by having a community physically near him in his mourning.

One troubling aspect of the death of one spouse in a mixed marriage is that Jewish cemeteries under the control of most synagogues do not permit the burial of a non-Jew. Some have made provision for non-Jewish relatives to be buried in an adjacent burial ground. Most cemeteries owned by Reform congregations or by secular Jewish fraternal organizations will permit burial of a non-Jewish spouse. Christian cemeteries, like the one in which Becky was buried, usually do not object to the burial of a Jewish spouse, so Larry, who had never before given the matter much thought, arranged shortly after Becky's death to have a plot in that cemetery himself. Though some people consider the subject too macabre for discussion, it is very wise for an intermarried couple to make inquiries, at least, as to where they might be buried together. For the survivor, having these arrangements in place in advance can mean the difference between experiencing the normal pain of grief or living through the additional cruelty of searching for an appropriate burial ground in an urgent situation. In one family where the matter was discussed very openly, the parents of the Jewish husband in an intermarried couple decided that they and their son should be buried in the ancillary area of their Jewish cemetery, so that when their non-Jewish daughter-in-law died they could all be buried together in the same area. Their daughter-in-law was enormously touched.

In the tragic situation where a child dies, if the parents have not resolved the child's religious identity while he or she was alive, there may be reason for having to make that determination after death, when a burial plot is being arranged for. To avoid precipitating a crisis between the husband and wife in what is already an emotionally overwrought situation, burial in any non-sectarian cemetery in which both spouses can later be buried too would be a feasible solution, sparing the parents from confronting their religious differences at a time when the relationship might not be able to tolerate additional strain.

Life-cycle transition points—some joyous, some heartbreaking—along with religious ceremonies and celebrations provide opportunities for intermarried couples to find concrete ways of binding their disparate lives together. "We're making memories," is how one man phrased his family's efforts. While they can also be used to drive a wedge between the partners, these events can allow partners to find ways for each to include the other in marking occasions with rituals to enhance both the occasion and the relationship.

# 10

# *Conversion to Judaism*

Ⓘf you love me so much, why do you want me to become
something different?

—*Protestant husband to his Jewish wife*

My fiancé isn't religious at all, and if he starts to tease or
mock me when I'm studying Judaism in the conversion class,
forget it—I'll just quit.

—*Catholic-born woman*

Conversion to Judaism is a serious process. It requires the
ability to sever without guilt any link to one's past religion. It
requires the steadfast courage to accept Judaism despite the
awareness of the role of anti-Semitism in Western history.
While every individual's synthesis of Jewish values and
practices will be unique, one who elects Judaism must affirm
its basic beliefs, must live its traditional patterns, and must
identify with the dreams and destiny of the Jewish people.

—*Rabbi Stephen C. Lerner in a brochure for the Center for Conversion*
*to Judaism*

"There's no doubt," one Jewish man said succinctly, "that in a
perfect world my wife would be Jewish." The conversion of one
spouse to the religion of the other may bring the possibility of
that perfection closer. It undoubtedly makes many of life's decisions and rhythms smoother if husband and wife, father and
mother, are of the same religion. Since there's no real way to
ensure that in an open society people will choose mates of their
own faith, conversion can create that harmony.

Sometimes viewed as an obvious solution to the "problem of intermarriage," conversion may indeed bring a couple closer together. However, even when it is an acceptable or even desired solution, it is rarely a simple one. For one thing, the term is not even correct. Considering the emotions that are involved when a person moves from one religious identity into another, the word *conversion* is something of a misnomer. The convert is not changing into something else, one hopes, but is doing something that feels consonant with the person he or she already is. Without this feeling of consonance, conversion might be an extremely uncomfortable, even jarring, experience. Nancy Kleiman, a former nun, lives in a Jewish home with her Jewish husband, and is committed to her work within the synagogue. Yet she remains a Christian: "I can't convert to Judaism. During the conversion ceremony, one publicly relinquishes prior religious ties and commitments. For me that statement would deny an integral part of who I am."[1]

Some couples—and in-laws—see conversion in the context of intermarriage as the act that will solve all problems, either with their families or between themselves, and resolve any of the uncertainties the partners might have had about a dual-faith household. Some of these hopes are realized when one partner converts to the religion of the other. But some of the duality persists, of course, regardless of what faith the couple chooses, simply because conversion does not bring about an actual change in who the person is. A change in faith does not immediately "recolor" all the images from a past lived under other assumptions. Both partners need to understand that, even after one converts to share the other's faith, the real differences that will still exist (as they do between any two people) need to be respected.

In the Middle Ages and earlier, state laws against intermarriage were so stringent that Jews who converted to Christianity under these circumstances usually did so to escape persecution and sometimes literally to save their own lives. In eighteenth-century Western Europe there was a high incidence of conversion of Jews to Christianity, particularly in cosmopolitan centers. Men converted usually for economic advancement—to ensure that they'd get ahead in business, the professions, or the social sphere. As a rule, Jewish women converted to Christianity in order to marry men whose elevated social position precluded marriage to a Jew. In the nineteenth century, conversion associated with intermarriage almost invariably meant that the Jewish partner became a Christian, usually to ensure social acceptability rather than to avert physical attack. Today few Jews married to Christians formally leave Judaism to enter another religion. They may raise their children in the Christian faith of a spouse, they may never walk into a synagogue themselves, but they very, very rarely convert.

Historically, there have been two attitudes toward seeking or accepting converts to Judaism. The earlier was a positive one. In biblical times, converts were honored. Ruth converts to the Judaism of her mother-in-law Naomi, saying ''Thy people shall be my people, thy God, my God,'' and is so admired that, according to the biblical account, King David (and subsequently the Messiah) comes from her line. According to one traditional Jewish source, ''The Holy One only dispersed the Jews among the nations so that converts would join them.''[2] Before the Christian era, Judaism welcomed converts quite readily, and proselytizing was not uncommon.

In the early years, Judaism and Christianity became competitive about conversions. When Jews were persecuted for proselytizing, notably by Constantine in the fourth century, conversion was discouraged by rabbis for obvious reasons—loss of life being among them. For about 1,600 years, Jews made no effort to convert non-Jews to Judaism and actively discouraged converts. Christians who converted to Judaism after the formative years of Christianity must have been very highly motivated, since there was a great deal to lose from joining one's fate to that of the Jews.

Especially as many Jews experienced attempts at forced conversions by Christians, proselytizing gained a bad name among Jews. The current wave of interest in converting the non-Jewish spouses of Jews to Judaism is an indication of how powerfully the trend toward intermarriage has affected long-held Jewish practice. While there are no laws against conversion per se, there have always been sanctions against those who converted for an ulterior motive—for example, in conjunction with marriage to a Jew. Under some Orthodox interpretations of Jewish law, one who converts for the sake of a marriage cannot marry a Jew, because the conversion is considered invalid. In all but the most traditional Orthodox segments of Judaism today this stricture no longer holds. Quite the contrary; conversion has become the strategy of choice in responding to Jewish-Gentile intermarriages—encouraged by many rabbis and by the family of the Jewish partner as well.

Conversion has been at the center of outreach efforts in almost all branches of Judaism. Partly as a result of the upsurge in intermarriage since the 1960s, Jews have again been talking about reaching out to "new audiences," including the "unchurched" and Christian partners married to Jews. The talk, in private conversation and public proclamations, is of conversion. This outreach, in combination with a greater acceptance of Jews and Judaism in Western society generally, has led to surprisingly large numbers of conversions of non-Jews to Judaism. Whereas in the past, Jews were more likely to convert to Christianity, today Christians married to Jews or planning such a marriage often consider conversion. About one in three Jewish-Christian intermarriages involve the Christian partner's taking on the Jewish faith.[3] Most of the rest remain mixed marriages.

The number of converts to Judaism has been climbing along with the intermarriage rate—approximately 10,000 to 12,000 per year in the United States.[4] Until the 1970s, conversion to Judaism was the only path the spouse of a Jewish partner could take that might "take the curse off the intermarriage."

In recent years the conversion rate has not quite kept up with the intermarriage rate. The slight slowdown may be caused by the fact that Jews feel less uncomfortable with intermarriages, so there may be less pressure on the Christian partner to convert. Along with the greater acceptance of intermarriage, the Reform movement's decision that any child with *one* Jewish parent can be considered a Jew eliminated an external motivation for conversion for the spouses of Reform Jews. Conversion today may thus be more sincere, not something attempted as a way of placating others or alleviating the anxiety of one partner.

Until now, women have been more likely to convert than men. Perhaps because under Conservative and Orthodox interpretations of Jewish law a child is only considered Jewish if born to a Jewish *mother*, Christian-born wives have been the ones converting. That very few Christian men convert to Judaism may be explained by the widespread acceptance of the idea of matrilineal descent; it may also be explained by the fact that women were traditionally more likely to shape themselves to their husbands' desires. One Christian man gave another reason for the willingness of women to convert; he told his fiancée: "I give up my self if I convert. You only give up your family if we marry." Yet Rabbi Stephen C. Lerner, a Conservative rabbi who has officiated at the conversion of hundreds of Christians to Judaism, sees a slight rise in the number of male converts over the past few years and attributes this not only to the rising number of Jewish women intermarrying but also to "women's new assertiveness. They're now willing to ask a partner to convert. They say, 'This is something that matters a great deal to me.'" There is no longer the automatic assumption—at least among Jews—that the father will determine all choices within the family. But Christian women still do not appear to be pressing the Jewish men they marry to convert to Christianity. The tropism is still toward Judaism.

There are many types of and responses to conversion—making it one of the most complex facets of an intermarriage. Obviously the issues an intermarried couple confronts differ if it is being contemplated as a premarital event, early in the marriage, or before or after the birth of children. Conversion can take place at any time in life—one Protestant-born man in his late sixties converted to Judaism recently after having nearly forty years of marriage to his Jewish wife. More than one-third of all converts adopt Judaism after they have been married for some time[5]; the marriage itself and a sense of being an "associate" Jew or a fellow traveler ease the way for making what can be a genuine transformation. Because Judaism is a religion of dailiness, of sanctifying time and giving instructions for all aspects of life, one can accept these instructions one by one as one feels a growing sense of familiarity and comfort with one's new identity as a Jew.

No one wants to be coerced into making a decision about matters so potentially all-encompassing as religious identification and affiliation. Some Christian partners decide to convert after being exposed to Jewish practices in a noncoercive fashion by a spouse and in-laws, drawn in by something they have seen or experienced in their spouse's family or spouse's own observances or feelings. The decision is often described as a slow process of "approaching." Dolores, a psychotherapist from a churchgoing Congregationalist family, who converted to Judaism after being married for seven years to a Jewish man, says, "It probably sounds a little macabre, but it was going to Jewish funerals that first attracted me to Judaism. There was no open casket, which I liked, and the *shiva* seemed very civilized and psychologically sensible."

Obviously, not everyone who appreciates Judaism chooses to become a Jew. Most interfaith marriages remain religiously mixed, but in about 20 percent of intermarriages where there has been no conversion, the non-Jewish partner "assimilates" into the Jewish community anyway.[6] This state has been defined as "adhesion to the Jewish community rather than conversion to the Jewish religion."[7] There are cases where conversion is not a viable option, such as intermarriages involving Christian clergy, when each spouse has a strong faith and at least one of them has a public identity rooted in that faith. However, for some intermarried Christians, being very devout in the faith of their birth has made them very good candidates for conversion—their religious faith becomes transferrable into a devout Judaism.

Not everyone responds positively to the opportunity to convert. Power plays between the partners are as likely to be enacted over this issue as over others. A Catholic woman who is angry with what she sees as her fiancé's "high-handedness" protests that her religious feelings aren't given equal time. "It's like a dirty word if you suggest to a *Jew* to convert, and yet there's this subtle pressure that the non-Jew should do it." The "subtle pressure" is often due to the fact that conversion is now viewed by many Jews as the last possible mechanism for turning a mixed marriage into a Jewish family, a device—or a resource—for making the couple, their home, and their children authentically Jewish. The conflict may not be so great for the Christian partner intermarrying, since he or she can still be a practicing Christian without having a "Christian" home and regardless of the faith of the other family members. Because a good deal of Jewish observance is home centered—the Sabbath and the laws concerning kosher food are but two examples—and because the Jewish identity of a child of an intermarriage depends, in Orthodox and Conservative Judaism, not on personal faith but on the religion of the mother, there is an assymetry that in itself leads to more pressure for conversion from the Jewish relatives and spouse than from the Christian.

When one spouse or one set of in-laws seems to be pushing relentlessly for the religious conversion of the other spouse, even in the face of reluctance or opposition, it is a sign that other power issues are surfacing in the guise of religious questions. The paradox of the partner who has found someone he or she cares about enough to want to marry, yet who presses for her or his transformation into a Jew, is evident in the question opening this chapter: If you love me so much, why do you want me to become something different? There is a real struggle here for all couples in which one partner feels he or she (usually he) cannot marry someone out of his or her faith, yet who has fallen in love with just that impossible person. Some couples can spin this problem around and around for years, prolonging the courtship phase for what seems to outsiders to be an eternity.

The circular pattern goes like this: He says he cannot marry someone who is not Jewish, so she must convert. She says that she doesn't want to be forced into anything, or to be manipulated by him, and that he loves her enough to be engaged to marry and that should be that. He fears that she will actually leave him, so he weakens a bit. She begins to make wedding plans. He feels (even if not consciously) that he has the advantage and presses again for her to convert before the wedding. Sometimes a situation like this goes on until an external factor changes. One man, who had wanted his fiancée to convert to Judaism so as not to wound his aging mother (though he always told his fiancée that the desire for conversion was his), never uttered another word about her converting after his mother died. They were then married in a secular ceremony.

No one wishes for a death in the family in order to help the couple come "unstuck" from their irresolute state. A better solution would be for the Jewish partner simply to realize that a choice is involved. Some issues never get resolved in life, and one must move on anyway. The negative response to a suggestion that one partner consider converting to the religion of the other can be explored openly and honestly. In this case, the Christian woman could have said, "I am not rejecting the possibility of conversion in the future, but I just cannot have my own religious status be a precondition for our marriage. I want *unconditionally* to marry you, and I would hope you felt the same." It would also be important to add, "I pledge always to honor and respect your religious traditions and practices and I'd like you to do likewise."

For couples who are exploring the possibility of an intermarriage without a conversion, one rabbi suggests creating an intermarriage prenuptial pact.[8] As with any such agreement, even an oral one, the salient point is that the very act of discussing such a pact gets out in the open the ways in which the partners view their own religious attachments: What ritual objects do they cherish and want in their new home? Would they like to live in a neighborhood with a distinct religious or ethnic flavor? How much money do they plan to set aside for church and synagogue membership dues or religious charities? Where and how would they like to be buried? The answers to these questions, and in fact just the discussion of the questions themselves, provide an opportunity to make clear a baseline of knowledge of one another's attitudes about the marriage and the ways they will live together. Couples attending conversion classes together have a formal context in which to share some of these thoughts; for the couple uneasy about conversion, setting out their expectations formally helps them to clarify—and even demystify—some of their differences. One of the most useful clauses in the intermarriage prenuptial pact does concern conversion: a statement of mutual respect with a pledge that it the partners decide that conversion is not an option no pressure will be applied regarding conversion after the marriage.

The marriage can certainly take place without conversion, if the partners want it, and the couple can then negotiate how they will live together, how they will celebrate, and how they will raise any children. However, putting off making these decisions until after the marriage, without trying to understand the underlying dynamic, may mean that the same circular disputes take place over holiday celebrations or circumcision of a son, for example, that dogged the earlier conversion discussions. The problem arises when the implacable demand for conversion is really a statement of terminal incompatibility, and sometimes a couple can only find this out through premarital or couple-oriented counseling.

To consider conversion under pressure is no way to enter a new faith or a marriage. If the Christian partner has serious misgivings, predominantly angry and rejecting feelings toward his or her own family or faith, or feelings of resentment toward a partner who has been coercive, it is far wiser, suggests a pastoral counselor, to put off the conversion until such time as it has hopes of being a genuine statement of religious feeling. Of course, every convert has doubts, and some do not feel fully at home in their new faith until they have lived it for some time, but what we are speaking of here are conversions motivated by duress. These conversions—and the intermarriage ''problems'' they are supposed to be ameliorating—are probably doomed from the start. People report having been "forced" to go through "quickie" conversions at the insistence of Jewish in-laws who, among other reasons, wanted their own rabbi to be able to perform the marriage ceremony. This approach hardly does credit to the allegedly religious sensitivities involved. One man to whom this happened, and who acquiesced to his in-laws' wishes because he had compelling reasons to proceed with the marriage quickly (he was about to be sent to Vietnam), stated unequivocally that "inauthentic conversions create bad feelings, bad Jews, and bad marriages."

The smell of hypocrisy does emanate from many such conversions, where in-laws who themselves have been apparently only marginally Jewish press strongly for conversion of a child's prospective spouse. A "bad" conversion pressed by the parents of the Jewish partner may only be so because the family is expressing through the demand for conversion a pathology that is in fact independent of the intermarriage situation. But not all families are alike. What seems in one family to be an inexplicable and manipulative upsurge of Jewish feeling when faced with a child's intermarriage may in fact be the surfacing of genuinely felt ties to Jewishness that the parents never needed to express before.

While some partners convert before a marriage to placate in-laws or to help alleviate a spouse's guilt, others want very much to convert and become part of the Jewish people, even in the face of surprising opposition from their Jewish partners. Assuming that in most cases the conversion is a willing and authentic one, several factors motivate an individual to choose to live in a faith other than the one that he or she was born into. Some non-Jews who choose Jewish partners say that they always felt close to Judaism and had contemplated conversion even before meeting their mate; others are profoundly religious Christians who would never have thought about converting before marrying a Jew, yet who find that their religious feelings are in some ways transferrable from Christianity to Judaism.

The attitude of the Jewish partner is probably the most significant factor influencing whether or not a Christian partner will consider converting to Judaism. Both a statistical survey of interfaith couples[9] and several rabbis have pointed out that in an extraordinary number of cases neither the Jewish family nor the prospective spouse even mentioned conversion as a possibility. For 71 percent of the nonconverts polled, the question of conversion had not ever entered their minds! The Jewish family's resistance to the religious adherence of the Christian-born partner, combined with their trying to foster in their child and his or her mate some positive feelings about Judaism, does have a positive influence on conversion. Converts who report that they are happy about marrying a Jew, and who believe that their partner is "not happy" that they're not Jewish themselves are the likeliest to convert to Judaism. For these people, conversion is probably seen as a way of solidifying the love relationship, of growing closer to a spouse.

Certainly a born Christian who responds favorably to a suggestion that she or he convert to Judaism has every right to be distressed when the Jewish partner seems unwilling to learn more about Judaism or to appreciate fully the Christian partner's efforts to become Jewish. Such ambivalence on the part of the Jew—encouraging conversion but disparaging the process or the faith itself—will lead to conflicts between the partners and to resentment on the part of the Jew by choice. Some of this potential conflict is eliminated if both partners attend conversion classes together—a good idea even if the Jewish partner is already knowledgeable. The very discussions themselves are likely to bring the partners closer, and at least they will have a common body of information, especially important if, for example, the conversion is being conducted under Orthodox or Conservative auspices but the Jewish partner identifies with the Reform wing of Judaism, more liberal in its interpretations of Jewish law. Especially in cases like this, the Jewish partner's attendance at the classes or instruction sessions should be mandatory, so that the partners start out with a body of shared knowledge.

Having a united approach to the practice of Judaism after the conversion is helpful to all couples, but is particularly useful in cases where the conversion feels to one or both partners as if it had been orchestrated by, or occurred because of, pressure from the family of the Jewish-born spouse. Jewish in-laws may push for conversion before marriage, sometimes to ensure that future grandchildren will also be Jewish. A prospective spouse may acquiesce in his or her parents' wishes about a prenuptial conversion. And yet, even when the non-Jewish partner is interested in considering conversion, Jewish parents—and sometimes the Jewish partner too—feel uneasy.

Conversion, while it has many advantages for the couple and

the family unit they are forging, may still not ease all conflict with the Jewish in-laws: For the parents, focusing on the "unsuitable" religious background of a child's mate may have been a way of exerting control over that choice, and where control is the issue the opportunity to exercise it is unlikely to arise as clearly once there has been a conversion. Sometimes the Christian partner converts at least in part to help alleviate what are perceived as problems the Jewish partner is having within his or her own family; if this is the case, it may come as a surprise to all when the problems don't disappear magically after the conversion.

Marriage to a Jew is frequently a significant part of the motivation when a non-Jew considers converting to Judaism. But the desire to move closer to a loved person does not address fully the basic question of what conversion is and means, and to what extent it actually signifies a change *away* from the person one was before, or a growth into a state in which one is more truly oneself. These personal religious feelings—of taking on a slightly different persona, or seeing the world through slightly different lenses—are highly idiosyncratic and vary dramatically from person to person, but one common thread in many authentic conversions seems to be that the conversion itself puts the seal on a state to which the Jew by choice had been moving for some time.

Rachel Cowan, a born Protestant who is now a rabbinical student, recognized a compelling need to convert to Judaism after fifteen years of marriage: "It was finally obvious to me that I was deeply engaged with Judaism. It was no longer simply enough to identify with Jews, it was time to become one."[10] Another woman, a practicing Methodist before her marriage to a Jew, could not decide after seven years of marriage whether or not she was ready for conversion. A clergyperson asked her: "Do you believe in Jesus Christ?" "No." "Do you believe in Judaism?" "Yes." The conclusion: "So, convert. You are living as a Jew in fact already, so you might as well become so in name too."

For some, the desire to convert may actually come first, and then the choice of a Jewish mate. Jewish mystics believe that every convert to Judaism is someone who was Jewish in a previous life. Whether one accepts this view or not, it seems obvious that there are people who have always felt attuned to Judaism, and for whom finding a Jewish mate did not seem accidental. "I never felt connected to my parents' religion. They're Baptists from Louisiana. I was always drawn to the few Jews in my school—they were smarter, funnier. And I used to spend a lot of time talking to the local rabbi when I was in high school. I didn't convert until just before my marriage, but I must say that the conversion—and even my marriage to a man who's not only Jewish but whose family is a pillar of their Conservative congregation up North—had the quality of inevitability about it." A woman with a similar background, from a small town in Texas, tells an almost identical story. It is possible, actually, that Judaism's rootedness in present realities and emphasis on how to live through everyday events, its stress on repairing the world we live in rather than focusing on rewards in a world to come, may have a particular appeal to women growing up in Christian fundamentalist homes where their own aspirations in the here and now were trameled by a combination of religious traditionalism and rural circumstances.

Another woman, who grew up in a nonpracticing Protestant academic family in Massachusetts, asks, "How could anybody *not* want to be Jewish? I converted before my wedding twenty years ago, and I love it—the ritual, the rhythm of the calendar, but especially the rigorous intellectual approach to problems, with legal precedents playing an important part in decisions. It turns me on that it's a religion based on thought rather than just belief." For others, conversion provides its own opportunity for genuine spiritual renewal and change. One rabbi noted that "Judaism represents a very special value in American life. The creative use of alienation attracts many non-Jews to Judaism. . . . It is often the person for whom all religious symbols have become transparent who converts to Judaism."[11] Jews have always been a people apart; unlike most other nations, for example, until this century they have never exercised political hegemony over large numbers. The small size of the Jewish community, the exiled quality of much of Jewish life, and the resulting marginality from the idealized Norman Rockwell version of mainstream American culture have doubtless contributed to the attraction many converts say they feel for Jews and Judaism, apart and aside from feelings of attachment to a Jewish spouse.

Until someone is ready to convert—or even if a person never converts but lives as a Jew (usually in an intermarriage)—a special category has been suggested. A Jew "in potentia" was historically termed *ger toshav* ("the stranger who lives among you"). In the sixteenth century, when the Jewish law code known as the

*Shulkhan Arukh* was set forth, there was a category for those who identified with Jewish concerns and lived as Jews among Jews. They themselves were not considered Jews but their children were to be considered such. This category no longer exists. Today, to be a formal participant in the Jewish community, or to have the right to call oneself a Jew if one was not born so, one must undergo a formal conversion to Judaism.

The process itself varies, depending on which branch of Judaism is approached and which rabbi is consulted therein. According to the strictest interpretation of Jewish law, a prospective convert to Judaism should be turned away at least twice. Those who persist and come back a third time are to be considered likely candidates. Officially, Orthodox rabbis are not supposed to officiate at a conversion linked to a marriage; the argument is that where there are external motivations the convert is not sincere in wanting to embrace Judaism for itself. (This is the argument used by some Orthodox rabbis as to why they will not perform an intermarriage even when the Christian spouse converted well before the marriage ceremony.) The traditional conversion process involves a period of study—weeks to months—followed by immersion in a *mikvah* for men and women and circumcision for men, both with proper witnesses. If the man has been circumcised before, a symbolic drop of blood is taken from the penis at the time of conversion. Orthodox and Conservative conversions follow this formula; Reform and Reconstructionist do not insist on circumcision. With the performance of these rituals, and an appearance before a court of three learned Jews (or *beth din*) to renounce previously held religious beliefs, the conversion itself is complete, at least in its formal manifestation. The Jew by choice takes on a Hebrew name, sometimes Ruth for women, which will be used on religious occasions, for example when she or he is called up to the Torah or to perform other ritual honors in synagogue. Orthodox rabbis—and sometimes the courts in Israel, governed by the Orthodox interpretations of Jewish law—do not recognize as valid any conversion that does not adhere to the full set of rituals. Some Orthodox rabbis refuse to accept as valid even a ''complete'' conversion supervised by a Conservative rabbi. This makes for considerable confusion among Jews. The disputes about conversion (and power) among Jewish denominations have led to odd situations.

Dorothy, a California woman long active in Jewish life in her city, converted to Judaism before her marriage thirty years ago. She was horrified when her son's prospective in-laws tried to stop him from marrying their daughter because Dorothy's conversion had been supervised by a Reform rabbi and hence—in Orthodox eyes—was not valid. In the end, her son refused to convert to Judaism to please his future in-laws, telling them that he was a Jew already; the young couple then arranged to be married by a Reform rabbi, over her parents' objections.

Tina, who before her marriage to Dick had converted to Judaism under the supervision of an Orthodox rabbi who led a Conservative congregation, asked the rabbi to rewrite the conversion documents on a plain sheet of paper rather than on the letterhead of his synagogue, lest the rabbinate in Israel or elsewhere challenge the validity of her conversion! These differences in interpretation, which may have little relevance at the time of conversion, may matter later if the child of a woman convert to Judaism wants to marry an Orthodox Jew, or if a Jew by choice wants to "make *aliyah*"—that is, go to Israel to live and to become an Israeli citizen. In the first instance the Orthodox rabbi or community may not allow the marriage because of doubts over the validity of the mother's conversion and hence the child's Jewishness. In the second case, a convert may not be eligible for automatic and immediate Israeli citizenship under the Law of Return because his or her Jewishness is not considered authentic. In many cases, there will be no "investigation," although given the schisms over the "Who Is a Jew?" question within the Jewish community in the 1980s, close examination of such documents may become the norm.

Because there is no prescribed course of study and no standard examination testing a prospective convert's understanding of Judaism, the actual prerequisites for conversion differ greatly, not only from denomination to denomination, but also among rabbis within denominations. There are occasional cases of "quickie" Orthodox conversions, adhering to the letter of the law but not its spirit, whose chief characteristics are that for a hundred or two hundred dollars one can be educated, immerse in a *mikvah*, say the appropriate blessings, have a symbolic circumcision if necessary, and be done with the process in a few hours. Clearly a "conversion" of this sort makes a mockery both of the *halakhah* (Jewish law) and of the psychological processes by which a person actually takes on what amounts to a new religious or spiritual identity. But even among rabbis who take their responsibilities very seriously in this area there are differences. Some require attendance of both partners at an Introduction to Judaism course lasting several weeks, as a prerequisite for undertaking the conversion process. Sometimes interfaith couples who attend courses like this just to inform themselves do find them to be a motivating factor in the Christian partner's decision to convert.

Rabbi Stephen C. Lerner, of the Center for Conversion to Judaism, like some other rabbis around the country, works with prospective converts individually for a period of many months (usually nine or ten); invites the partners (or the relatives) to services and family celebrations of Jewish events, and holds weekend retreats to expose them to experiential aspects of Judaism in addition to the study of history, traditions, prayer, and Hebrew. The academic approach of most conversion classes, often stimulating in and of itself, is not necessarily adequate or sufficient preparation for crossing the ethnic divide.

Rabbi Lerner's procedure for conversion might be a useful model for other programs. Sensitive to the ethnic issues in a conversion, Lerner tries to give prospective converts some of the *experiences* that can help them identify with the ethos of the Jewish people, as well as teaching them formally about the more intellectual aspects of the Jewish religion. He does this by enriching a rigorous course of study with, among other things, walking tours of New York's Lower East Side and suggested readings of Jewish fiction.

"Judaism is not in the business of saving souls," Lerner reminds people. "What you do—how you practice the religion—is important, not just that you have gone through the formal process of conversion." For this reason, he refuses to convert babies at birth unless the child's mother (who by definition is not a Jew, or the child's conversion would be unnecessary in the first place) takes courses in Judaism, so that she will be able to impart something of Jewishness to the child she is committed to raising as a Jew.

This same commitment to the quality of the Jewish home the couple will create is evident in conversion classes that include the Jewish partner, too. In the twenty-five or thirty sessions that the most demanding conversion classes require, couples learn a lot about their own feelings and backgrounds as well as about Judaism, though these classes are not therapy groups. "They spend time talking about life processes," notes Rabbi Lerner. "Not many couples of any religion usually spend this much time in the course of a year talking to each other about these things. This should make their marriage *better*, and in fact people do say that the learning and discussion process has strengthened their relationships."

Uniformly, professionals involved in organizing groups for prospective converts, or classes in Judaism that prospective converts are urged to take, make the point that the Jewish partner really should attend also. In one case, the Jewish partner was a senior rabbinical student whose longtime girlfriend, a Jamaican anthropologist, took a thirty-week course about Judaism at his suggestion while they were considering what their lives would be like were they to marry. He attended every class with her, although, said the instructor, "he could have been teaching the course himself." But his attendance meant a great deal to his girlfriend, who took it as a gesture of support and solidarity with her efforts to understand more about Judaism. Such classes should also present some basic material on Christianity, so the partners share a body of information and the Jewish partner has a sense of the roots of the Christian partner's approach to religion.

Among the questions Lerner's prospective converts respond to in writing are these: "If you were raised in another religion, in what ways do you feel that Judaism differs from that religion? In what ways do you think Judaism is more appropriate for you?" This approach—and this direct query—contrasts sharply with the thoughts expressed by many non-Jews who say that they will feel comfortable creating a Jewish household or raising their children as Jews "because Christianity and Judaism are so similar; the differences really don't matter." Lerner comments that "When," in his classes for prospective converts, "I hear too much of the 'blending' I know I've got a problem—that person wants to remain Christian."

One way of handling this denial of differences is to face it directly, talking with the prospective convert about what the differences are between Christianity and Judaism—theological and practical—and what he or she will be giving up in becoming a Jew. One aspect the convert gives up is a sense of continuity with certain past experiences and the wholeness that comes with repeating these experiences at different stages of life. Another is the forfeiture of a religious link to the birth family that comes through being an active participant in religious ceremonies with parents, siblings, and the extended family. This sense of continuity, though abstract, should not be minimized. It plays a large part in peoples' fantasies, and needs to come out into the open if a conversion is going to feel like a comfortable choice. A woman about to appear before the rabbinical court as part of the last phase of her conversion to Judaism said that for her the stumbling block was the idealized Christmas celebration dancing around in her head, one in which her children (as yet unborn) attended Mass with their grandparents, and everyone had a fine time together at home afterward. "I finally realized," she said, "that this TV version of Christmas was not going to be mine, just as realities changed and I became a sound engineer and not a nurse, the way I'd planned to as a kid. I am just going to have to figure out other ways of staying close to my family, because I love my husband, and I love Judaism, and I want all this to work. There's no way that it can if I keep going on about Christmas."

Many people who convert to Judaism have a strong sense of religious identity to begin with. They start out different from those partners in interfaith marriages who do not convert in that they often feel a personal attachment to spiritual matters and to prayer, and in general have positive feelings about religion. A devout Protestant man, shocked to hear that some people would consider converting to Judaism simply to please a spouse or a family member, said, "If I converted it would certainly not be for convenience! My religious feelings are very deep. But, in a way, that makes me open to other religions, and I could convert to Judaism because of *that*. I'm a religious person already, so maybe for me it's easier to convert to Judaism than it would be for someone who had no faith at all."

Based on the hundreds of people he has seen in his conversion (or preconversion) classes, Rabbi Lerner concludes that "if a person is not religious, it's hard to break through, although they may go through the conversion. If a person is a good Christian, and they can break away from Christian beliefs, they make better Jews than the converts who were nonbelievers." Since Christians who convert to Judaism give up the certainties of belief that they had known all their lives, a clear and symbolic recognition of the new status and identity are helpful in sealing this transition, and giving recognition to the effort involved. Too often in the past the conversion marked the end of a process, rather than being acknowledged as the beginning of a lifelong affiliation. Just as there are now ceremonial welcoming ceremonies—where practically none existed a generation ago—for newborn Jewish daughters, so converts, their rabbis, and their families are finding ways of welcoming these new Jews, sending a strong message both to the individual and to the Jewish community that their presence is a cause for rejoicing. Many converts, however, are so absorbed in the learning and the effort involved in approaching a new religion that they have little chance to plan for these important personal ceremonies. Part of integrating into a new community is making a public statement that one is "there."

Many converts mention that they wished they had experienced a conversion that was more ceremonial than just presenting themselves before three rabbis (often strangers to them) and testifying as to their intentions. Some rabbis involve their entire synagogue populations in a ceremonial welcoming of converts to Judaism, which may include the rabbi's blessing of the convert(s) at a regular Sabbath service, or at Shavuoth, the spring holiday at which the Book of Ruth is traditionally read. (Ruth is considered the quintessential convert to Judaism, so Shavuoth, the festival marking the first of the year's harvests, is sometimes set aside as a time to honor "first-generation Jews.")

Rachel Cowan marked her conversion to Judaism during a synagogue service at which her non-Jewish relatives were present, and in which her children also participated. Other converts report wishing that they had done something like this. Lydia Kukoff, describing her own conversion in a *Choosing Judaism,* a book that has become standard fare in Reform conversion classes, said with regret that she wished she had had some guidance from others in planning such a ceremony, because she herself felt too new to Judaism to create one to celebrate the very moment of her becoming a Jew, yet the intense excitement of that marker event called out for some ceremonial correlative to the spiritual moment.[12] A woman in Vermont expressed similar feelings about her Conservative conversion.

> I went the whole nine yards, but so, so much was missing! Just as people plan their bar and bat mitzvah ceremonies, they should plan their own special conversion ceremony. Time and effort would increase their understanding and sense of connection with the Jewish community. A special

celebration should follow the final vow of commitment. I don't think another decision could affect my life more than conversion, including marriage! And everything is *so* new it cannot be the responsibility of the convert to apply pressure for these changes. Converts are too nervous; they need, at least, the guidance of other Jews.

Often the Jewish partner is shy about creating the celebration—or ignorant, perhaps, since conversion is not a ceremony familiar to him or her. It should be a cause for celebration; just as Jews celebrate a *siyyum*, the completion of a tract of study, the Jewish partner might want to arrange a postconversion *siyyum*, complete with festive meal. This helps to make the event sacred, respectable, joyous, and public all at once—nothing at all to be embarrassed about, as some converts report having felt when the conversion was not marked with special fanfare. A public celebration will help the new Jew feel like a full Jew. And if the couple has children, they should definitely be part of the welcome-to-becoming-a-Jew committee.

Rabbi Albert S. Axelrad, Hillel rabbi at Brandeis University since the 1960s and counselor to numerous interfaith couples, suggests an adult bar or bat mitzvah ceremony for converts at some time after the conversion itself, as a way of providing "a heightened sense of belonging and a greater feeling of authenticity." He commented: "Few and far between are the conversion courses that prepare a convert to accomplish liturgically what the bar or bat mitzvah achieves. At the same time, many a convert craves such an accomplishment, so as to feel more like a bona fide Jew."[13]

There are pitfalls in the conversion process that do cause some converts to doubt their choice, and indeed to feel unlike "bona fide Jews." Women in particular have reported feeling alienated from aspects of Judaism that exclude women or deny them full participation in ritual obligations. Some of the objections of women converts dissipated after the Conservative movement adopted more nearly egalitarian practices in stages since the early 1970s; now women are counted in the prayer quorum, called before the congregation of the synagogue to bless or read from the Torah, and, most recently, ordained as rabbis. But objections still surface from women who are in the process of converting to Judaism under Orthodox auspices.

215

Being aware of the denominational differences in women's rights (and rites) in Judaism can go a long way to sidestepping this pitfall in the conversion process. If a Christian woman who wants to become a Jew considers herself a feminist, or even an egalitarian, she should be prepared to deal with a certain amount of cognitive dissonance during instruction for an Orthodox conversion. If the tenets of Orthodoxy (which mandates, among other things, that women and men sit in separate sections during worship and that women cannot testify before a religious court) are unacceptable to her, she might want to consider converting under Conservative, Reform, or Reconstructionist tutelage.

People vary widely in their responses to the change in identity entailed by conversion. Converts report feelings ranging from the lukewarm to the positively ecstatic, depending on a number of variables, including the convert's feelings about religion generally, the quality and nature of the conversion experience itself, and the attitudes of the Jewish partner and in-laws. Some of the most serious issues arise after the conversion itself. How to relate to the birth family of the faith now set aside? How to practice Judaism in the family itself? How to really "feel" Jewish? A thirty-year-old woman from Vermont protested that "the process has been addressed but not the ensuing difficulties."

One of the most complicated identity issues that arises when an individual decides to convert to Judaism is the "ethnic" component to Jewish identity. The convert does not automatically acquire ethnicity in one tidy learning session or even in a nine-month conversion course. Intellectual or factual understanding about Judaism is much easier to come by than the feelings of "Jewishness" that entail political responses, a backlog of Jewish memories, an identification with a minority, and so on. "I have a sense that I could go through the whole conversion procedure and not only would I not totally feel like a Jew, but I think my husband and his family would still see me as not Jewish," predicted a Chicago woman who was quite sincere about her desire to become Jewish. Some of these feelings of ethnic identification will come to exist over time. Just as a new relationship with another person creates its own history, so does a new relationship with a faith group. This is one reason why religious practice is so important in the lives of Jews by choice; as distinct from intellectual understanding, ritual experiences themselves help create the "felt" history that makes identification possible. Even conversion classes contribute to the convert's socialization as a Jew.

Time was the most important factor in the integrated conversion experience of Ruthanne, the daughter of an Episcopalian minister; she had been on a spiritual search of sorts since the age of eight. ("My mother was a Fundamentalist before she married my dad," she said by way of explanation of her early interest in different religious traditions.) Her conversion to Judaism came five years after her marriage to a Jew. "I felt Jewish long before I converted. I didn't want to convert and *then* grow to understand Judaism. You have to be very confident about religion, or the conflict will show with your children." (Her two young children were converted to Judaism at the same time she was.) "Conversion was the *finale* for me. It's like marriage—the wedding ceremony is the fireworks, but the substance comes first. Going before the *beth-din* (court of three rabbis) as part of my conversion was very meaningful for me. It seemed like hours. They battered me with questions, but nothing practical; it was purely philosophical. A big question was how did *I* feel personally about *Shabbat!* For the first time I had to articulate my own perceptions about on time and off time and to really get in touch with how different *Shabbat* is from the busy-ness that Sundays in church had represented to me. I could actually sense as I was speaking not just what was different about Judaism but how enriched I felt by Jewish observances. It was one of the most interesting times of my life."

Assuming that the prospective convert has found a congenial milieu in which to study and experience Judaism before converting, negative reactions of the Jewish spouse may impede a comfortable conversion. Unless the rabbi instructing the convert makes a point of including the Jewish partner in conversion instruction, he or she is likely to feel excluded. The non-Jewish spouse may be learning more about Jewish matters than the Jewish partner, and may even feel closer to the rabbi than the born Jew does. Conversion stresses the importance of the religious affiliation and its role in the identity of the convert. Ironically, said one observer, "this often evokes hostility from the Jewish partner who is so minimally Jewish that he feels threatened when the non-Jew takes it seriously."[14]

There has probably been too little respect from individuals and religious institutions for what the convert gives up. In her groups for interfaith couples, psychotherapist Esther Perel hears "a lot of talk about the compromises converts or Jewish-affiliated Christians have made. They need validation and acceptance by their Jewish partners. They don't need to hear, 'I'd like you to meet my *shiksa* wife.' Some men may still need the thrill of announcing that they've married someone from another group, but the people making the sacrifices and compromises will feel less guilt and resentment if they feel fully accepted as Jews by their own partners."

Perhaps a Jew who denigrates a partner's conversion efforts has uneasy feelings about his or her own Jewish identity. The man who always introduces his wife, who converted to Judaism many years before, as "my *shiksa*" is just an extreme example of what some Jews are, consciously or not, struggling with when a non-Jewish spouse becomes a Jew. The refusal of some Jews to engage themselves religiously at all creates the unbalanced situation of the Jew by choice (usually female) being more observant religiously and even more involved in the Jewish community than the born-Jewish spouse.[15]

For the Jewish partner the ambivalence about conversion may have its basis in the fact that part of the attractiveness of the non-Jewish partner is precisely his or her difference from, or distance from, what is known and what is Jewish. Conversion signifies "the formal acceptance of a new identity,"[16] and the born Jew may also have a hard time accepting this new identity in his or her spouse, though the conversion may initially have been earnestly desired by the Jewish partner. "Often there is conflict between the expectations of the Jewish partner, who really wants a non-Jewish mate, and the increasingly Jewish attitudes and practices of the convert."[17] One man said to his wife shortly after she converted from Catholicism to Judaism. "My God, I feel like I married my mother!" Actually, one of the family patterns created when the Jewish husband is reluctant to practice Judaism in any way is that his wife and his mother form a close alliance, with the son left out in the cold.

Useful in getting over the born Jew's discomfort in reaction to the conversion is finding a community in which both feel comfortable with the style of worship and celebration. This is not as easy as it may sound, since the convert often has a more formal appreciation of Jewish history and liturgy, while the born Jew may be more familiar with the trappings of the celebrations, the holiday customs, or the Israeli folk tunes that often accompany both. A "traditional *chavurah*" style of worship may work well for such couples, combining relaxed participation (which the born Jew may experience for the first time) with a serious approach to the texts themselves (comfortable for the born Christian, who has just learned about the texts and the prayers).

While growing to feel relaxed among other Jews in such settings, the convert may experience discomfort with some Christians. One of the most painful issues for a convert to face is the potential rejection of his or her birth family. Even those whose conversion is not linked to a marriage may feel this, but the situation is more complicated for people who are embracing Judaism at the same time that they are being embraced by a whole new family. Parents of the convert may feel that their child is not only abandoning their religion but going over to another *family* as well. A New York man who converted to Judaism twenty-two years ago, just before his marriage to a Jew his parents had known and liked for years, said that his parents' first response was to ask "Why do *you* have to be the one to give something up?"

One rabbi who often meets with and counsels the non-Jewish parents of the people in his conversion program tells them that the conversion is in no way a "giving up" but is "a change of religious perspective," an admittedly euphemistic explanation that nevertheless seems to reassure. In reality, of course, there *are* sacrifices and forfeitures, as we have seen. But the person converting is moving toward something new and potentially very fulfilling, and some parents are able to recognize and acknowledge this.

Ruthanne's father, the Protestant religious leader, returned from a Christian tour to Israel with a *kippah* (skullcap) for himself, to wear when he visits his daughter's house, and a *tallith* for her. (The *tallith* is a prayer shawl until recently worn only by Jewish men at prayer, now being worn or adapted by women too.) Her community of birth and her community of choice appear to be dwelling together harmoniously where religious pluralism is concerned, but, she says, "It's hard for my mother because she wants her grandchildren close by for Christmas, and I can't give that to her." Instead, they celebrate Thanksgiving as their big annual family get-together holiday, more neutral than any occasion with a more specific religious agenda.

To keep confusion at a minimum for all the parties involved, one rabbi counsels converts *not* to go "home" at Christmas and Easter. This advice is a departure from the common wisdom, which says that one should simply make it clear to all involved that one is there simply as a guest and to help "the others" celebrate "their" holiday. Each interfaith family must decide this one on its own. There is a validity to this approach of not approaching because some people find it is too unsettling to witness family religious traditions in which they no longer feel comfortable participating (such as caroling, giving children an Advent calendar, or attending Midnight Mass at Christmas). This separation approach is most likely to succeed if the families of origin are close and can understand fully the reasons for the absence at, say, Christmas or Easter. Otherwise there is a real danger that the rejected parents will feel so awful that they will precipitate a complete cutting off from the younger family or simply seethe or suffer with a resentment or hurt that emerges in subtle and not-so-subtle ways.

Holiday visits to the Christian relatives can also be awkward for the Jewish spouse and children. Children are less clearly aware than the adults that this is "just a visit." Rabbi Lerner counsels: "If you must go, plan to get there at two in the afternoon of Christmas Day, so that you're there for the family but not for the religious services or for the exchange of presents. You can certainly give other people Christmas gifts, but now that you're a Jew it would be inappropriate for them to give you a present at Christmas."

Explaining to grandparents in advance what would make the visiting family feel most comfortable is obviously necessary if holiday visits are going to run smoothly. Similarly, explaining about Jewish customs and religious events as they arise can help the non-Jewish members of the family feel more comfortable and involved. For example, at a Jewish wedding ceremony, where the bride had recently converted to Judaism, each wedding guest received a small printed program at the door to the sanctuary of the synagogue where the wedding took place. In this program Jewish wedding customs were explained, so that the Christian parents and all the other relatives who were there to help celebrate would know the order and significance of the ceremony. Such explanations can also enhance the experience for many Jews present who may not be well versed in all the traditions of their own religion. Thus the printed program is a nice equalizing gesture. The non-Jews feel less alien and the Jews less uncomfortable.

The "otherness" of the convert's birth family always exists, however it may manifest itself. One woman who had converted to Judaism and was planning a Jewish baby-naming ceremony for a newborn daughter alerted her Protestant mother about what to expect in the way of blessings, prayers, songs, and good wishes. Her mother, who listened attentively and asked appropriate questions, came to the ceremony wearing a huge gold crucifix on a chain around her neck. She seemed to respect her daughter's choice, but she clearly felt the need to make a statement about who she herself was, and hence about her daughter's origins, too.

Giving advice on how to handle parents who are more aggressive in fighting a child's conversion, a woman who is herself a Jew by choice tells people, "You are marrying one another; you are *not* living your parents' lives. Other people will see your bond and know it's real." Once the individual him- or herself feels comfortable with the choice of Judaism, parental objections may diminish or at least feel less threatening. Most parents ultimately do try to act on their earlier declarations that they only want their children's happiness. Nevertheless, dealing with parental objections or discomfort can require more than asserting one's separateness. Often a convert may be defending to his or her own parents the choice to convert while at the same time wrestling with internal doubts over how to "live" or "feel" Jewish. Parents' expressions of concern may resonate with those internal doubts. Addressing and resolving—or making peace with—those doubts then becomes the more central task.

Some converts lay to rest their own doubts (or even residual feelings of guilt over being "not Jewish enough") by expressing "Jewish" views even more strongly than their Jewish-born cohorts. Consider, for example, a California woman who complained that her teenage son refused to date Jews, dated only *"shiksas."* Nothing so unusual until one realizes that the woman lived through the situation before, only the last time *she* was the *shiksa*. She converted to Judaism before her marriage and has adopted the same fervent anti-intermarriage stance as many of her Jewish-born friends. Her ethnic identification with this "Jewish" issue would seem to be complete, and she sees no contradiction or dissonance between her expressed views on interfaith dating and the example of her own marriage.

The convert has to build many levels of comfort with a new identity and perform many small tasks that will help Judaism to feel this familiar—even in its biases! The tasks are performed in order, moving from the innermost soul-searching before the conversion through the ethnic and familial issues in gaining one's parents' and in-laws' acceptance of the new status, to finding a niche in a new community. For converts who have been "associate Jews" for some time, the community may already be familiar. But for people whose conversion to Judaism coincides with a new marriage, and sometimes also with a household move, anomie can be averted if the couple is lucky enough to locate a synagogue or group of supportive friends who provide a matrix of Jewishness in which the new Jew can grow. One woman, commenting about a retreat weekend she attended just before her conversion, disclosed that "until I had a chance to spend a weekend in the company of other Jews like that, I didn't feel authentically Jewish. Now I feel that I can *be* a Jew rather than the 'acting as if' I was doing before."

Finding a compatible community in which to practice Judaism is crucial, and so of course are the practices themselves, which make concrete the convert's knowledge of Judaism and resolve to live as a Jew. A questionnaire that Rabbi Stephen Lerner entitles "Some Concluding Responses Before Conversion" highlights the commitment a convert makes to practicing Judaism and living— as an observant Jew is supposed to—within a community of Jews. He asks participants in his classes to write out detailed answers to such questions as "What positive practices have you assumed to make *Shabbat* a special day, and what commonplace activities do you commit yourself to avoid to enhance the holiness of *Shabbat?*" "Of what synagogue do you pledge yourself to become a member immediately after conversion?" "What are your plans for further Jewish study?" "The more demands we make on a potential convert," says Lerner, "the better the conversion will be." His instincts are borne out by the reports of converts themselves. One man, married for twenty years to a Jewish woman, became a Jew in a Conservative conversion before their wedding. He understood that he was becoming Jewish in far more than name only, took very seriously his obligations as a Jew, and has since that time grown increasingly observant and active in his wife's family's synagogue. "The observance of Judaism made me a Jew, much more so than the conversion itself," he says now.

Many rabbis help students integrate into a local synagogue and expect that they will meet regularly with their community rabbi. Ensuring the convert's continued connection with the faith community is ideally part of the conversion process. Remember the convert in Vermont who said that she and others like her "need the guidance of other Jews." Synagogues are now recognizing this and training lay leaders in outreach to interfaith couples, especially those recently converted to Judaism, so that they can help develop the friendship networks and "secular" Jewish support systems that many born Jews take for granted, helping to shore up the Jewish identity of the Jews by choice in matters other than religion itself.

With the increase in conversions over the past two decades, synagogues (and their members) are more sensitive to the needs of Jews by choice than they used to be. A Colorado woman who converted to Judaism before her marriage nearly thirty years ago still tells the tale of a conversation with an older man after services one *Shabbat* in the synagogue she had been attending regularly for more than ten years. The man, himself not a regular attendee on Saturdays, commented, "You look just like a *shiksa!*" She replied: "I am, but I'm trying to get over it." The distance that a remark like this engenders is obviously destabilizing or at least unsettling. Comments like this—and the feelings that underlie them—probably stem not from a desire to wound but from the simple fact that "Jewish experience has almost entirely been directed toward assimilating into other groups rather than in integrating outsiders into their own."[18]

One woman created her own synagogue environment. Converted to Judaism early in her marriage, she is now the president of a major East Coast synagogue that offers programs for interfaith families. At least as far as religious observance and community participation go, it does seem to be the case that converts make the best Jews. Perhaps in part because they cannot rely on ethnic identification, biology, or memories for their sense of themselves as Jews, converts are generally more religious than born Jews. They are often more committed to ritual and synagogue attendance while less involved in Jewish organizations and friendships than born Jews. Born Jews may *feel* more Jewish, but converts *act* more Jewish.

In surveys, converts score higher on measures of Jewish behavior (synagogue attendance, home rituals, and so on) than do born Jews, but they score lower on questions that measure attitudes about Jewishness (friendship patterns, or a sense of being responsible for all other Jews, for example).[19] When a convert to Judaism begins to feel as born Jews do, reacting to Jewish charitable appeals, identifying with historical Jewish suffering, the Jewish identity then begins to reside "in the gut as well as the brain," as one man, a Jew for the twenty-five years of his marriage, described his own feelings of identification with the Jewish people.

For many converts being Jewish may mean taking on a different religious identity from the one they were born into, but because a sense of real identification with Jewish peoplehood depends in large measure on the connections that the convert makes within the Jewish community, it is important not to permit recent converts simply to fade away or fade into a congregation but instead to find ways to help them integrate into the fabric of Jewish life in more ways than just the formally religious. Examples include encouraging synagogue members to invite converts for Sabbath meals or integrating them socially into organizations with a Jewish political or social-action focus. In fact, especially for former Christians who were active in church groups before converting, social action (arranging programs for the elderly, lobbying for better housing, staffing a synagogue shelter for the homeless) might be the most appropriate entry point into the community. The issues may well feel familiar, and the Jews by choice may have skills or experience that are needed by the synagogue. Nothing helps achieve integration more rapidly than the feeling of being needed by the organization the convert is approaching.

Some skills are transferable from one religious culture to another. One woman says that she just marched into the synagogue she joined after her conversion and volunteered for several committees. "I became active in the synagogue right away because I'd always been active in church groups. I felt comfortable in the role of an active volunteer; it's just my way." Needless to say, not all transitions are this smooth. Each of us brings into a new situation some residue of the past. Previous beliefs do not evaporate overnight. One formerly devout Catholic, now a Jew, reported saying "Hail Marys under my breath one night when my teenage son was out late and we didn't know where he was. Although I'd totally renounced the *beliefs* of Christianity when I converted, I guess some of the superstitions remained." A man who converted to Judaism from Protestantism before his marriage twenty years ago describes how on his first trip to Israel he walked along the Via Dolorosa, following what is believed to be Christ's route before his crucifixion. His comment: "It was so touching. I really understood what *my religion* is all about [italics added]."

Conversion is more than an exchange of one set of religious rules for another. An authentic conversion to Judaism means a real change of identification, an engagement with a people who have a specific history and a multifaceted community. The task of the Jew by choice is not merely to become a Jew in name and in deed, but to begin the process of becoming a Jew in the heart and the viscera as well. One of the things that happens when a Christian married to a Jew becomes a Jew is that their marriage is no longer an intermarriage. While some differences remain, of course, the fact that under Jewish law one does not refer to a convert as anything less than a full Jew means that formally, at least, an entire area of conflict has been wiped out for the couple. Ethnic differences remain and can be cherished; personality differences remain and can be a source of delight or annoyance; but the chasm of religious difference, with its potential for misunderstanding and fractiousness, has been bridged and the possibilities for marital harmony and integrated child rearing significantly enhanced.

## 11

◆

# Adult Children
# of Intermarriage

There was a Jewish child lurking in my Christian skin. . . .
I always felt like a Jew among the *goyim* and a *goy* among
the Jews.

> —*New York foundation executive Madeline Lee, raised by an*
> *Episcopalian mother and a Jewish father*

The adult children of interfaith marriages, particularly the offspring of "mixed" or nonconversionary marriages, seem to live
their lives in a constant state of irony, always able to see both
sides at the same time—a kind of double vision. Whether one
parent converted to the religion of the other or the parents decided that religion didn't matter at all to either of them, adults
reared by parents of different religious backgrounds say that they
always feel as if they have the two parts "inside" them. Because
the parents' differences were not in religion alone, but in culture
and ethnic identity and experience as well, conversion of one parent doesn't always alter the adult child's sense of "doubleness,"
or of having alternative identities.

This is not the same situation as might obtain, say, for an American adult who has one parent from the rural South and another
from the urban North. In this day and age differences between
North and South don't usually permeate all aspects of one's life.
Trying to find an exact analogy, a Massachusetts woman, raised
by a Jewish father and a Methodist mother, faltered: "It's not like
being a Democrat or a Republican. The feelings are there all the
time. Every day something arises that reminds me of the fact that
I'm two things, split."

In the words of one man raised in a Christian-Jewish family who is now a Protestant minister, "I see everything with two sets of eyes." When asked (by a young Jewish man, married to a Catholic woman and trying to figure out how to raise their own small child), "Do you mean how you react to the holidays?" he replied, "Holidays? No! How I react to the *newspaper*—Israel, Washington, New York, AIWACS. I react from two different perspectives. It *is* confusing."

Adults in this situation nod in agreement with the statement made by a member of Pareveh, an organization formed in the early 1980s that calls itself The Alliance for Adult Children of Jewish-Gentile Intermarriage: "You're more *one*, but you *always* have the other in you." The Hebrew word *pareveh* (or *pareve*) refers to Jewish dietary laws and denotes a food that is neither meat nor dairy: "neutral" or "neither one nor the other." The word for the organization does not, in its original meaning, suggest the yoking of two disparate materials, but rather something itself undefined that can be served with either meat or dairy meals.

The literal meaning may indeed be the correct emblem for the group's members, who report having a sense of strangeness, of not having a single identity, or of "being afloat in a middle ground." "The children of intermarriage can go either way. That sums up the situation we're in," according to Leslie Goodman-Malamuth, one of Pareveh's founders. "We all have two halves, regardless of how we live or raise our children." The feeling of isolation is probably stronger for those adult children of intermarriage who were born before the late sixties, when intermarriage rates began to rise. Many of them were the only "mixed" people they knew growing up.

In one Midwestern city, with a population of about half a million in the 1940s and 1950s, only two or three families were identified as having one Jewish parent and one Christian parent. The children of those marriages, now in their thirties and forties, report feelings ranging from interest to discomfort at their own situation. One woman, with a recognizably Jewish surname, said that she experienced anti-Semitism from Christian classmates because of her name but was ostracized by her Jewish classmates because she had a Christmas tree in her living room. She wasn't considered a suitable date by the families of Jewish *or* non-Jewish boys! "I always had the feeling I wasn't as good as the other kids," she said.

Even when a Christian-born mother converts before the child is born, or when the mother is born Jewish, the children may have been reminded directly, by their own relatives, that they are "not really Jewish." One woman in her forties described her mother's conversion to Judaism before marriage, her own Orthodox Jewish upbringing which included a *yeshiva* (Orthodox day school) education, and then added, "I never felt comfortable dating Jewish guys. I always felt I wasn't Jewish enough."

The Protestant minister remembers feeling as a child the "loneliness of being the only half-half" he knew. "I had no role models growing up." This has led to a degree of concealment. People who send out material for Pareveh have commented on how many of those who request information want anonymity. They want the proverbial "plain brown wrapper." Most of today's adult children of intermarriages are the offspring of those people who wanted to dispose of their own past rather than explore it. Both from the parents and from friends and cohorts, the dominant mode for dealing with the adult children of intermarriage in the past was silence.

This is not the case today, with even elementary schools sometimes offering courses in interfaith matters or in "comparative religion." And interfaith marriages are now so common that in most cities, at least, children are likely to be acquainted with others whose background is mixed. Which is not to say that parents in an interfaith marriage don't still hear comments that make them anxious about how people see their children; one man, a Jew living with his Protestant wife and their two teenagers, whom they've raised as Jews, says that his ultra-Orthodox next-door neighbors in Brooklyn have never allowed their children to play with his (although the neighbors might have reacted similarly to a "fully Jewish" but totally unobservant family).

Sheer numbers may change some of these attitudes, since Pareveh's founders estimate that there are now about as many children of intermarriage as there are Orthodox Jews in America. Still, many who identify themselves with Orthodox and Conservative Judaism will continue to raise questions about the Jewish identity of children born to a mother who is non-Jewish, or who hadn't yet converted at the time of the birth.

Angered by this, Robin Margolis, a founder of Pareveh, claims that "by the year 2000 parevehs (that is, children of Jewish-Christian marriages) will be 50 percent of all Jews. They'll *have* to change the *halakhah* on who is a Jew—*we'll* be paying the rabbis and supporting the synagogues and reforesting Israel!" Jewish law presumably will not change its tune based on who's paying the piper, but Margolis is correct in assuming that if present intermarriage and conversion rates hold there will be adult children of interfaith marriages in every area of Jewish life (that is, assuming that the same percentage of them choose to identify as Jews as is now the case). Drawing on American Jewish Congress data suggesting that there are now at least a half million children of intermarriage, Leslie Goodman-Malamuth predicts that "they will comprise the majority of American Jews by the year 2050."[1]

Margolis's own case reveals how much underlying conflict there was about intermarriage a generation ago. Now in her thirties, Margolis did not discover until a few years ago that her late mother had been a Jew. Only while going through some papers after her mother's death did she discover that her "Mayflower" father had—apparently unwittingly—married a Jew. After the discovery, Margolis (who took her mother's maiden name) decided, as she put it, "to live as a Jew," much to the distress, she said, of her father and the rest of the family, who had never suspected that her mother was Jewish. Like many adult children of intermarriage, Margolis speaks of "living as a Jew" or "living as a Christian," as though this were an *assumed* identity (which it is, though in a way that is unfamiliar to someone born of two Jewish or two Christian parents). Robin Margolis does not say of herself, as she might if she had been raised by her intermarried parents in Judaism, "I am a Jew." Instead she says, "I have chosen to live as a Jew."

Granted, this situation is unusual—and it becomes more complex when Margolis reveals that she had tried to convert to Judaism some time before she learned that she was, according to Jewish law, a Jew. Discovering that her mother indeed had been Jewish and that she herself is therefore a Jew did not alleviate any problems. Instead, it introduced a doubleness into her life. "Half of me is the enemy, the *goyim*—my halves are at war." She view herself as the persecutor and persecuted all in one. The issues for her, as for her counterparts, are essentially different from those of the intermarried couple themselves; adults reared in a mixed marriage are living out the sense of self-and-other that their parents could negotiate between them; in this case the struggle is within one person. Or as Margolis put it, "We are the *living* bridge between two traditions."

A fourth-grade student at Manhattan school that counts many interfaith couples as parents of its students began a sentence off-handedly with, "Well, when you have families that are *split* . . ." Yet, even in families where a conversion has taken place and there is officially *no* split, some of them doubtless remain uncertain. A Montreal woman in her early twenties said, "I don't know if I'm Christian or Jewish. My mother converted to Judaism before I was born, but we always spent Christmas and Easter with my mother's family. I felt like something was erupting for me when I was in my late teens. It didn't matter that I was considered a Jew by Jewish law. *I* am not sure which I am. It feels to me different—and worse—than what must be the conflicts between the two people who are getting married."

Rabbi Lavey Derby, who cotaught classes for interfaith children for several years at Trinity School in Manhattan, commented: "All the ecumenical and interfaith dialogue in the world doesn't prepare you for this—these kids really *are* both. Their issues are different from what happens when two separate individuals are trying to resolve these differences in a marriage." Some adult children struggle very hard with the theological issues around each religion in order to discover what it is they really believe—can they accept the idea of Jesus as the Messiah? Do they accept the ideas of a covenant between the Jewish people and a singular God? But most adult children decide by "feel" rather than by a intellectual process. Rabbi Derby believes the choice is made "by who they fall in love with" as much as by any thorough analysis of religious traditions.

A successful resolution of the struggle comes to some people quite naturally, although it often still incorporates that doubleness that adult children of intermarriage returned to again and again in conversations. One twenty-eight-year-old woman, reared by a Jewish father and a mother who was born Protestant and converted to Judaism when Maureen was twelve, said that she simply considers herself Jewish and was considered Jewish by her parents. Describing a Catholic wedding she attended, Maureen mentioned that the priest announced that "no one who feels uncomfortable about doing so needs to kneel." Her comment: "I guess he knew he had a Jewish girl in the audience."

And yet, despite her self-identification as a Jew, Maureen never learned much about Judaism, either in her parents' home or in her adult life. She has struck a balance between being able to "say who she is" and her reluctance to betray something in her mother's heritage by being "too" Jewish. She is engaged to marry Marc, a man whose own parents have a Protestant-Catholic intermarriage, reflecting what observers and statisticians agree upon: that the children of intermarriage "marry out"—that is, away from the religion that is their primary identity—thus maintaining the structure of their adult lives the duality they knew growing up in a dual-faith household. In the new household Maureen and Marc will form no religion is likely to be practiced. A Protestant minister confessed to being very concerned about this possibility. "When interfaith children choose other interfaith people as marriage partners, they'll never do the worshiping. The two faiths will remain only as ideas in their heads and not as religions being practiced."

Maureen is typical of other children of intermarriage both in her marriage to a Christian and in making no suggestion that her fiancé convert to Judaism. While the Jewish children of conversionary marriages marry non-Jews at about the same rate as do other American Jews, their non-Jewish spouses do not usually convert to Judaism.[2] In one study of the children of interfaith marriages in which the non-Jewish partner had *not* converted to Judaism, two out of three married non-Jews.[3] About a third of the children of two Jewish parents marry out. Thus those who take a gloomy view of intermarriage may be correct when they say that the Jewish community will have to look at the third generation to see the full effects of intermarriages.

What are some of the issues that these adult children face in their own lives? Those who recall their own parents giving them ambiguous and downright confusing messages about their own and their children's religious-cultural identity feel some anger at their parents. With just such a background himself, a man in his mid-thirties asked, "What's so wrong with rabbis wanting people to marry within their own group? Maybe it's a *good* thing. Look at how confusing it's been for us." One way of avoiding the hurt, anger, and confusion is by distancing themselves from their parents, living at a physical distance from them, and calling infrequently. The children of conversionary families, as adults, keep in closer touch by phone and visits with their parents than the children of mixed marriages—perhaps because the latter prefer to avoid a situation that caused them confusion growing up. "The children of conversionary marriages [to Judaism] seemed to follow the more characteristically Jewish pattern of frequent visiting and phoning, and the children of mixed marriages seemed to follow the more characteristically Gentile pattern of less frequent visiting and phoning (except for . . . frequent telephone contact with their Jewish mothers)."[4] The distance is one way of not having to choose a faith or a parent—or, if a choice has been made, to keep it at a remove from the parents in order not to wound the parent whose faith has not been chosen.

Let us return to Maureen here, because in her own experiences and expressed feelings she manifested many of the concerns of the adult children discussed here. Her father (Jewish) and mother (Episcopalian) met at college in the 1950s, married, and had four children. The children all say that they are Jewish but express a good deal of conflict with their father over this, especially the two daughters, perhaps because their father always talks about how good the Jews are and disparages his wife—and, in fact, all Christians—all the time. The daughters ask each other, "If Jewishness matters so much to Daddy, why didn't he just marry someone who was Jewish, instead of making Mom crazy all these years?"

It turns out that this experience is not uncommon. Many adult daughters of interfaith marriages have negative feelings toward their Jewish fathers, especially if their mothers were put down like this. Perhaps this is a phenomenon more characteristic of earlier intermarriages, in which the male Jew had higher education and economic status than the father of the Christian woman he married. Needless to say, their father's domineering attitude toward their mother—combined with the relentless sense of Jewish superiority he felt he had to express (perhaps to assuage his own guilt at marrying out)—made him a complicated and difficult person for his children to relate to. Maureen's father is not unique. Other adult children reported hearing from a Jewish father such phrases as "my *shiksa* wife"—a comment perhaps intended to be amusing and not disparaging, but nonetheless, having the effect of emphasizing the differences between the parents. It may be, as one observer pointed out, that "such men may have been sexist and obnoxious to begin with, and may have married Christian women to begin with because they found them more subservient."

One of Maureen's brothers, Brian, active in radical political causes, says that he sees in his father a "bourgeois" who "doesn't believe in God, just in Jews. He thinks Jews are better at everything, and he supports Israel no matter what the Israel government does." Brian brings out renewed evidence of the finding that the children of intermarriage do not have the same visceral responses when Israel's survival is perceived to be in danger or to the Holocaust or to other Jewish survival issues as those with two Jewish parents. "My father's attachment to Israel is so *irrational*," Brian complains.[5]

Because the father considers himself a "cultural" Jew, he did nothing to educate the four children Jewishly. As is often the case in families where the father is the Jew, the mother, sensing from his parents and from him, too, that Judaism was important to him, made sure that the children had some religious education available to them. But Maureen's younger sister, Lynn, asked poignantly with real confusion and anger at not having been given adequate resources to answer her questions: "What's going to happen to *my* generation of Jews? How can we be Jews? We don't have memories of persecution or anti-Semitism to hold us together."

Rather than expressing anger toward her parents, a forty-five-year-old Midwestern woman seemed to view her parents from afar, describing them as seeing themselves in the vanguard of social change by intermarrying. Their method of child rearing had been to deny any distress at their having to sustain the ideology of a "successful" intermarriage. She said that she and her siblings had the burden of "being happy, very happy," in order to justify their parents' choice, "to prove that love, damn it, triumphed over differences."[6] This strong denial came through initially in interviewing these adult children; Robin Margolis characterized this as the "no big deal" response, after which one hears that it *was* a challenge to live as the child of interfaith parents.

Particularly in families where the parents did not consciously raise their children as both Christians and Jews, but where the drift was toward this duality, when the adult children finally do decide to move toward one of the two faiths, they may be plagued by feelings that they are choosing one parent over the other rather than one religion over the other. The consensus among adult children of intermarriage is that while every one of them indeed incorporates two traditions within him- or herself, each is "more" one religion than the other.

Children of intermarriages usually do not sustain this duality throughout their lives. So how to reassure the parent whose religion is not chosen is a very real dilemma—and the problem is not only that the parent might feel hurt but also that the adult child still feels a sense of guilt and responsibility. The religious explorations of the adult child are much less threatening to the parents if they themselves understand and accept each other's religions and have consciously raised their children with access to both faiths. If either parent has been able to answer the child's religious queries and has treated the other parent's faith with *genuine* respect, religion is less likely to be seen by the adult child as a battleground, or the choice of one faith over the other as a preference for one parent over the other.

In choosing, adult children sometimes choose the religion one parent has converted *out of*—almost as if the child were acting out something for the parent, going back into a situation that might have been left with unexamined feelings of loss and sadness on the part of the converting parent. Decisions about religion made by interfaith parents for their children (in which the parents choose what faith the child will be raised in, what religious rituals will have dominance in the household, and so on) are not etched in stone. The children may want to explore aspects of their own parents' backgrounds that the parents have long set aside. Perhaps when a parent converts out of his or her birth religion and into another faith the child has less access to that part of his or her background, and that mysterious, hidden part of his or her heritage, therefore becomes, in some ways, more attractive than what is more openly expressed. The search may be motivated by the same kind of personal need to know one's heritage that drives some adopted children to seek out their birth parents.

When a parent is ambivalent or negative about his or her religious background, the explorations of adult children may feel very threatening. For the adult child, the "mystery" has allure and significance. One woman, now in her forties, reported having had no knowledge of her father's Jewish identity until she was out of college. He hadn't wanted her to know, he said, because he didn't want her to think that as a Jew she was entitled to "special treatment." Her father's ambivalence may have contributed to her current practice of writing regularly for Jewish periodicals. In a sense, she was forced to come to terms with Jewish identity issues because her father was unable to. Another woman, raised by a Jewish stepfather and a Catholic mother (and hence a child of intermarriage not by birth but by upbringing) decided to convert to Judaism following her marriage to a Jew. In the eyes of her stepfather, who had negative feelings about his own Jewish identity, this was "a calamity." Neither of these examples is typical, perhaps, in its specifics, but each highlights the struggle to come to terms with parents' attitudes about their own backgrounds—surely as much of a factor for the interfaith child as the effort not to offend each parent's tradition.

Within families where the parents wanted to "expose the children to both and let them choose; it's a personal thing . . ." siblings may not always make the same ultimate choice in religious identification. Siblings may act out various aspects of the parents' ambivalence about their own religion. This happens even with children of endogamous marriages—for example, a son from a Jewish family marries a non-Jew and has nothing to do with Judaism while his sister marries a very observant Jew and chooses to lead a strictly religious life. This phenomenon is even more likely to occur among children of interfaith couples, where several choices are seen as available within the family context. When siblings make different religious choices, they then face the same kinds of issues that their parents might have had to deal with a generation earlier: who celebrates what holidays with which relatives in attendance, and so on.

It is no surprise that in measuring their degree of comfort with themselves, sociologist Egon Mayer has found that the adult children of dual-faith marriages do not feel "close fellowship with a group" and often feel that "no one really understands me."[7] He also found that some of these feelings of alienation or marginality may persist, surprisingly, even in children who are the offspring of conversionary marriages.

Once the adult child of an interfaith marriage has made a conscious choice to live in one faith or the other, there may still be a struggle to gain others' acceptance. Religious institutions are often uneasy about the ambiguities and complexities in the lives of offspring of intermarriage. Leslie Goodman-Malamuth, co-founder of Pareveh, says that the synagogue wants people like her "to go underground," pretending that there isn't another side to their identities and backgrounds even if they now choose to identify wholeheartedly as Jews. Understandably, synagogues may want the children of intermarriage to identify completely as Jews, and press them to convert and forget the non-Jewish "part" of themselves entirely, making no reference to it and eschewing any Christian celebrations in their homes. Some of this institutional nervousness, expressed in social conversation with active synagogue members or in discussions with synagogue personnel about including non-Jewish relatives in Jewish ceremonies, will be likely to diminish as the children of the current wave of intermarriages (post-1970) mature into adulthood themselves. Since their numbers will be far greater than those of their predecessors, rabbis and congregants will doubtless have heard it all before and may have more inclusive models on which to base their responses.

Whether they identify as Jews or not, some children of Jewish-Christian intermarriages do feel their fate is linked to that of all (other) Jews. Some adults in this situation seem more concerned with the risks of being part Jewish than are people who fully identify as Jews, referring to the Nazi persecutions even of people who were only a fraction Jewish. For some converts, also, deliberately linking their lives to the Jewish people may feel risky—most know that the Nazis and the Spanish Inquisition saw "partial" Jews as Jews, period. Most Jews with two Jewish parents grew up taking in this fact with their mothers' milk. Children of interfaith marriages may sometimes feel that they incur an unnecessary risk by having the Jewish part of their identity known.

In addition to negotiating the complexities of their relationship and feelings toward whichever faith group they were raised in, children of intermarriage are often simultaneously negotiating between the Jewish and Christian communities. Not only the marriage choices but also the friendship patterns of the children of interfaith marriages (even if conversionary marriages) are not quite like those of children in endogamous families. Interfaith children tend to have many more non-Jewish friends than children of two born-Jewish parents. About two out of three of American Jews as a whole report that half their closest friends are Jews. Fewer than half of the children of intermarriage report that half of their closest friends Jewish.[8]

The adult children of interfaith marriages who consider themselves Jews may be the largest "alternative" constituency in recent Jewish history. Their presence means not only that there are many, many people of diverse heritage who consider themselves allied at some level with the Jewish community, but also that that community, in its own diverse manifestations, will have to come to terms with the changing nature of its constituents.

## 12

———◆———

# Seeking and Building Community

Insofar as the continuity of the Jewish family will depend increasingly on converts, the part played by communal organizations and educational institutions can be expected to expand. These will then overshadow the family as a bearer of Jewish norms and values.

—*Bernard Farber and Leonard Gordon,*
*in* Contemporary Jewry (*Spring-Summer 1982*)

The danger of support groups for mixed-marriage couples is that this still keeps them out. They should be integrated into study groups and events. We don't want *hyphenated* Jews!"

—*Rabbi Avis Miller,*
*at a conference on intermarriage (May 1988)*

The Jewish community of secular organizations, religious denominations, and social service agencies has set itself the contradictory tasks of "deterrence and reconciliation"[1]—trying to discourage intermarriages with one hand yet trying to bring the interfaith couple closer with the other. On an individual level, the Jewish community includes people who see interfaith couples as a significant population to reach out to, and those who reject them. These opposing goals and responses have caused considerable debate in the Jewish community. Interfaith couples are reaching toward a community at the same time as the arms of various communities are reaching out to them. An almost unbearable burden is placed on any couple deciding to survive alone. The American frontier ethic of self-sufficiency notwithstanding, couples and families need the support of other people around them. Whereas

239

twenty years ago intermarriage was most often seen as a ticket out of one's own community, many couples today are looking for a comfortable place to be *whatever* they have decided to be (converts, fellow travelers, a mixed household)—but they do not want to be unusual alone. Especially for interfaith couples, their goals and the goals of those who are reaching out to them may not be perceived as similar, at least at the moment of contact.

For the couple searching for a community, one possibility is to find a group of like-minded interfaith couples and restrict their minicommunity to these people. But a community of so-called hyphenated individuals creates a slightly distorted reality, plus an unrealistic view of religious choices for the children. More satisfactory in the long run seems to be the choice many couples are making—to find, albeit with "special status," a niche within the Christian or Jewish communities.

However, in the Jewish community especially, the seekers and providers of this sense of community very often view one another with suspicion, each regarding the other as a source of problems. One or both members of an intermarrying couple is likely to be struggling with issues of loyalty and betrayal; any community agency that extends a welcoming hand must understand that an approach that smacks of disapproval, rejection, or dogmatism is likely to turn them away. One possibility is to offer—both for couples and their children—programs, classes, and various hands-on "exposure" opportunities making explicit the fact that the events are not for Jews only, but rather a way of providing an enriched sense of Jewish background for interfaith families. One such program is Denver's Stepping Stones, a free education program for any child of an interfaith marriage whose parents want him or her to learn about the Jewish values and traditions that make up half of his or her own family history. Another is Derekh Torah in New York City: classes and Jewish experiences that attract both interfaith couples and unaffiliated Jews.

These programs—and others of a similar nature—usually go out of their way to show a noncritical attitude toward whatever choices the couple has made. The danger of a rejectionist attitude—from Jews *or* Christians—is that interfaith couples who hear cries of woe and despair in response to their marriage are likely simply to turn their backs on the faith that is the source of the utterances. People will "vote with their feet" and make no attempt to find a comfortable spot in a religious or communal structure that has expressed inhospitable attitudes. Many Jewish partners say they sense subtle or sometimes overt anti-Semitism in the Christian community, even if there has been no statement of objection to a Christian's intermarriage; other partners have commented on what to some feels equally alienating—church hierarchies that are very Establishment-oriented and not geared for social action and social change. Within the Jewish community the predominant mode, even among traditional thinkers, is to declare that interfaith marriages are regrettable because they are likely to weaken the fiber of Jewish life, yet paradoxically to provide a whole range of services for intermarried couples, in the hopes of drawing them in and keeping them affiliated with a group of Jews.

When we consider the seekers, the couple on its way to finding a congenial spiritual or communal "home," it is time to ask how an interfaith couple is going to fit into a community or find one. This is an especially poignant question for people whose *own* community—parish, synagogue, or peer group—seems to be rejecting them for having chosen one another as mates.

Family and friendship networks may change after an intermarriage, with the couple drawing closer to some family and friends and feeling more distant from others. Because traditional alliances may no longer feel comfortable, this shift also underlines the need to find a community for genuine support. This is what happened to a man from New Jersey who had been an active member of his synagogue until his marriage to a Christian woman. Once the board of the synagogue discovered that his wife did not plan to convert and that the children would be raised as Christians, he was asked to step down from the committees he sat on. As a punitive measure, his congregation had decided that a member who married out of the faith could hold no synagogue office. Unhooked from the religious and friendship community he had been part of for fifteen years, he was left to seek out a different set of alliances and friendships.

When incidents like this occur, just as when a devout rabbi says that he cannot perform a couple's wedding because of religious scruples, the people involved feel extremely alienated. Whether justified or not, this alienation and anger leads to what a social worker who has led groups for interfaith couples calls the "scapegoating of the Jewish community." Turning away from the larger community, intermarried couples may then turn inwards, at times believing that nonintermarried families have found for themselves the perfect community. "I tell them there is no such thing, that even people in endogamous marriages feel estranged from a lot of what goes on in synagogues or in Jewish organizations, or in church services," said one group leader.

In fact, it is often evident from conversations with Jews and non-Jews, in interfaith marriages and in the community at large, that the issues interfaith couples are dealing with in their search for community are not very different from what many Jews are feeling also. Thus, programs developed specifically to address the needs of interfaith couples will benefit all the seekers. These efforts take several forms, most commonly discussion groups for intermarried couples (and in some cases for their extended families as well). The burgeoning number of these groups, whether based in synagogues or in more "neutral" settings like community centers or people's homes, tend to explore issues of identity, how one sees one's own past, and would like to see one's future. The issues discussed, such as the "December dilemma," are often not so much about religion as they are about loyalty and family and belonging; uncertainties about these feelings also exist for many Jews and Christians who are not intermarried. (Intermarried couples seeking a community undeniably have specific problems, but they are not as isolated—even in their alienation—as they might think.)

Some partners—Jews and Christians alike—would never, ever attend a group for intermarried couples, either because they feel themselves intellectually above such encounters or because they are afraid of the buried conflicts that might surface. The Orthodox Jews (*modern* Orthodox, that is, those who work at secular careers and look and dress like other Americans) are very successful at drawing couples into considering a connection to Judaism, perhaps because of the authenticity of their experience with texts and ritual. The emphasis from Orthodox groups (the few that do reach out to interfaith couples) is on conversion, but even with this bias their rigorously intellectual approach to Judaism has been magnetic for couples who were not afraid to consider a Jewish affiliation.

Under the general sponsorship of a Jewish entity, some groups for interfaith couples have managed to attract such families, often by way of providing programs for their children. However, these groups may in fact be imbalanced toward Judaism since, even if they are not held under the roof of a synagogue, in most cases one of their goals is to reinforce the couples' Jewish identity, not necessarily to press for conversion but to provide a Jewish presence in their lives. "Enhancement" of the marriage is how it is sometimes phrased. The Jewish component is not a hidden part of the agenda; it is simply a reflection of the fact that intermarriage is of greater concern to Jews than to Christians, because of their sheer disparity in numbers.

Ironically, the rising intermarriage rate has turned out to be a good thing for Jewish women professionals, who are being hired to run outreach programs across the continent. Women, stereotypically seen as the ones with good intuition and good communication skills, are being called upon to provide professional services for a whole new "market" under the Jewish communal umbrella. Though these programs differ in approach and quality, in general they are viewed as crucial attempts to keep intermarried couples linked to the Jewish community while at the same time respecting the partners' own divergent backgrounds.

Among the guidelines that have been developed for how these groups should operate is a set of instructions that says.

> A workshop for the intermarried is not likely to be an easy project. The sponsoring agency cannot—and should not—mask its own Jewish identity, and any attempts to present a neutral or "value-free" position on the issue will probably be regarded with suspicion. Some couples may view the workshop as an opportunity to vent pent-up resentments; others may come to seek a *hekhsher,* or community approval, for a decision they have already made. Most, however, are likely to recognize that it offers them an opportunity to grapple with personal, cultural, religious, and communal ambivalences in their lives, and to learn how to come to terms with some very troubling issues.[2]

The paradox that needs to be understood is that some in the group may be seeking approval and at the same time feeling resentful of the community they have in some ways chosen not to affiliate with. One rabbi, a woman who has sat in on several groups, says quite honestly that "a rabbi can screw up the group—his or her presence can block the open feelings from coming out." This situation is a paradigm for how the Jewish community as a whole is trying to respond to interfaith couples. On the one hand, this woman has a vested interest in having such couples draw closer to Judaism; on the other hand, she is committed to providing an open environment in which they can come to that point themselves.

Some in the Jewish community have been more hospitable to Christian spouses than others. An executive in the women's division of a nationwide Jewish fundraising organization said: "We're not bound by Jewish law. We can take anyone in, so we're reaching out more and more to the Christian wives of Jewish men." Another observer noted that volunteer groups in the Jewish community that attract working women—usually called Business and Professional Women in the organizational structure—are "a haven" for Jewish women who have intermarried, because "they can come without their husbands, and they can feel connected to the Jewish community themselves without the hassle of a synagogue situation where their husbands wouldn't join, or where they feel they'd be uncomfortable."

Just as the formal responses to intermarriage differ from Christian and Jewish groups, so, too, do the needs of individual couples. A Jew who has often attended church services with her Lutheran husband said that she felt she would be accepted in his faith community if she could accept the spiritual goals of Protestantism, or even if she were interested in Christianity in general. "Although I sometimes hear comments about non-Baptized individuals, by which I assume they are referring to me, the Jew, I've never been made to feel unwelcome. It's different in the Jewish community. I have a feeling that there's resentment against my husband, and that some of this might continue even if he were drawn to Judaism spiritually." Birth, conversion status, and deep-seated identity are often at issue, and the "outsider" may never *feel* fully accepted in the Jewish community. Some of this has to do with the fact that Jewishness includes an ethnic and not only a religious component, and while the religious identification may come more easily to some than to others, other factors—such as a sense of being responsible for other Jews, or feeling a strong commitment to the survival of the State of Israel—may always be different for those raised in different faiths.

Except for occasional premarital counseling under church auspices, there are no discussion groups per se for interfaith couples sponsored by Christian organizations. In general, Christian discussions of intermarriage have been theoretical or theological, and seem to be subsumed under the category of interfaith dialogue rather than interpersonal interactions. While churches are frequently involved in formal dialogues with Jews and Jewish groups under the rubric of ecumenical explorations, Christians tend to regard these occasions as evidence for the rapprochement or blending of the two traditions rather than an opportunity to help bring interfaith partners into greater harmony as individuals. For example, the Episcopal church, among others, has made statements about the need to reevaluate relations between Christians and Jews from the vantage point of a new approach to Hebrew and Christian Scriptures, moving toward seeing the two religions in a more equal light. It is at this level that the Christian community responds to the issue of "relations between Christians and Jews," while the Jewish community organizes groups for interfaith couples in the hopes of keeping one or both partners interested in Judaism.

Protestant theologian Harvey Cox of the Harvard Divinity School said with enthusiasm that "Christian theologians are now more appreciative of the rabbinic tradition. They used to lose interest after the Torah." He went on to say: "There's a future which may surprise all of us in terms of its possibilities."[3] No Jewish theologian has spoken warmly of the "possibilities" inherent in greater interfaith mixing, although many see outreach to interfaith couples as a necessity.

Those in the Jewish community who express only concern and little hope that good things will emerge from the newly permeable boundaries between Christians and Jews are reacting to feelings that Jewish life will change drastically (some say it has already) as interfaith couples and their children are increasingly counted under the broadest definition of a Jewish community. Here is one very simple example of a change in the communal nature of Jewish life in the wake of intermarriage: In its simplest form of signaling a meaning or an identity, such a telling indicator as having what demographers call a "characteristic Jewish surname"—used even by mailing houses to sort through lists and provide organizations with addresses for individuals with distinctively Jewish last names—no longer guarantees that the bearer of the name is a Jew. A brother and sister named Cohen reported that they often found themselves in the awkward position of having to announce to Jews that they are not Jews, having been raised as Christians by a Protestant mother and a Jewish father.

The presence of interfaith couples within the Jewish community—and the uneasiness expressed by many Jews about a possible weakening of the fabric of Jewish life as a result—has had its positive aspects. Jewish institutions are beginning to be clearer about what kinds of programs they need to create to strengthen the Jewish identity of born Jews, not so much to "prevent" them from intermarrying as to help them feel more comfortable with themselves as Jews no matter whom they marry.

Jewish life is changing in the wake of widespread intermarriages. For example, the fairly homogeneous political stance of Jews—who as a group have consistently expressed more liberal sentiments in voting patterns and opinion polls than have other white Americans—may well change as the Jewish community grows to encompass people who were not raised by Jewish parents. Liberalism is now and has been, for American Jews, "not merely a characteristic, but a major component of their understanding of what it means to be a Jew."[4] The presence of converts is changing what it "means" to be Jewish. Often more religious than many born Jews, converts do not take their Jewish identity from inchoate feelings of "being" Jewish, or from shared liberal political and social ideologies, but from religious practice and belief—the latter being somewhat alien to many North Americans who were born Jewish and who would define themselves as Jews but whose orientation is more secular. By the same token, those born Jews who would be hard-pressed to define what being Jewish means to them now find themselves having to, as one man put it, "explain more." All the things that did not have to be made explicit, from certain Passover traditions to certain political tendencies, now have to be thought out and talked about, since *not* "all" Jews can intuit them anymore.

In the extended-family network, more Jewish families will number Christians among their relatives, and vice versa. The Christian relatives can end up being responsive allies and supporters of Jewish causes and of Israel, on the one hand, or their presence at family gatherings can dilute Jewish observances even in the home of a conversionary couple. Whatever the reverberations in the individual family, neither community will be as insular in the next decade as was the case in the past. It may still be possible in North America to encounter Christians who have never, to their knowledge, laid eyes on a Jew, but outside ultra-Orthodox enclaves it will be increasingly rare to find a Jew who does not have close ties to non-Jews via an intermarriage somewhere in the extended family. Synagogues and Jewish community agencies will have considerable numbers of non-Jews as participants and, in some cases, as members. At least on the level of the breaking down of stereotypes, Harvey Cox is perhaps correct that better times are on their way for interfaith relations generally, although the resulting loss of cohesiveness will be felt almost exclusively by the Jewish community.

Intermarriage will uniquely affect the Jews because of its role in creating schisms among Jewish groups. The presence of more mixed marriages than ever before, combined with a rise in the number of non-Orthodox conversions (or of conversions supervised by rabbis ordained in other-than-Orthodox denominations) has raised the question of Who is a Jew? argued both in North America and in Israel (where every Jew has a right to settle under the Law of Return). Disputes come on the heels of—and may derive from—the disagreements among Jews over the policy of "patrilineal descent" of Reform and Reconstructionist Judaism. This is a policy that derives directly from the numbers of mixed-marriage families who are affiliated in some way with Judaism; it states that a child born to a couple where one parent is Jewish will be considered Jewish if the child decides to identify as a Jew.

These community-wide controversies stemming from interfaith marriages may be healthy in spurring organizations to change. The dilemmas of "living with differences" that individual couples experience are writ large for community entities. The solutions have not yet been worked out on a larger scale, but the early returns tell us that a Jewish community with greater diversity than ever before is de facto being created by interfaith couples. As a community, Christianity and its denominations are not undergoing anything like this change. This diversity has enormous positive potential to draw back into the Jewish fold those who were turned off or alienated (including many nonintermarried Jews) by their perception that "all" Jews acted or thought in a certain way. A more diverse community allows more people to feel more comfortable within it, whether these people are single parents, homosexuals, the never-married or the intermarried, or members of any other group that have at various times felt closed out from

247

full participation and recognition in Jewish life. The liability, for a Jewish community that has lost some of its cohesion, is that the comfortable feelings of familiarity and dependability that many Jews have characterized as an intuitive part of their positive response to things Jewish will clearly not be there in the same way.

As communities, Christian denominations are not undergoing anything like this change. Characteristically, since we have seen that Christian identification is religious rather than secular, one response to Christian-Jewish intermarriages has been an exploration of some of the theological issues involved when the two faiths come together in one couple. As they have had to think them through in concert with a Jewish partner, Christians are learning to understand better some of the theological implications of their own faith, including an exploration of how Christianity is trying to redefine its relationship to Judaism, moving away from an earlier belief that Judaism was superseded by Christianity. A couple striving for mutual respect of one another's faith groups must struggle with all these discontinuities.

The challenge of living with differences, whether for an individual couple or a nationwide "community," is to make creative use of those differences to learn and grow, respecting divergent views without feeling threatened, loving one's partner while also remaining loyal to one's own past.

# Notes

## Chapter 1
### What We Talk About When We Talk About Intermarriage

1. Richard L. Rubenstein, "Intermarriage and Conversion on the American College Campus," in *Intermarriage and Jewish Life: A Symposium*, Werner J. Cahnman, ed. (New York: Herzl Press and Jewish Reconstructionist Press, 1963), p. 122.

2. Statistics extrapolated from the work of Egon Mayer, *Love and Tradition: Marriage Between Jews and Christians* (New York: Plenum, 1985), p. 10.

3. Mayer, *Love and Tradition*, p. 73.

4. *National Jewish Population Study* (New York: Federation of Jewish Philanthropies, 1971); U. O. Schmelz and Sergio Della Pergola, *Basic Trends in American Jewish Demography* (New York: American Jewish Committee, 1988), p. 22; and elsewhere.

5. Egon Mayer and Amy Avgar, *Conversion Among the Intermarried* (New York: American Jewish Committee, 1987).

6. Schmelz and Della Pergola, *Basic Trends in American Jewish Demography*, p. 23.

7. Some very conservative Orthodox rabbis and communities refuse to marry a convert to a born Jew and do not accept such unions as valid.

8. Animal sacrifices were once a part of Jewish tradition; substitute forms of worship developed. Polygamy, once practiced by Jews, was banned largely because it was at odds with normal practices of medieval Christianity. When geographic dispersion within a community meant that Jews would have had to violate the Sabbath in

order to carry young children to synagogue services, or to carry keys or medication or eyeglasses, the law was reinterpreted to provide for these needs that flowed from the fact that Jews no longer lived very close to the synagogue.

9. Steven M. Cohen, *American Modernity and Jewish Identity* (New York: Tavistock, 1983), 6–22.

10. Calvin Goldscheider and Alan S. Zuckerman, *The Transformation of the Jews* (Chicago: University of Chicago Press, 1984), p. 178.

11. Rela Geffen Monson, in Susan Weidman Schneider, *Jewish and Female: Choices and Changes in Our Lives Today* (New York: Simon & Schuster, 1984), pp. 335–37.

12. Francine Klagsbrun, *Married People: Staying Together in the Age of Divorce* (New York: Bantam, 1985).

13. *Mother Jones,* January 1977, pp. 11–12.

14. Mayer, *Love and Tradition,* p. 151.

15. Edwin H. Friedman, "Systems and Ceremonies: A Family View of Rites of Passage," in *The Family Life Cycle: A Framework for Family Therapy,* ed. Elizabeth A. Carter and Monica McGoldrick (New York: Gardner, 1980), p. 430.

## Chapter 2
## Who Marries Out—and Why

1. This is the percentage cited by Egon Mayer, Sidney Goldstein, and others, and most recently by Goldstein in his report to the World Jewish Population Conference in Jerusalem, December 1987.

2. Rosemary Ruether, *Faith and Fratricide: The Theological Roots of Anti-Semitism* (New York: Seabury Press, 1979), p. 209.

3. Deborah Hertz, *Jewish High Society in Old Regime Berlin* (New Haven: Yale University Press, 1988), p. 222.

4. Hertz, *Jewish High Society,* p. 214.

5. Ibid., p. 238.

6. David Kaplan, "South Africa Has World's Lowest Jewish Intermarriage," *Western Jewish Bulletin* (July 31, 1986), p. 4.

7. Calvin Goldscheider and Alan S. Zuckerman, *The Transformation of the Jews* (Chicago: University of Chicago Press, 1984), p. 180.

8. Eric Rosenthal, "Divorce and Religious Intermarriage: The Effect of Previous Marital Status Upon Subsequent Marital Behavior," *Journal of Marriage and the Family* (August 1970):435–40.

9. Gary A. Cretser and Joseph J. Leon, "Intermarriage in the U.S.:

An Overview of Theory and Research," *Marriage and Family Review* (Spring 1982):6. Also, although some have acknowledged a few other categories of intermarriers, Louis A. Berman, in *Jews and Intermarriage: A Study in Personality and Culture* (New York: Thomas Yoseloff, 1968), sets forth the idea that Jews who marry out of their faith want to reject their own backgrounds.

10. A set of distinctions set forth in 1933 by Reuben B. Resnik, discussed in Cretser and Leon, "Intermarriage in the U.S."

11. Graenum Berger, *Black Jews in America* (New York: Federation of Jewish Philanthropies, 1978), p. 122.

12. Egon Mayer, *Love and Tradition: Marriage Between Jews and Christians* (New York: Plenum, 1985), p. 91.

13. These intermarriages are examined from the perspective of black families in William H. Grier and Price M. Cobbs, *Black Rage* (New York: Basic Books, 1968).

14. Edwin Howard Friedman, "Conversion, Love and Togetherness," *Reconstructionist* 39(4)(May 1973):17.

15. "The Myth of the Shiksa," in *Ethnicity and Family Therapy*, ed. Monica McGoldrick, John K. Pearce, and Joseph Giordano (New York: Guilford Press, 1982), p. 506.

16. Friedman, ibid.

17. Egon Mayer, "Processes and Outcomes in Marriages Between Jews and Non-Jews," *American Behavioral Scientist* 23(4)(March-April 1980):508.

18. I am grateful to Naim Kattan, Head of the Writing and Publication Section of The Canada Council in Ottawa, Ontario, for sharing with me his view of philo-Semitism in Europe today and for reviewing with me the literature in French on this subject.

19. Richard Rubenstein, "Intermarriage and Conversion on the College Campus," in *Intermarriage and Jewish Life*, ed. Werner J. Cahnman (New York: Herzl Press and Jewish Reconstructionist Press, 1963), pp. 133–36.

20. Fred Masarik, *Intermarriage: Facts for Planning* (New York: Council of Jewish Federations National Jewish Population Study, 1971), p. 7.

21. Vicki Rosenstreich, personal communication.

22. Bernard Farber and Leonard Gordon, "Accounting for Jewish Intermarriage: An Assessment of National and Community Studies," *Contemporary Jewry* 6(1)(Spring-Summer 1982):60.

23. See Mayer, *Love and Tradition*, p. 90, for a discussion of status exchange.

24. Mayer, "Processes and Outcomes," p. 500.

25. Steven M. Cohen, "Education and Intermarriage," *Moment*, November 1986, pp. 17–20, see also Calvin Goldscheider, *Jewish Continuity and Change* (Bloomington: Indiana University Press, 1986), p. 20.

26. James L. Peterson and Nicholas Zill, *American Jewish High School Students: A National Profile* (New York: American Jewish Committee, 1984).

27. Goldscheider, *Jewish Continuity and Change*, p. 20.

28. "The deaf, Jews who live in silence," *Sh'ma* 16(307)(February 7), 1986:52.

29. Mark Winer, "A Study of Mixed Marriage in One Congregation," in *The Threat of Mixed Marriage*, ed. Rabbi Sheldon Zimmerman and Barbara S. Trainin (New York: Federation of Jewish Philanthropies, 1976), p. 77.

*Chapter 3*
## Jewish Women and Jewish Men: What's Going On?

1. Salo W. Baron, Arcadius Kahan, and others, *Economic History of the Jews*, ed. Nachum Gross (New York: Schocken, 1975). See also Deborah Dash Moore, *At Home in America: Second Generation New York Jews* (New York: Columbia University Press, 1981).

2. Rela Geffen Monson, *Jewish Campus Life* (New York: American Jewish Committee, 1984), and James L. Peterson and Nicholas Zill, *American Jewish High School Students: A National Profile* (New York: American Jewish Committee, 1984).

3. Monson, *Jewish Campus Life*, p. 5.

4. Corinne Azen Krause, *Grandmothers, Mothers and Daughters: An Oral History Study of Ethnicity, Mental Health, and Continuity of Three Generations of Jewish, Italian and Slavic-American Women* (New York: American Jewish Committee, 1978).

5. *Beliefs and Values of American Jewish Women: A Survey* (Washington, D.C.: B'nai B'rith Women, 1985).

6. For example, *The Bagel Baker of Mulliner Lane* by Judith Blau (New York: McGraw-Hill, 1974), a children's book in which the grandmother berates the grandfather for dancing with his bagels all night.

7. Erica Jong, *Parachutes and Kisses* (New York: New American Library, 1984), p. 358.

8. Reported in several articles under the heading of " 'JAP'-Baiting on Campus," *Lilith* 17 (Fall 1987).

9. Livia Bitton-Jackson, *Madonna or Courtesan: Jewish Women in Christian Literature* (New York: Seabury Press, 1983).

10. Karl Abraham, cited in Lewis A. Berman, *Jews and Intermarriage: A Study in Personality and Culture* (New York: Thomas Yoseloff, 1968), p. 129.

11. Gwen Gibson Schwartz and Barbara Wyden, *The Jewish Wife* (New York: Peter Wyden, 1969).

12. Ibid.

13. Judith Weinstein Klein, *Healing Wounds Through Ethnotherapy* (New York: American Jewish Committee, 1979).

14. Ibid.

## Chapter 4
## Trying to Say . . .

1. Calvin Goldscheider and Alan S. Zuckerman, *The Transformation of the Jews* (Chicago: University of Chicago Press, 1984), pp. 168–69.

2. See, among others, Paul Cowan's comments on Choate in *An Orphan in History* (New York: Bantam, 1983), and Bob Lamm, "Christian God and Jewish Man at Yale," *Response* 8 (3)(Fall 1974):7–16.

3. Barry Roger Friedman, "Different People, Different Needs," *Compass* 8 (No. 1), (Fall 1984):19.

4. Ibid.

5. Judy Richter, quoted in Barbara Pash, "Does Interdating Mean Intermarriage?" *Baltimore Jewish Times*, May 20, 1988, p. 80.

6. Steven M. Cohen, *American Modernity and Jewish Identity* (New York: Tavistock, 1983), p. 44; see also "Redbook's Survey on Religion," *Redbook* (April 1977):129. Two out of three of the Catholic and Protestant women who responded attended church at least once a week, while only 6 percent of Jewish women went to synagogue that frequently. The results are not strictly comparable because synagogue attendance is viewed as a male activity in some branches of Judaism, and many Jewish observances take place at home; even allowing for these distinctions, however, with the exception of those who make annual appearances at the High Holidays each fall, most Jews do not attend synagogue services regularly.

7. Albert S. Axelrad, *Meditations of a Maverick Rabbi* (Chappaqua, N.Y.: Rossel Books, 1985), p. 74.

8. Lori Santo, *Ethnicity and Parenting* (American Jewish Committee, 1984).

9. Paul Cowan with Rachel Cowan, *Mixed Blessings: Marriage Between Jews and Christians* (New York: Doubleday, 1987).

10. Susan Weidman Schneider, *Jewish and Female: Choices and Changes in Our Lives Today* (New York: Simon & Schuster, 1984), p. 348.

11. See, among others, Carol Gilligan, *In a Different Voice: Psychological Theory and Women's Development* (Cambridge, Mass.: Harvard University Press, 1982) and Lillian B. Rubin, *Intimate Strangers: Men and Women Together* (New York: Harper & Row, 1983).

12. According to the Jewish Education Service of North America, which published data on the 1983 census of enrollment in Jewish schools in the United States and Canada; see also a survey of Jewish education conducted by the Conservative movement, reported on in *United Synagogue Review* (Spring 1980):9.

13. Judith Weinstein Klein, *Healing Wounds Through Ethnotherapy* (New York: American Jewish Committee, 1979).

## Chapter 5
## *Living with Differences*

1. In some families Passover has become a generalized holiday of liberation; "freedom" and feminist seders exist in print, and black spirituals have become part of the seder song repertoire, with "Go Down, Moses," for example, popular at some celebrations even in Jewish schools.

2. Egon Mayer, "Processes and Outcomes in Marriages Between Jews and Non-Jews," *American Behavioral Scientist* (March-April 1980).

3. Edwin H. Friedman, "The Myth of the Shiksa," in *Ethnicity and Family Therapy*, ed. Monica McGoldrick, John K. Pearce, and Joseph Giordano (New York: Guilford Press, 1982), p. 503.

4. Friedman, "The Myth of the Shiksa," p. 516.

5. Edwin H. Friedman, "Systems and Ceremonies: A Family View of Rites of Passage," in *The Family Life Cycle: A Framework for Family Therapy*, ed. Elizabeth A. Carter and Monica McGoldrick (New York: Gardner Press, 1980); Friedman tends to focus on how the intermarrying child can attempt to change the behavior or a parent, almost always the mother. For a discussion considerably more sympathetic to the mother's responses, but focusing also on the family dynamic, see Harriet Goldhor Lerner, *The Dance of Anger: A Woman's Guide to Changing the Patterns of Intimate Relationships* (New York: Harper & Row, 1985), pp. 180–188.

6. Lerner explores this triangle very powerfully in a chapter entitled "Thinking in Threes," pp. 154–88.

7. Dr. Robert Seidenberg, quoted in Judy Oppenheimer, *Private Demons: The Life of Shirley Jackson* (New York: Putnam, 1988), p. 73.

8. Jay Brodbar-Nemzer, "Marital Relationships and Self-Esteem: How Jewish Families Are Different," *Journal of Marriage and the Family* 20(1988):91.

9. Gruzen is the author of *Raising Your Jewish-Christian Child: Wise Choices for Interfaith Parents* (New York: Dodd, Mead, 1987).

10. Led by psychotherapist Esther Perel.

11. Mark L. Winer, "The Divorce-Intermarriage Connection," *Reform Judaism* (Summer 1984):20. The work that supports this claim was based on marriage license information in Iowa and Indiana, where the religious backgrounds of groom and bride are noted. The work is reported in Eric Rosenthal, "Divorce and Religious Intermarriage: The Effect of Previous Marital Status Upon Subsequent Marital Behavior," *Journal of Marriage and the Family* (August 1970): 435–40. Rosenthal comments: "Previous widowhood strongly encourages subsequent endogamy, while previous divorce leads to such a high level of subsequent intermarriage that it must be considered a leading factor in the formation of religious intermarriages" (435).

12. Graenum Berger, *Black Jews in America: A Documentary with Commentary* (New York: Commission on Synagogue Relations, Federation of Jewish Philanthropies, 1978), p. 22.

13. Because Jewish-Christian intermarriage is not seen as a threat or a matter of particular concern to Christians as a group or to individual Christian denominations, no exclusively Christian-context discussion groups or support communities appear to have developed. Individual churches or other Christian institutions have cosponsored the occasional program with a Jewish institution or clergyperson.

14. A useful tour through the differences (and the sometimes erroneous assumptions of similarities) between groups is to be found in McGoldrick, Pearce, and Giordano, eds., *Ethnicity and Family Therapy;* and Joel Crohn, *Ethnic Identity and Marital Conflict: Jews, Italians and WASPs* (New York: American Jewish Committee, 1985).

15. Crohn, *Ethnic Identity and Marital Conflict,* p. 49.

## Chapter 6
### Parents of Interfaith Couples

1. Richard L. Rubenstein, "Intermarriage and Conversion on the American College Campus," in *Intermarriage and Jewish Life: A Symposium,* ed. Werner J. Cahnman (New York: Herzl Press and Jewish Reconstructionist Press, 1963), p. 125.

2. Steven M. Cohen, *Unity and Polarization in Judaism Today* (New York: American Jewish Committee, 1988).

3. The traditional bias against Jews sees them as richer than others, more powerful than others, in possession of inside information unavailable to others, and so on. While prejudice against other groups often accuses them of having diminished capabilities—being shiftless, lazy, lacking in morals, and so on—Jews are seen as having greater powers. See Rosemary Ruether, *Faith and Fratricide: The Theological Roots of Anti-Semitism* (New York: Seabury Press, 1979). p. 205ff.

4. Harriet Goldhor Lerner, *The Dance of Anger: A Woman's Guide to Changing the Patterns of Intimate Relationships* (New York: Harper & Row, 1985), p. 182.

5. Among others, Steven M. Cohen, *The Political and Social Attitudes of American Jews, 1988* (New York: American Jewish Committee, in process).

6. Edwin H. Friedman discusses the reactions of parents as part of a complex system of family interactions that includes the grandparents in "Systems and Ceremonies: A Family View of Rites of Passage," in *The Family Life Cycle: A Framework for Family Therapy*, ed. Elizabeth A. Carter and Monica McGoldrick (New York: Gardner Press, 1980), pp. 429–60.

7. Derived from *Jewish Parents of Intermarried Couples: A Guide for Facilitators* (New York: Union of American Hebrew Congregations, 1987).

8. Reported in *Reform Judaism* (September 1987):18.

9. Sherri Alper, quoted in *Jewish Parents of Intermarried Couples*, p. 44.

10. For a lucid discussion of status exchange in intermarriage, see Egon Mayer, *Love and Tradition: Marriage Between Jewish and Christians* (New York: Plenum, 1985), pp. 102–3.

11. *Jewish Post* (Winnipeg), December 12, 1984, p. 5.

12. Edwin H. Friedman, "The Myth of the Shiksa," in *Ethnicity and Family Therapy*, ed. Monica McGoldrick, John K. Pearce, and Joseph Giordano (New York: Guilford Press, 1982), p. 506.

13. Marshall Sklare, *America's Jews* (New York: Random House, 1971), pp. 191–93.

14. From "Love and Tradition," a video produced by Ilana Bar Din and Lydia Kukoff for the Union of American Hebrew Congregations, 1987.

15. Egon Mayer, "From Outrage to Outreach," *Women's League Outlook* (Fall 1987):12.

16. Egon Mayer, *Children of Intermarriage: A Study in Patterns of Identification and Family Life* (New York: American Jewish Committee, 1983). p. 41.

17. Psychotherapist Esther Perel, in discussion groups for parents of intermarried couples, has participants act out the roles of members of their own birth families to see this continuum. For a literal example of how transmission of religious customs and values changes from one generation to the next, as a patchwork quilt is used for a sabbath tablecloth, a wedding canopy, and more, see Patricia Polacco's book for children, *The Keeping Quilt* (New York: Simon and Schuster, 1988).

18. Lerner, *The Dance of Anger*, p. 183.

## Chapter 7
## The Wedding

1. Celia Deutsch, in *A Dictionary of the Jewish-Christian Dialogue*, ed. Leon Klenicki and Geoffrey Wigoder (New York: Paulist Press, 1984), p. 177.

2. Maurice Lamm, *The Jewish Way in Love and Marriage* (San Francisco: Harper & Row, 1980), p. 230.

3. Ibid.

4. Albert S. Axelrad, *Meditations of a Maverick Rabbi* (Chappaqua, N.Y.: Rossel Books, 1984), p. 65.

5. Ibid., p. 71.

6. Ronald Osborne, ''Marriage of Christians and Jews,'' in *Times and Seasons: A Jewish Perspective for Intermarried Couples* (New York: Union of American Hebrew Congregations, 1987), p. 152.

7. Ronald M. Brauer, ''Ger-Toshav: Reviving an Ancient Status,'' *Reconstructionist* (April 1982):29.

8. Quoted in Mark Winer, ''Should Rabbis Perform Mixed Marriages?'' *Jewish Advocate* (Boston), January 22, 1987, p. 24.

9. ''The Children of Noah,'' in Anita Diamant, *The New Jewish Wedding* (New York: Summit, 1985), pp. 239–42.

10. Winer, ''Should Rabbis Perform Mixed Marriages?'' p. 24.

11. Rabbi Alfred Miller, quoted in the *Chicago Jewish Sentinel*, March 19, 1987, p. 11.

12. Egon Mayer, *Conversion Among the Intermarried* (New York: American Jewish Committee, 1987).

13. Rebecca T. Alpert and Jacob J. Staub, *Exploring Judaism: A Reconstructionist Approach* (New York: Reconstructionist Press, 1985), p. 61.

14. ''The Roman Catholic party is asked by the Roman Catholic Church to promise to do what he or she can to see that the children of this marriage will be baptized and educated in the Roman Catholic

Church.'' *Anglican-Roman Catholic (New York) Joint Statement on Marriage*, published by the Roman Catholic Archdiocesan Ecumenical Commission *Forum*, September 1984, p. 7.

15. Sister Rose Thering, *Jews, Judaism, and Catholic Education* (New York: Anti-Defamation League of B'nai B'rith, American Jewish Committee, and Seton Hall University, 1986).

16. Edwin H. Friedman, "Systems and Ceremonies: A Family View of Rites of Passage,'' in *The Family Life Cycle: A Framework for Family Therapy*, ed. Elizabeth A. Carter and Monica McGoldrick (New York: Gardner Press, 1980), p. 448.

## Chapter 8
## Raising Children

1. Rosemary Ruether, *Faith and Fratricide: The Theological Roots of Anti-Semitism* (New York: Seabury Press, 1979), p. 205.

2. So common is this situation that an anthology is now in preparation collecting the stories of individuals who learned they were Jewish when they were adults.

3. Philip Rosten, "The Mischling: Child of Jewish-Gentile Marriage,'' undergraduate honors thesis, Harvard University, Cambridge, Mass., 1960.

4. U. O. Schmelz and Sergio Della Pergola, *Basic Trends in American Jewish Demography* (New York: American Jewish Committee, 1988) p. 23.

5. Leonard J. Fein, "Some Consequences of Jewish Intermarriage,'' *Jewish Social Studies* 33(1971):44–58.

6. For the comments of Jews involved in workshops dealing with Jewish identity and self-esteem, see Judith Weinstein Klein, *Healing Wounds Through Ethnotherapy* (New York: American Jewish Committee, 1979).

7. Steven M. Cohen, *Political and Social Attitudes of American Jews* (New York: American Jewish Committee, 1988).

8. *Times and Seasons: A Jewish Perspective for Intermarried Couples* (New York: Union of American Hebrew Congregations, 1987), p. 151.

9. Two children's books treat this theme—both, interestingly, with girls as the protagonists, perhaps because they are thought to be more sensitive in general than boys. In *Mixed-Marriage Daughter*, by Hila Colman (New York: William Morrow, 1974), Sophie denies much of her "Jewish half'' until it's awakened when she sees rank discrimination against Jews at a resort hotel. The heroine of the novel *Kate* by Jean Little (New York: Harper & Row, 1971) senses that there

are secrets in her Jewish father's past; through her, the father is reconciled with a dying parent and family rifts are healed. See also Judy Blume, *Are You There God? It's Me, Margaret* (New York: Dell, 1970).

10. Michael Lerner, quoted in Ari L. Goldman, "In Dual-Faith Families Children Struggle for a Spiritual Home," *New York Times*, August 18, 1988, p. C1.

11. Schmelz and Della Pergola, *Basic Trends in American Jewish Demography*, p. 22.

12. Egon Mayer, *Love and Tradition: Marriage Between Jews and Christians* (New York: Plenum, 1985). In a chapter entitled "The Tenacity of Jewishness," Mayer elaborates on the ways in which the interfaith couples he has studied did "something" Jewish, whether celebrating Jewish holidays or maintaining contact with Jewish relatives.

13. Mayer, ibid.

14. Egon Mayer, "Processes and Outcomes in Marriages Between Jews and Non-Jews," *American Behavioral Scientist* 23 (4)(March-April 1980):510.

15. Ronald M. Brauner, "Ger-Toshav: Reviving an Ancient Status," *Reconstructionist* (April 1982):28.

16. Dan Wakefield, "Spreading the Gospel at Harvard," *The New York Times Magazine*, May 22, 1988, p. 24.

17. Mayer, "Processes and Outcomes in Marriages," p. 514.

18. Sanford Seltzer, "Intermarriage and the Courts," *Humanistic Judaism* (Autumn 1982):28.

19. Ari L. Goldman, "In Dual-Faith Families Children Struggle for a Spiritual Home," *New York Times*, August 18, 1988, p. C1.

20. Schmelz and Della Pergola, *Basic Trends in American Jewish Demography*, p. 23.

21. This is put forth in Lee F. Gruzen, *Raising Your Jewish-Christian Child: Wise Choices for Interfaith Parents* (New York: Dodd, Mead, 1987); and in Paul Cowan with Rachel Cowan, *Mixed Blessings: Marriage Between Jews and Christians* (New York: Doubleday, 1987).

22. Ari L. Goldman, ibid.

23. For a straightforward articulation of the differences and similarities between modern-day Judaism and Christianity, see *A Dictionary of the Jewish-Christian Dialogue*, ed. Leon Klenicki and Geoffrey Wigoder (Ramsey, N.J.: Paulist Press, 1984); and Trude Weiss-Rosmarin, *Judaism and Christianity: The Differences* (New York: Jonathan David, 1943).

24. See Chaim Potok's *Davita's Harp* (New York: Ballantine, 1985).

25. Helen Latner, "Ask Helen Latner," *Atlanta Jewish Times*, March 25, 1988, p. 23A.

26. For example, see Samuel P. Oliner and Pearl M. Oliner, *The Altruistic Personality* (New York: Free Press, 1988).

27. Among others: Jessica Lynn Cohen, "A Comparison of Norms and Behaviors of Childrearing in Jewish and Italian Mothers," Ph.D. thesis, Syracuse University, Syracuse, N.Y., 1977; and Corinne Azen Krause, *Grandmothers, Mothers and Daughters: An Oral History Study of Ethnicity, Mental Health, and Continuity of Three Generations of Jewish, Italian, and Slavic-American Women* (New York: American Jewish Committee, 1978).

28. Joseph Giordano and Irving M. Levine, "White Ethnic Groups," *Encyclopedia of Social Work*, 1987, p. 866.

29. Andrew Chernin and Carin Celebuski, "Are Jewish Families Different?" *Journal of Marriage and the Family* (November 1983):906.

30. Joel Crohn, *Ethnic Identity and Marital Conflict: Jews, Italians and WASPs* (New York: American Jewish Committee, 1995), p. 21.

## Chapter 9
## Cycles, Ceremonies, Celebrations

1. There are no religious consequences from doing it differently if the mother of the child is Jewish. Under some interpretations of Jewish law, if the child is born to a non-Jewish mother, he would have to convert formally to Judaism if he wanted to be considered a Jew; one of the requirements of that conversion is a ritual circumcision, which could be waived if the ceremony had been performed in infancy according to Jewish law.

2. Mary Jane Frances Cavolina Meara, Jeffrey Allen Joseph Stone, Maureen Anne Teresa Kelly, Richard Glen Michael Davis, *Growing Up Catholic* (Garden City, N.Y.: Doubleday, 1985), p. 144.

3. Egon Mayer, *Children of Intermarriage: A Study in Patterns of Identification and Family Life* (New York: American Jewish Committee, 1983). p. 19.

4. Adapted from *Guidelines for Outreach Education: Developing Sensitivity to the Needs of Children Who Have Non-Jewish Relatives* (New York: Union of American Hebrew Congregations, 1986), p. 48.

5. To begin the inquiry, contact the Coalition for the Advancement of Jewish Education and the National Chavurah Institute, both in New York City.

6. Fredda M. Herz and Elliott J. Rosen, "Jewish Families," in *Ethnicity*

and Family Therapy, ed. Monica McGoldrick, John K. Pearce, and Joseph Giordano (New York: Guilford Press, 1980), p. 382.

7. Egon Mayer, *Love and Tradition: Marriage Between Jews and Christians* (New York: Plenum, 1986), p. 29.

8. While Reform Judaism eschewed the bar mitzvah ceremony from the mid-nineteenth century, the event has been reinstated in almost all Reform synagogues today.

9. Mayer, ibid., p. 28.

10. The Reconstructionist movement made this decision even earlier, but since it affected only the small percentage of American Jews who identified with that movement, it had little effect on most interfaith families.

11. *Guidelines for Outreach Education* (New York: Union of American Hebrew Congregations: 1986), p. 51.

12. Ibid., p. 61.

13. *Choosing Judaism* (New York: Union of American Hebrew Congregations, 1981), p. 83.


*Chapter 10*
## Conversion to Judaism

1. "To Instruct and Challenge: An Interview with Nancy and Ed Kleiman," *Compass* 8(1)(Fall 1984):3.

2. Rabbi Eleazar, *Pesachim*, 87b.

3. Egon Mayer, *Love and Tradition: Marriages Between Jews and Christians* (New York: Plenum, 1985), pp. 212–13.

4. Ibid., p. 213, and demographic studies by others.

5. Ibid., p. 233.

6. Ibid., p. 55.

7. Richard L. Rubenstein, "Intermarriage and Conversion on the College Campus," in *Intermarriage and Jewish Life*, ed. Werner J. Cahnman (New York: Herzl Press and Jewish Reconstructionist Press, 1963), p. 128.

8. Sidney J. Jacobs and Betty J. Jacobs, *122 Clues for Jews Whose Children Intermarry* (Culver City, Calif.: Jacobs Ladder Publications, 1988), pp. 136–38.

9. Egon Mayer and Amy Avgar, *Conversion Among the Intermarried* (New York: American Jewish Committee, 1987).

10. Cited in Susan Weidman Schneider, *Jewish and Female: Choices and*

*Changes in Our Lives Today* (New York: Simon & Schuster, 1984), p. 350.

11. Rubenstein, "Intermarriage and Conversion," p. 141.

12. Lydia Kukoff, *Choosing Judaism* (New York: Union of American Hebrew Congregations, 1981), p. 16.

13. Albert S. Axelrad, *Meditations of a Maverick Rabbi* (Chappaqua, N.Y.: Rossel Books, 1985), p. 64.

14. Rosalyn Hirsch, cited in *Outreach Programs to Intermarried Couples* (New York: American Jewish Committee, 1985), p. 13.

15. Mayer and Avgar, *Conversion Among the Intermarried*, p. 28.

16. Marshall Sklare, *America's Jews* (New York: Random House, 1971), p. 204.

17. Rubenstein, "Intermarriage and Conversion," p. 129.

18. Sklare, *America's Jews*, p. 206.

19. Mayer and Avgar, *Conversion Among the Intermarried*, p. 2.

## Chapter 11
## Adult Children of Intermarriage

1. From a presentation to a convention of B'nai B'rith Women in Miami, Florida, in 1988.

2. Egon Mayer, *Children of Intermarriage* (New York: American Jewish Committee, 1983), p. 34.

3. Mayer and Amy Avgar, *Conversion Among the Intermarried* (New York: American Jewish Committee, 1987).

4. Mayer, *Children of Intermarriage*, p. 38.

5. Egon Mayer, in *Children of Intermarriage,* provides a quantification of the differential attitudes toward the Jewish people from children of conversionary families and children of mixed marriages. Other studies, frequently conducted by sociologist Steven M. Cohen for the American Jewish Committee, measure the attitudes of American Jews toward Israel and toward other Jewish survival issues. There appears to be a sliding scale here, with endogamous Jews the most supportive, followed by children of conversionary marriages, followed by children of mixed marriages.

6. Lee Gruzen, *Raising Your Jewish-Christian Child: Wise Choices for Interfaith Parents* (New York: Dodd, Mead, 1987), p. 78.

7. Mayer, *Children of Intermarriage*, p. 37.

8. Ibid., p. 22.

◆

*Chapter 12*
## Seeking and Building Community

1. Jonathan D. Sarna, "Coping with Intermarriage," *The Jewish Spectator* (Summer 1982), p. 27.

2. Andrew Baker and Lori Goodman, *Working with the Intermarried: A Practical Guide for Jewish Community Workshops* (New York: American Jewish Committee, 1985), p. 3.

3. Harvey Cox, personal communication, 1988.

4. Steven M. Cohen, *The Political and Social Attitudes of American Jews, 1988* (New York: American Jewish Committee, in draft), p. 3.

# Bibliography

AXELRAD, ALBERT A. *Meditations of a Maverick Rabbi*. Chappaqua, N.Y.: Rossel Books, 1985.

BAKER, ANDREW, and LORI GOODMAN. *Working with the Intermarried: A Practical Guide for Jewish Community Workshops*. New York: American Jewish Committee, 1985.

BARON, MILTON L., ed. *The Blending American: Patterns of Intermarriage*. Chicago: Quadrangle Books, 1972.

BERMAN, LOUIS A. *Jews and Intermarriage: A Study in Personality and Culture*. New York: Thomas Yoseloff, 1968.

BLUME, JUDY. *Are You There God? It's Me, Margaret*. New York: Dell, 1970.

CAHNMAN, WERNER J., ed. *Intermarriage and Jewish Life: A Symposium*. New York: Herzl Press and Jewish Reconstructionist Press, 1963.

COHEN, J. SIMCHA. *Intermarriage and Conversion: A Halakhic Solution*. Hoboken, N.J.: Ktav, 1987.

COHEN, STEVEN M. "Education and Intermarriage." *Moment*, November 1986, pp. 17–20.

———. *American Modernity and Jewish Identity*. New York: Tavistock, 1983.

COHEN, STEVEN M., and CHARLES S. LIEBMAN. *The Quality of American Jewish Life: Two Views*. New York: American Jewish Committee, 1987.

COLMAN, HILA. *Mixed-Marriage Daughter*. New York: Morrow, 1968.

COWAN, PAUL, with RACHEL COWAN. *Mixed Blessings: Marriage Between Jews and Christians*. New York: Doubleday, 1987.

CRETSER, GARY A., and JOSEPH J. LEON. "Intermarriage in the U.S.: An Overview of Theory and Research." *Marriage and Family Review*, Spring 1982, pp. 3–15.

CROHN, JOEL. *Ethnic Identity and Marital Conflict*. New York: American Jewish Committee, 1985.

DIAMANT, ANITA. *The New Jewish Wedding*. New York: Summit, 1985.

## Bibliography

FARBER, BERNARD, and LEONARD GORDON. "Accounting for Jewish Intermarriage: An Assessment of National and Community Studies." *Contemporary Jewry*, vol. 6, no. 1 (Spring/Summer 1982), pp. 47–75.

Federation of Jewish Philanthrophies. *Intermarriage: The Future of the American Jew.* New York: (Proceedings of a Conference, December 1964.)

FISHER, EUGENE. *Homework for Christians: Preparing for Jewish-Christian Dialogue.* New York: National Conference of Christians and Jews, 1982.

FRIEDMAN, EDWIN H. "The Myth of the Shiksa," in Monica McGoldrick, John K. Pearce, and Joseph Giordano, eds., *Ethnicity and Family Therapy.* New York: Guilford Press, 1982, pp. 499–526.

——. "Systems and Ceremonies: A Family View of Rites of Passage," in Elizabeth A. Carter and Monica McGoldrick, eds., *The Family Life Cycle: A Framework for Family Therapy*, pp. 429–460. New York: Gardner Press, 1980.

——. "Conversion, Love and Togetherness," *Reconstructionist*, vol. 39, no. 4 (May 1973), pp. 13–21.

GLAZER, NATHAN, and DANIEL P. MOYNIHAN. *Beyond the Melting Pot*, Cambridge, Mass.: MIT Press, 1970.

GRUZEN, LEE F. *Raising Your Jewish-Christian Child.* New York: Dodd, Mead, 1987.

GOLDSCHEIDER, CALVIN. *Jewish Continuity and Change: Emerging Patterns in America.* Bloomington: Indiana University Press, 1986.

GOLDSCHEIDER, CALVIN, and ALAN S. ZUCKERMAN. *The Transformation of the Jews.* Chicago: University of Chicago Press, 1984.

GORDIS, ROBERT. *Love and Sex: A Modern Jewish Perspective.* New York: Farrar, Straus & Giroux, 1978.

HERTZ, DEBORAH. *Jewish High Society in Old Regime Berlin.* New Haven: Yale University Press, 1988.

JACOBS, SIDNEY J., and BETTY J. JACOBS. *122 Clues for Jews Whose Children Intermarry.* Culver City, Calif.: Jacob's Ladder Publications, 1988.

KUKOFF, LYDIA. *Choosing Judaism.* New York: Union of American Hebrew Congregations, 1981.

LERNER, HARRIET GOLDHOR. *The Dance of Anger: A Woman's Guide to Changing the Patterns of Intimate Relationships.* New York: Harper & Row, 1985.

LIEBMAN, CHARLES S. *The Ambivalent American Jew: Politics, Religion, and Family in American Jewish Life.* Philadelphia: Jewish Publication Society, 1973.

MAYER, EGON. *Love and Tradition: Marriage Between Jews and Christians.* New York: Plenum, 1985.

——. *Children of Intermarriage: A Study of Patterns of Identification and Family Life.* New York: American Jewish Committee, 1983.

——. "Processes and Outcomes in Marriages Between Jews and Non-Jews." *American Behavioral Scientist,* vol. 23, no. 4 (March/April 1980), pp. 487–518.

MAYER, EGON, and AMY AVGAR. *Conversion among the Intermarried: Choosing to Become Jewish.* New York: American Jewish Committee, 1987.

MEARA, MARY JANE FRANCES CAVOLINA, JEFFREY ALLEN JOSEPH STONE, MAUREEN ANNE TERESA KELLY, and RICHARD GLEN MICHAEL DAVIS. *Growing Up Catholic.* Garden City, N.Y.: Doubleday, 1985.

NEUSNER, JACOB. *Christian Faith and the Bible of Judaism.* Grand Rapids, Mich.: Eerdmans, 1987.

PETSONK, JUDY, and JIM REMSEN. *The Intermarriage Handbook: A Guide for Jews and Christians.* New York: William Morrow, 1988.

REUBEN, STEVEN CARR. *But How Will You Raise the Children?* New York: Pocket Books, 1987.

RUETHER, ROSEMARY. *Faith and Fratricide: The Theological Roots of Anti-Semitism.* New York: Seabury Press, 1979.

SCHMELZ, U. O., and SERGIO DELLAPERGOLA. *Basic Trends in American Jewish Demography.* New York: American Jewish Committee, 1988.

SELTZER, SANFORD. *Jews and Non-Jews: Falling in Love* and *Jews and Non-Jews: Getting Married.* New York: Union of American Hebrew Congregations, 1984.

SILBERMAN, CHARLES E. *A Certain People: American Jews and Their Lives Today.* New York: Summit, 1985.

SKLARE, MARSHALL. *America's Jews.* New York: Random House, 1971.

STERNFELD, JANET. *Homework for Jews: Preparing for Jewish-Christian Dialogue.* New York: National Conference of Christians and Jews, 1985.

Union of American Hebrew Congregations. *Jewish Parents of Intermarried Couples: A Guide for Facilitators.* New York, 1987.

WEISS-ROSMARIN, TRUDE. *Judaism and Christianity: The Differences.* New York: Jonathan David, 1943.

WILLERMAN, LEE. *The Psychology of Individual and Group Differences.* San Francisco: Freeman, 1979.

ZIMMERMAN, SHELDON, and BARBARA TRAININ, eds. *The Threat of Mixed Marriage: A Response.* (Proceedings of a conference, 1976.) New York: Federation of Jewish Philanthropies, 1978.

ZUROFSKY, JACK, ed. *Intermarriage: The Psychological Implications.* (Proceedings of a conference, April 1966.) New York: Federation of Jewish Philanthropies.

# Resources
# for Intermarried Individuals
# and Interfaith Families

This list, while far from complete, suggests the kinds of programs and groups available across the United States and Canada. Because of the ephemeral nature of some discussion groups, the best way to determine if there are programs in your area is to contact synagogues, the local Jewish community center or YM-YWHA, or the Jewish Federation (umbrella organizaton for Jewish agencies) in your locale. The resources listed here are largely under Jewish auspices because, as has been stated elsewhere in this book, intermarriage, at least on the level of community programming, is usually a matter of greater public concern to Jews than to other groups. They are listed alphabetically under each subheading.

## Weddings

### JEWISH

For names and addresses of rabbis in your area, call any local synagogue or contact:

Central Conference of American Rabbis (Reform)
21 East 40th St.
New York, NY 10016
(212) 684-4990

Rabbinical Council of America (Orthodox)
275 Seventh Ave.
New York, NY 10001
(212) 807-7888

Rabbinical Assembly (Conservative)
3080 Broadway
New York, NY 10027
(212) 678-8060

Reconstructionist Rabbinical Association
31 East 28th St.
New York, NY 10016
(212) 316-3011

## "ECUMENICAL" OR INTERFAITH

All Souls Unitarian Church
Rev. Richard Leonard
1157 Lexington Ave.
New York, NY 10028
(212) 535-5530

Associated Interfaith Rabbinical Marriage Counseling
460 13th St.
Brooklyn, NY 11215
(718) 645-3915
Interfaith marriage counseling and marriage ceremonies.

Community Church of New York
Rev. Tracy Robinson Harris and Rev. Bruce Southworth
40 East 35th St.
New York, NY 10016
(212) 683-4988
In many of their ceremonies "individuals want to honor both traditions."

Ethical Culture Society
2 West 64th St.
New York, NY 10023
(212) 874-5210

Rabbinic Intermarriage Counseling
Rabbi Irwin Fishbein
128 East Dudley Ave.
Westfield, NJ 07090
(201) 233-0419
Rabbi Fishbein maintains a list of rabbis in the U.S. and Canada who perform interfaith marriages with descriptions of what preconditions, if any, each sets.

The Society for Humanistic Judaism
28611 West Twelve Mile Road
Farmington Hills, MI 48018

## SECULAR

The Unitarian Church publishes a booklet of suggested readings for a secular marriage ceremony (all written by Christian men), given to all couples who inquire, "but especially interfaith couples."

Unitarian Universalist Church
United Nations Office
777 United Nations Plaza, 7D
New York, NY 10017

## Programs for Interfaith Couples

Adas Israel Congregation
5502 Western Ave.
Chevy Chase, MD 20815
(202) 362-4433

Commission on Outreach of Intermarrieds
Council on Jewish Life
Jewish Federation Council

6805 Wilshire Blvd., Suite 702
Los Angeles, CA 90048
(213) 852-1234, ext. 2982
Publishes a resource guide listing programs, courses, and activities for intermarried couples and their families.

Discussion/Support Group for Interfaith Couples
Congregation Shaare Tefilah
556 Nichols St.
Norwood, MA 02062
(617) 762-8670
One may join the group without an affiliation with this synagogue or any other.

Interfaith Couples Workshops
Nancy Tamler
c/o Jewish Community Federation
655 Arastradero, Suite 100
Palo Alto, CA 94306

Interfaith Support Group
Jewish Family Services
P.O. Box 13369
(704) 366-5007
Charlotte, NC 28211

Project Joseph
Joint Committee on Intermarriage and Singles Programming
(Conservative)
Nancy Caplan

910 Salem Ave.
Hillsdale, NJ 07205
(201) 353-7035
New Jersey–based programs, largely through Conservative synagogues.

Task Force on Interfaith Marriages
Jewish Federation of Greater Seattle
1904 Third Ave., Suite 510
Seattle, WA 98101
(206) 622-8211

"Times and Seasons"
A program of discussion groups for intermarried couples "seeking to explore differences in their backgrounds" held in Reform synagogues nationwide.

Outreach Programs
Union of American Hebrew Congregations
838 Fifth Ave.
New York, NY 10021
(212) 249-0100

The Reform movement has outreach programs for interfaith couples across the continent. For information:

Canadian Council
534 Lawrence Ave. West, Suite 210
Toronto, Ontario, Canada
M6A 1A2
(416) 787-9838

Great Lakes Council/Chicago Federation
Mimi Dunitz
100 West Monroe St., Room 312
Chicago, IL 60603
(312) 782-1477

Mid-Atlantic Council
Elizabeth H. Farquhar
2027 Massachusetts Ave. NW
Washington, DC 20036
(202) 232-4242

Midwest Council
10425 Old Olive Street Road
Suite 205
St. Louis, MO 63141
(314) 997-7566

New Jersey/West Hudson Valley Council
Dru Greenwood
One Kalisa Way, Suite 108
Paramus, NJ 07652
(201) 599-0080

New York Federation of Reform Synagogues
Carolyn Kunin
838 Fifth Ave.
New York, NY 10021
(212) 249-0100

Northeast Council
Nancy Kelly Kleiman
1330 Beacon St., Suite 355
Brookline, MA 02146
(617) 277-1655

Northeast California Council/Pacific Northwest Council
Rabbi Morris M. Hershman
703 Market St., Suite 1300
San Francisco, CA 94103
(415) 392-7080

Northeast Lakes Council/Detroit Federation
Kathy Cohn
25550 Chagrin Blvd., Suite 108
Beachwood, OH 44122
(216) 831-6722

Pacific Southwest Council
Arlene Chernow
6300 Wilshire Blvd., Suite 1475
Los Angeles, CA 90048
(213) 653-9962

Pennsylvania Council/Philadelphia Federation
Sherri Alper
2111 Architects Building
117 S. 17th St.
Philadelphia, PA 19103

Southeast Council/South Florida Federation
Rabbi Rachel Hertzman
Doral Executive Office Park
2785 NW 82nd Ave., Suite 210
Miami, FL 33166
(305) 592-4792

Southwest Council
13777 N. Central Expressway, Suite 411
Dallas, TX 75243
(214) 699-0656

## Resources for Parents of Interfaith Couples

Support groups for parents are held nationwide in synagogues and other settings, largely under the auspices of the Reform movement. For information on local groups, which are of several weeks' duration, contact:

Outreach Program
Union of American Hebrew Congregations
838 Fifth Ave.
New York, NY 10021
(212) 249-0100

Support group for Jewish parents whose children have intermarried:

United Jewish Federation of Tidewater (VA)
7300 Newport Ave.
Norfolk, VA 23505
(804) 489-8040

In addition to these, many of the locations listed previously as resources for couples from time to time hold groups for the parents of such couples.

## Resources for Children

Derekh Torah
92nd Street YM/YWHA
1395 Lexington Ave.
New York, NY 10028
(212) 427-6000
Programs for families (and individuals) wanting to incorporate some Jewish experience into their lives; not exclusively for interfaith families, but large numbers of intermarrieds participate.

Directory of Jewish Resources for Intermarried Families
Project in Intermarriage
Jewish Family Services
5750 Park Heights Ave.
Baltimore, MD 21215
(301) 466-9200, ext 297

The Jewish Family Connection
Outreach Program
Temple Israel
Longwood Ave. & Plymouth St.
Boston, MA 02215
(617) 566-3960
Maintains a network to refer callers to personal contacts in the community.

"Stepping Stones"
Temple Emanuel
51 Grape St.
Denver, CO 80220
(303) 388-4013
An experimental curriculum for children of interfaith marriages (K–high school), charging no fee and describing itself as "an enriching program for young people leading to a Jewish identification."

## Adult Children of Interfaith Marriages

B'nai B'rith Hillel Foundation
University of Washington
Seattle, WA 98101
(206) 527-1997
Outreach program for the children of intermarriage on the campus.

Pareveh
The Alliance for Adult Children of Jewish-Gentile Intermarriage
3628 Windom Place NW
Washington, DC 20008
(703) 761-5070

## Conversion

B'nai Abraham
(postconversion support group)
Temple Israel
Longwood Ave. & Plymouth St.
Boston, MA 02215
(617) 566-3960

The Center for Conversion to Judaism
Rabbi Stephen C. Lerner

752 Stelton Ave.
Teaneck, NJ 07666
(201) 837-7552

Jewish Converts Network and Interfaith Couples
Lena Romanoff, Director
1112 Hagysford Road
Narbeth, PA 19072
(215) 664-8112

The network has lists of support groups and can often put people in touch with individual converts in locations where no formal group exists.

Rabbi Steven E. Foster
Temple Emanuel
51 Grape St.
Denver, CO 80220
(303) 388-4013
Groups for prospective converts.

Rabbinical Assembly
3080 Broadway
New York, NY 10027
(212) 678-8060
Can refer prospective converts to Conservative rabbis in the United States and Canada.

Reform Commission on Outreach
Lydia Kukoff
6300 Wilshire Blvd., Suite 1475
Los Angeles, CA 90048
(213) 653-9962

## Congregations

Chavurah for Interfaith Couples
c/o Rabbi Yehiael Lander
Helen Hills Chapel
Smith College
Northampton, MA 01063
(413) 585-2754
The chavurah (fellowship group) meets in Amherst, Massachusetts, and is composed of interfaith couples all of whom have identified with the Jewish community.

Jewish Reconstructionist Congregation
Rabbi Arnold Rachlis
303 Dodge Ave.
Evanston, IL 60202
(312) 328-7678

Rabbinic Center Synagogue
128 East Dudley Ave.
Westfiled, NJ 07090
(201) 233-0419

Temple B'nai Torah
6195 92nd S.E. St.
Mercer Island, WA 98040
(206) 232-7243

Temple of Universal Judaism (Da'at Elohim)
Rabbi Roy A. Rosenberg
1010 Park Ave.
New York, NY 10028
(212) 535-0187
Congregation described as "organized primarily to meet the needs of interfaith couples."

# Index